AN AMBITIOUS WOMAN
The Third book in the 'Redwoods Series'

Kate Loveday

Copyright © 2018   Kate Loveday

The right of Kate Loveday to be identified as the author of this work has been attested to under the *Copyright Amendment (Moral Right) Act 2000*

Published in Australia in 2019 by Scribes Ink Publishers, South Australia

This work is Copyright. Apart from any use as permitted under the *Copyright Act 1968*, no part may be reproduced, copied, scanned, stored in a retrieval system, recorded or transmitted in any form or by any means, without the prior written permission of the publisher.

National Library of Australia Catalogue-in-Publication entry
A823.4
Loveday, Kate
An Ambitious Woman/Kate Loveday
ISBN: 978 0 646 98685-2 (pbk)

Typeset in 12/16 Garamond

Scribe's Ink Publishers
* * * *

Also, by Kate Loveday
Inheritance
Black Mountain
The Trophy Wife
Reflections

The Redwood Series
An Independent Woman
A Liberated Woman
An Ambitious Woman

Acknowledgements

I'd like to thank Jacqui Winn for her critiques, editorial suggestions and encouragement, to say nothing of her time spent over numerous cups of coffee.

Thanks to Janice and Roger, Kay and Melissa for their supportive assessments, and to Leonie Bell for loaning me her copy of 'The letters of Rachel Henning' which first sparked my interest in the early days of Bulahdelah.

I thank my publishers for help in getting it all right.

I must also thank Peter for all his listening, support and encouragement.

And last, but not least to all my readers and particularly those who have told me they are eagerly awaiting my next book, thank you all

*For Brenda, Sally, Margie, Wendy, and Rhonda,
with thanks for help, support
and encouragement over the years,
and for being the only sisters I have known.*

Chapter One

Bulahdelah   1900

Tears of frustration pricked Joy Barron's eyes as she looked at her fiancé. Normally she admired his tenacity, but not when it was turned against her.

'David Cavanagh, why do you have to be so stubborn? I don't want to wait until the new house is built. I want us to be married now, and I'll be just as happy in the little cottage. After all, what does it matter if we don't live in a big house?'

'It matters to me.' His level voice held the steely determination she knew lurked beneath his calm exterior. 'I won't have you starting our life together in circumstances less than you've been used to.'

'But it would only be until the big house can be rebuilt.'

'No.'

Joy's heart plummeted. She tried once more.

'Don't you want us to be married?'

'You know I do. The last thing I want is for us to have to wait.' His face tightened. 'But I didn't count on Redwoods being burnt to the ground. And if you don't want us to go to live with my parents until the house is rebuilt, we'll just have to wait.'

Joy blinked back the tears. She didn't want to wait. She loved him so much, she wanted them to be married, and she ached to make a start on their plans. She must convince him.

'What about all this?' Her sweeping gesture took in the stables and the paddocks that stretched down to the river – the Redwoods property. 'We need to get everything ready for the horses. We must build new stables, a store, clear the paddocks. If it's to become a first class stud, we can't afford to waste time, and Riverside's too far away for us to be able to come and work here every day.'

'I can stay here in one of the cottages and do all that, while you stay down in Sydney with your mother and Rufe.'

'Then I'll stay here in one of the other cottages by myself.'

'You can't do that. Not if I'm living here too. It wouldn't be right. It'd cause a scandal.'

'You're not very anxious to be married to me if you want me down in Sydney.'

David wrapped his arms around her, pulling her close. He tilted her head back and looked into her face. 'You know that's not true. It's agony for me waiting, I want you so much, but I want it all to be right for us. For you.' He raised a hand and smoothed the hair back from her face, then bent his head to kiss her.

As the kiss became longer, and deeper warmth flooded Joy's body and her knees became weak. She kissed him back fiercely, loving the feelings he roused in her, until finally he pushed her away, holding her at arm's length with his breath coming in gasps.

'No,' he panted. 'No, we mustn't do this. It's too hard.' He dropped his hands from her shoulders and turned away. 'Come on, we need to get back.'

He grasped her hand to walk to their horses tethered nearby. Joy let him lead her, but she wasn't happy. She loved him so much, why did he have to be so stubborn? She wanted them to be married right away, and she wanted to be here at Redwoods so she could be part of the preparations to bring the horses here – the horses that were the nucleus of their thoroughbred breeding programme. She wanted them here. Now. Determined to have her way, a plan began to form in her mind.

When, three months later, Joy stood at the altar alongside David feeling very nauseous, she wasn't so sure it had been the brilliant idea she'd thought. She was afraid she was going to be sick, in front of them all, the minister, the Markham church choir, all those who come to see her married and all over her bridal gown. Or perhaps faint, which might be even worse. But if she hadn't done it, she would've had to leave and go to Sydney. Instead, here she was, marrying the man she loved, and able to stay with him and continue their work at Redwoods with the horses.

The minister asked if she took David to be her lawful wedded husband, and she managed to utter, 'I do.' David took her hand and slipped the ring on her finger, and the minister pronounced them man and wife, and it was all over.

Her new husband took her arm to lead her into the vestry to sign the register, and when she looked up at him she saw his eyes full of concern. She managed a weak smile, and after they signed and walked down the aisle, and she felt the fresh air coming in from outside, she started to feel better.

Looking back at the congregation following them, she saw her mother Kitty with Rufe Cavanagh, her stepfather and David's uncle. Her own father drowned before she was born, and she felt a little pang as she wished she'd known him, that he could be here today. But Mother was happy with Rufe, and Joy noticed how beautiful she looked in a stylish outfit of soft green that set off her honey-gold hair and green eyes to perfection. They shared the same colouring and everyone said Joy looked like her mother, which pleased her immensely because she'd always thought her mother was beautiful.

Behind them came David's parents, Edward and Erin Cavanagh with their daughter Emma, whom she'd only just met. Behind them were her grandparents, Bella and Jack Morgan. Grandpa was her step-grandfather, who'd married Grandma before Joy was born. Patrick and Mary, who'd both been working for her mother for so long they were now regarded almost as family. They were followed by the general congregation—workers on Redwoods and people she knew from Bulahdelah.

As they left the small village church Joy knew her mother was disappointed her daughter didn't have a big wedding at St. James in Sydney, as planned. But Joy didn't mind. She'd had her way–they'd not had to wait for the house to be rebuilt.

And if she felt a twinge of guilty conscience for deceiving David, she managed to overcome it by telling herself it was all for the good of Redwoods. After all, she'd promised her mother she would make Redwoods the best, and she needed to be here to see that everything happened in the best possible way.

When Joy had announced she was pregnant, the family was upset, and that was a bit unpleasant, but as she and David were already engaged, an immediate marriage was arranged. It wasn't like her stepsister Lily, Rufe's daughter, who'd become pregnant when they were holidaying in England, and who'd refused to name the father and abandoned her baby at birth by running run away to America. Lily had left baby Benjamin behind for Rufe and Kitty to bring up as their own.

Actually, once they got over the shock of her pregnancy, Mother and Rufe were very good about it. They both told her what a silly girl she was, and Rufe told David he'd thought better of him. When she opened her mouth to say it had not all been David's fault, a sharp glance from David silenced her, and he took the blame like a gentleman.

Joy thought how easy her plan had been to accomplish. She pretended to acquiesce to David's insistence they wait for the house to be rebuilt. But she formulated her plan, and it all worked well. She studied a book about women's health she found on Grandma's bookshelves and worked out which time of the month she was most likely to fall pregnant. Then, on the first suitable day, she waylaid David as he headed towards the paddocks.

'Come with me.' She took his hand.

'But I'm busy. I've still got heaps of things I want to finish today.'

'I'm sure you have, but I'll help you later. Come on, I want to show you something.'

'What?'

'Just come with me.'

David let her lead him along the track that led to the base of the mountain. Covered in forest and with steep vertical cliffs at its top, it towered over Bulahdelah and loomed large beyond the house. She knew he was surprised when she urged him on to the path that wound upwards.

'Surely you don't want to go mountain climbing when we have so much to do.'

'Just come with me.'

They climbed up the narrow track until they came to a large boulder set in amongst the trees, with a plateau in front forming a small secluded clearing. Spread out below them was the whole of Redwoods estate. They could see over the treetops from one end of the property to the other, and beyond. The winding river far below formed one of the boundaries glinting silver in the sun. Dotted here and there were the workers' cottages, each surrounded by a small clearing. On the burnt-out site where the house was to be rebuilt workers scurried to and fro, shifting piles of debris into waiting carts ready to be pulled away and disposed of, and already marking out where the new house was to go. The partly completed stables seemed to beckon them in the warm sunlight.

'I've never seen it from this high before.' David's eyes shone. 'Look at all the new grass sprouting up through the burnt areas. You can see it so clearly from up here.'

Joy's heart leapt. He was going to agree to bring the horses here soon. She turned to face him. 'It's almost time to bring the horses home.'

'Yes. We'll have to supplement the feed for a while, but they can come as soon as the stables are complete.'

She threw her arms around his neck. 'Oh, David, it's the beginning of our dream. Isn't it exciting?' She pulled him closer.

'Yes, it is.' His mouth came down on hers and he kissed her.

Joy felt her ardour rise as she returned his kiss, fiercely, passionately. Pulling away from him she whispered. 'I love you, David.'

'I love you too,' he replied, his dark eyes incandescent as he looked down at her.

'Let's just sit down here for a few moments and look at our future home taking shape. We'll be able to remember this moment when we're an old married couple.'

When she urged him down on to the bed of grass and ferns at their feet, he offered no resistance. They sat for a moment or two, an arm around each other, watching the activity at the house site. Then she turned to him, raising her face to his.

'Kiss me again,' she murmured.

He bent his head and their lips met, gently. She clung to him, and as his kiss deepened, she eased him slowly back until they were lying down, kissing, and she gave full rein to the passion rising inside her and pushed against him, feeling his hardness.

After a moment he pulled away. 'No,' he said hoarsely, 'we must stop this before it's too late.'

But Joy was already undoing the buttons on the front of her gown. 'Please darling,' she begged, 'touch me. Just once. Please.'

'No.' He gasped, but his eyes were on her breasts, partly exposed beneath the opening.

'Just this once,' she urged, taking his unresisting hand and placing it on her chest, and as his hand slid down and stroked her breast softly, she felt her nipple rise to meet his fingers. Eagerly she pulled him closer, and his mouth was on hers, hungrily. He pushed back her clothing until both breasts were free, and his hands caressed her. She tingled all over with the ecstasy of it.

He attempted to roll away from her. 'No, no, we mustn't,' he muttered, but she pulled him back.

'It's all right darling. We love each other. We'll be married soon. Don't leave me now. Please.' She held him close as her hand slid down between them to feel his hardness. Her eyes widened at the feel of him, and she drew in her breath sharply.

'David, I love you. I want you. I want you so much.'

'I can't fight it any longer.' He groaned as he began to remove her clothes.

Afterwards Joy was surprised at how much she'd enjoyed it. She'd been prepared to be hurt, but after the first sharp pain she felt nothing but a mounting delicious tension, like a surging tide inside her, pulling her upwards until she felt as if she was reaching, soaring ever higher until finally she reached the summit, and an explosion of cataclysmic proportion shook her to her very soul. Her moans of pleasure turned into one exultant cry of ecstasy, followed almost instantly by David's own cry.

As they lay together, naked in the warm sunlight, covered in sweat, Joy felt a wonderful languor seep through her body.

David turned to her. 'Are you all right?' he asked, concern on his face.

'I'm more than all right, I'm in seventh heaven.'
'Was it…all right for you?'
She ran her fingers gently across his chest. 'It was wonderful.'
His face lit up. 'Really?'
'Really.'
She could tell he was pleased that he could give her such pleasure, but then his face clouded over again. 'We shouldn't have done this. It's too dangerous. It mustn't happen again until we're married.'

Joy looked at him wide-eyed and slid her hand behind her back and crossed her fingers. 'It's all right darling. I wouldn't have let you if I didn't know it's a safe time for me. I read all about it in Grandma's women's health book. I studied it carefully.'

'Are you sure?'
'Absolutely,' she replied firmly. 'There are a few safe days in every month, and this is one of them.'
'Well, that's a relief.'
'So as long as we stick to these days we can come here whenever we want.'
'Well, I don't know…'
'Don't you want to?' She stared down at her hands, before raising eyes full of misery. 'Wasn't it any good for you? Wasn't I any good?'

'Darling!' He clasped her close again. 'It was wonderful. You were…are…wonderful. That has nothing to do with it. I'm just worried for your sake, that's all. You know what happened to Lily, I wouldn't want that to happen to you…to us. That's all.'

'Oh well,' Joy smiled happily. 'If that's all, then I'll be very careful to make sure we only come here when it's very safe.'

And David agreed, if somewhat reluctantly at first. So they kept their tryst on all the days she selected. And once he accepted her word that all would be well, great enjoyment for them both ensued.

When her monthlies appeared at the end of the first month, she was dismayed. But at the end of the next month, there was no sign of it, and, to her great joy, she started to feel sick. And any time she felt she'd been wicked to deceive David she pushed the feeling firmly away.

Chapter Two

Joy felt happy with the world as she left the house and walked down towards the horse paddocks. It was a calm, bright morning. The sun shone down from a cerulean sky and a light breeze ruffled the leaves on the trees. They were all happily settled in the new house now, with Grandma and Grandpa living there too, and Grandma and Mary running the household, just as it had all been before the fire. Except that she and David were married and living here as well, of course. All as she had planned.

The horses were all at Redwoods and Joy loved nothing better than spending time with them. The thoroughbreds were in the same paddock with the Redwoods' horses, including Blaze, her own horse that had been a present from David when they returned from England. They had decided to let them all mingle for the time being, for company and to teach them to socialise.

Joy closed the gate behind her before she called to the horses, and as they ambled up to her she opened the bag she had brought with her.

'Oh yes, I know what you lot all want,' she laughed as she reached inside for the carrots. After she distributed them to the eager horses she turned to her filly, Joy's Dream.

'And how are you today, my beauty?' She stroked her neck, and the horse whinnied and pushed her nose into the bag dangling from Joy's arm.

'Oh no, Dreamer, no more, you cheeky thing! You think you should have preferential treatment, do you?' She tossed the bag back over the fence, away from the prying nose.

Joy's Dream, or Dreamer as she called her, was the filly Kitty presented her with in England. She was a foal too young to be separated from her mother, so mare and foal had both come to Australia on board ship with the other horses purchased by the Cavanagh family. They had been bought for the purpose of extending their horse breeding programme to include thoroughbreds, as well as the 'Walers' that were the mainstay of their stud.

It was while in England visiting her grandparents for a London Season that Joy attended Royal Ascot racecourse with the rest of the Barron family. She was overwhelmed by all the excitement of the races and the thrill of seeing those magnificent animals thundering down the track, giving their all in their battle to win. It was then that she formed the ambition to breed thoroughbred racehorses herself. Her ambition was applauded by her grandfather, Sir Alexander Barron. So much so that he bought her a mare, Gay Lass, whose bloodline went back to Iambic, an early English champion.

The mare was put to Starlight, Rufe's stallion, before the horses left Riverside, the property that both Rufe and his brother Edward owned, and where the horses had been kept until Redwoods was ready for them. The vet confirmed the pregnancy, but it was early days yet. Bending over, Joy ran her hand gently along Gay Lass's belly, but she couldn't feel any sign of the life inside. Straightening up, she patted the horse's neck.

'Good girl,' she told her as she rubbed her ears. As she leaned over to lift her front hoof and check it, a sudden pain brought an involuntary cry from her and forced her upright.

'Oh my God.' She clutched her stomach. 'I think it's my time, old girl. I'm going to beat you by a mile.'

Memories of the pain she'd seen Lily endure at the birth of her baby, Benjamin, lent wings to Joy's feet as she hurried back to the house. Once there she surrendered herself gratefully to the care of her grandmother, while Mary raced across to the mill to alert David, and to send Patrick for the midwife.

David had a mixture of thoughts when Mary arrived at the mill, breathless, to tell him Joy was about to have the baby–delight that his baby was about to arrive, but also concern, first for his wife's comfort, for he'd heard tales of the horrors of childbirth, and real fear for her safety. Women sometimes died in childbirth!

Hurrying home post-haste, he hadn't known what to expect. He sat next to her, holding her hand. At first it had been all right, they sat together, drinking endless cups of tea and talking about their child. If it's a girl, will she go down to Sydney to St Catherine's School, where Joy was educated? If it's a boy will he want to stay here and work with the horses?

As each pain came, he held her hand, flinching because he was the cause of the ordeal she was going through, the cause of her suffering. When the pains came more often, they sent him from the room.

Bella came out later and coaxed him into the kitchen, where she set a meal of cold meat and pickles in front of him, but he wasn't hungry, and after a few mouthfuls he pushed his chair back and resumed his pacing.

When he heard Joy scream, much later, he rushed to the room, fear making his legs weak, and threw open the door. Mary moved quickly to take him by the arm.

'It's all right David. She's all right.' She propelled him gently but firmly out into the hall again, and pulled the door closed behind them. 'She's doing well. It won't be much longer now.'

His heart raced. 'Are you sure? She didn't sound all right.' His stomach tied itself into knots. 'I'm frightened, what if...?' he couldn't continue, the words stuck in his throat.

'There now,' she soothed. 'The baby's well on its way and everything's fine. You'll be a father in no time now.'

He gulped, and his heartbeat slowed a little. 'I had no idea it would be as bad as this for her.'

'Don't worry,' she patted his arm. 'It'll be over soon.'

At that moment Jack came in.

'I think David's in need of some support,' Mary told him. 'Everything's fine in there,' she motioned towards the closed door, 'but I think the father-to-be can probably do with a stiff drink right now.'

'Come on, mate.' Jack took him by the arm. 'The women know what they're doing, they're the experts in this field, and we'd best leave it to them. We blokes just need to keep out of the way.'

Jack led David into the sitting room and closed the door behind them. After settling him, he crossed the room to where a decanter and glasses sat on a table. Pouring two generous measures of whiskey into glasses, he handed one to David.

'Here, get this into you,' Jack urged him. 'It'll make you feel better.'

David accepted it gratefully. 'Thanks.' He took a gulp and felt the strong liquid course through him. 'I never knew it'd be this bad. I can't bear to think of what Joy's going through.'

'Did they say if it's going to be much longer?'

'Not long, they said. But do they really know?'

Jack shrugged. 'Women seem to know these things.'

David stared into his drink, thankful it began to calm the sense of panic he'd felt on hearing Joy's scream.

Jack started talking about clearing a large clump of cedar in an out-of-the-way part of the property, and how difficult it was. David listened without taking it all in, his ears strained for any sound from the other room, but grateful to Jack for trying to take his mind off what might be happening in there. He finished his drink and was wondering whether to have another when the door opened and a smiling Bella came into the room.

'I think you should go and see your wife and baby now,' she said.

David jumped up, his mouth suddenly dry. 'Is she all right?'

'Quite all right. Why don't you go and see for yourself?'

When he entered the room, he stopped. His breath caught at the sight of Joy propped up against the pillows, looking as if she had not a care in the world, and smiling down at the swaddled bundle in her arms.

Her smile deepened as she looked up and saw him.

'Come over and say hello to your beautiful daughter.'

For a moment David could only look at her, his heart full of love, wondering how she could appear so serene after what she had endured.

'Are you...all right?' he asked, as he moved to stand beside the bed.

Joy smiled up at him, eyes shining. 'I don't think I've ever been better in my whole life.'

He felt weak with relief. Suddenly his heart felt too big for his chest. Tears pricked his eyes as he leant down and kissed her tenderly.

'Isn't she the most beautiful thing you've seen in your life?' Joy stroked the baby's head tenderly.

David swallowed as he turned his attention to the tiny scrap of humanity in his wife's arms. All he could see above the rug that wrapped her was a petite, rather red face, topped by a soft fuzz of dark hair, with blue eyes that gazed solemnly up at Joy.

All at once the world was wonderful.

'She's almost as beautiful as her mother.' He smiled broadly.

'Oh no, she's more beautiful than I've ever been. She's perfect, all over. I've checked every bit of her.'

'So she has all her fingers and toes?' he teased.

'I told you, she's perfect.' She held the little bundle out to him. 'Here, you hold her.'

Gingerly he took his daughter, awkward as he tried to make the bundle fit in the crook of his arm, and terrified he might drop her, or squash her, but with a sense of wonderment as he looked at his child.

'Now, I've been thinking,' Joy continued.

'Yes?'

'I think we should call her Alexandra Wilhelmina. Alexander after my grandfather, and William after my father. You don't mind, do you?'

'Of course not.' He traced his finger gently around the face of the tiny infant. 'Alexandra Wilhelmina Cavanagh, a very influential sounding name for such a small person, but your grandfather will be pleased.'

'Yes, he will. Dear Grandfather, I must write and tell him.' She turned and plumped up the pillows at her back, then settled herself back comfortably against them. 'And now I'm really rather hungry. I wonder what Mary cooked us for dinner?'

The next morning David went about his work whistling. The world looked good. Their baby had been born, and Joy was safe and well. When Joy offered him the baby to hold, he'd been frightened to take her in case he dropped her, but she'd insisted. As he gazed down into that little face he'd felt the most incredible wave of love and wonder. This was his child. He and Joy had made this little person between them. He even felt glad then that Joy made the mistake about the so-called safe days when they were making love.

He was angry with her when she told him, asking her how it could have happened when she'd been so sure—he'd even had the terrible suspicion that she engineered the whole thing on purpose, just to get her own way. But she'd been so contrite, hardly daring to look at him when she told him, just standing there with her eyes down, twisting her hands together while she told him she must have been a day out in her calculations. And when she looked up at him with such a woebegone look on her face and tears in her eyes, he had to forgive her. He pulled her into his arms and told her not to cry, everything would be all right. And now it had all turned out for the best.

He pulled his mind back to the job as he walked down to inspect the pasture in the furthest paddock, the one he was considering moving the horses into next. The grass recovered well after the fire, and he didn't want to risk depleting the feed in any one paddock by leaving the horses there for too long. Better to rotate them, there was plenty of room and he intended to continue supplementing their diet with hay. It was good for them. He collected the hay and took it to the horses. When they finished the lot he went in search of Patrick to help him move the horses to the next paddock.

Chapter Three

Emma Hardy walked from room to room in the empty house, where sadness hung heavy in the air. It looked bare and forlorn with the furniture gone. The new owners were due to move in tomorrow, and that would be the end of it, the end of a fairy story that had become a horror tale.

Her memory went back eight years, to the happy time when she moved here as a bride. She'd been happy to leave her parents, and her brother David, and the family home at Riverside. She was madly in love with Matthew, her new husband, and he made it clear with his every action how much he adored her.

Things looked so rosy for them. He had a good job as an accountant with an old established firm in Melbourne and his prospects for advancement were good.

As Emma walked into the lounge room and ran her fingers along the marble mantel piece, she sighed, recollecting how she'd enjoyed furnishing their house, and how she took pride in keeping the house perfectly. She'd spent many happy hours in the garden and she always had a perfectly cooked meal waiting for Matthew when he came home from work.

They'd been married for two years when Matthew caught a bad cold. It was better in a couple of weeks, but it left him with a cough.

Finally he agreed to Emma's urging to see a doctor, and when he mentioned the dreaded word 'consumption' Emma felt as if the bottom dropped out of her world. She he could tell Matthew was worried, although he tried to not to show it.

In spite of treatment with a new wonder drug Matthew's cough became worse. Weeks dragged into months, while Emma watched her husband become pale, listless, and thin.

They made love less, he just didn't seem to have the strength, and when they did there was urgency to their love-making, as if each felt it was the one thing they had left that was good in their lives.

One evening when he came home from work Matthew told her he no longer had a job.

'I had a coughing fit in the office today, and Mr. Witherspoon said he'd been worried for a long time that I was really sick, and it's become too bad for him to ignore any longer. He said he's got to think of other people's health. It's not fair on the others that work there.' He grimaced. 'And he's right, of course. This is contagious. You shouldn't be here with me.'

Emma rushed to him and put her arms around him. 'Don't think for one moment that I'm ever going to leave you. You're going to get better.'

He held her away from him, his eyes full of concern. 'Emma, my darling heart, we have to face facts. I might not get better. I've been thinking about it. I think you'd be better off at Riverside with your parents.'

'Don't even think about it. I'm staying right here. I love you, and I'm staying to look after you. What do you think you'd do all on your own?'

'The doctor told me there are places for people with TB, sanatoriums, where they have treatment and are looked after.'

'No! Never! He said the tuberculin would fix you. We just have to be patient.'

Matthew shook his head. 'He never said it's a sure cure, just that they're having good results with it. It'll work just as well in a sanatorium.'

Emma wanted to scream, to shout and rail against the cruel fate that sent this terrible illness that was draining Matthew's life away. Instead she took a deep breath and looked away, clamping her teeth tight on her tongue, holding her mouth shut until that pain overcame the other, which was taking over her body. Then she set her lips and looked Matthew in the eyes. Her voice held only the slightest quiver when she spoke.

'I'm not going anywhere, so forget it.' She forced her stiff lips into a smile. 'You don't get rid of me that easily.'

Matthew pulled her to him again and buried his face in her hair. 'Oh my darling. I love you so much. What are we going to do?'

Emma pushed away the panic that threatened to engulf her. 'I'm going to make us both a cup of tea, and we'll have a bite to eat, and then we're both going to have an early night.'

When they had rested in bed for a while Emma turned and ran her hands gently over Matthew's face, and kissed him. When he responded slowly to her kiss, she began to stroke his body–his arms, his chest, his legs, and then back to his chest. When she felt the first stirring of his arousal, her hands went lower and caressed him slowly, sensuously, her eyes never leaving his face. When she saw the passion flare in his eyes she smiled at him, and relaxed as he turned and pulled her close, his lethargy gone. That was the night their son was conceived. And it was the last time they made love.

Emma tried to pull her thoughts away from that memory, for it made her remember how it had been in the beginning. Virginal when she married, they'd both been delighted to find, once the first tentative coupling was over, that she responded to Matthew's overtures with enthusiasm. Their love-making swept her away on a tide of passion, opening her to a world of unsuspected delights. She revelled in this side of their life together. When Matthew became so ill that he lost all sexual feelings it left her with a niggling sense of frustration to add to her other worries. And the fire of desire hadn't left her, but sometimes kept her awake with longing.

Coming back to the present, she felt ashamed she should be thinking of such things at a time like this. She grieved for Matthew, of course she did, but for the last few years she'd felt as if he'd become her child rather than her husband, while she was still a woman, with a woman's needs.

Although it never occurred to her during those long years, perhaps Matthew had been aware of her feelings, for the day before he died she sat with him, holding his hand as she read to him, when he asked her to stop reading for a moment.

'There's something I want to say my darling,' he said, his voice weak. 'I'm sorry to have caused you so much unhappiness these last years.' He shook his head as she tried to stop him. 'No, hear me out.' He took a deep breath. 'I want you to promise me something.'

Her voice seemed to choke her as she replied. 'What is it?'

'When I'm gone I want you to find someone. Someone who'll love you and take care of you, and who'll be a father to Johnnie, as I've never been able to.'

Something sharp twisted inside Emma. 'Don't darling, don't talk like that. I'll never love anyone else.'

His voice became stronger. 'This is important to me. I want you to find love again. Promise me you'll try, so I'll know there's a chance for you to be happy again.' He squeezed her hand, struggling to sit up. 'Promise me, please.'

Emma swallowed the lump in her throat. 'All right. I promise I'll try.'

He relaxed back again. 'Good.' He closed his eyes. 'Go on now, read some more,' he said, 'I love the sound of your voice.'

And she continued reading until he drifted off to sleep.

As she finished her last check of the rooms, Emma was surprised to find tears running down her cheeks. She thought she had no tears left, thought they'd all been shed over the past years of Matthew's illness. She'd refused to send him to a sanatorium and had nursed him to the end.

Drying her tears, she took one last look around the rooms before walking through the front door and closing it firmly behind her. Her mother would be here in a few moments with a cab, the first leg of her journey to Riverside. And then what? What future was there for her, thirty-three years old with a young child? Could she ever find anyone to replace Matthew, as he wished, or was she destined to spend the rest of her life as a lonely widow?

Chapter Four

Joy crossed to the window as she heard the sound of a buggy outside. Delighted to see Rufe and Kitty alighting, she put Alexandra back into her cradle and hurried to meet them. She was even more pleased when she saw they were accompanied by Emma, David's sister, whom she met briefly at their wedding, and her little boy, Johnnie.

'What a lovely surprise,' she called as she ran down the steps. 'How wonderful to see you all.' She hurried to her mother and embraced her, and then turned to the others with a happy smile.

'I hope we haven't come at an inconvenient time?' Kitty asked, removing her gloves while Rufe unloaded the cases. Emma stood to one side, holding her son's hand as he looked around.

'Of course not. Your room is always ready.'

Joy turned to Emma. 'Oh Emma, how are you? I'm so pleased to see you.' She put her hand on the young woman's arm, not knowing how to show her sympathy. 'I was so very sorry to hear about Matthew, I know it must be terrible for you.'

'It's all right Joy. It's becoming easier all the time. And I have Johnnie for comfort.'

Joy squeezed her arm. 'Of course.' She bent down until she was on Johnnie's level.

'Hello Johnnie. I'm so pleased you've come to stay with us. Now we'll all be able to get to know each other, won't we?'

'Are we going to stay for a long time?' he asked seriously.

'I hope so.'

'Will Mummy be here too?'

'Yes.'

'Then I'll stay too.'

'Good.' Smiling at him, Joy stood up. 'Then let's go inside, you're just in time to relax a bit before dinner. And to see the baby.' She took Johnnie's hand. 'And you can come and meet your new cousin Alexandra.'

In the nursery Joy lifted Alexandra from her crib. She sat in a chair with the baby on her knee so Johnnie could see her properly.

'She's not very big,' he said, reaching out a tentative hand to touch the tiny arm that was waving around.

'No,' Joy told him, 'she's very young yet, but she'll grow bigger, and then you'll be able to play with her.'

He nodded and turned his attention back to the baby, holding out a finger to touch the waving hand. Alexandra curled her tiny pink fingers around it and gurgled, her eyes on his face.

Johnnie smiled. 'She likes me. See, she's wants to play now.'

'I'm sure she does.'

Johnnie turned his attention back to the baby. 'Do you want me to stay and play with you?' Taking her gurgle as consent he jiggled her hand. 'See, she does.'

Joy felt a surge of affection for the little boy. 'You're her only cousin, you know. I hope you'll always be good friends.'

'We will.' He nodded.

'You're older than her, so perhaps you'll take care of her when you're both growing up.'

'I'll have to 'cause she's littler than me.'

'Can you say her name? It's quite long, isn't it?' She articulated it slowly. 'Alexandra?'

Johnnie struggled but finally came out with it. 'Xandra,' he said proudly.

Joy laughed. 'Well done. Xandra it is.'

And somehow, very soon, she became Xandra to everyone.

It was a happy group that gathered around the dinner table. After discussions of the baby were over and Johnnie's progress commented on, Jack turned to Rufe.

'So, what's been happening down in Sydney?' he asked. 'We're not privy to the latest goings-on up here, you know. We only know what we read in the newspapers.'

The conversation turned to politics, with Rufe filling them in on the latest inside news from Sydney. Most of the talk concerned Federation, and how it was working now all the colonies were joined together under a central Federal government. But it was not without much wrangling between the States.

Finally Rufe spread his hands, smiling. 'Ah well, so much for politics.' He paused.' As a matter of fact, there's a matter of business I want to discuss with you, David, regarding Redwoods.'

Joy's interest quickened.

'Oh. What is it?' David asked.

'I had a look around as we drove in. Everything seems to have recovered pretty well from the fire.'

'Yes, the grazing land's re-grown, and I've seeded additional pasture. It's all coming on well.'

'Good. Do you think you could run extra horses in another month or so?'

'Why are you asking?'

'With the war in South Africa raging, I've had a request from the army to see if I can supply them extra horses each month. Our supply is getting low, but I've been in touch with a couple of the big stations up north, and they can supply whatever we want. It's a matter of having space to keep them while we work with them. Some of them have been more or less running wild, and they need a bit of gentling before they can be sent. How do you feel about taking some? It's a lucrative business, supplying the army.'

Excitement grabbed Joy. It would mean additional income while they were establishing the thoroughbred programme. She frowned when David hesitated.

'Well, I'm not sure, it'd mean a lot of extra work. I'm not sure we could cope.'

Joy turned to him. 'It's a wonderful offer, David. If we had an extra hand I'm sure we could manage.'

'I'm not sure if I could find anyone locally who knows enough about horses.'

'Perhaps we could find someone to help with the other work, and Patrick could spend all his time with you and the horses,' Joy suggested. 'It's such a good offer; we'd be fools to refuse.'

David looked a little cross by her intervention. 'I'm not sure...' he began hesitantly.

'There are plenty of local lads who'd be glad of a job.' She turned to Jack. 'And you could easily train one of them to help in the mill, couldn't you?'

'Yes, that wouldn't be a problem, and we often have enquiries for work.'

'So there you are,' Joy said, 'and we know Patrick likes working with the horses, so there's no problem.'

David wouldn't go against her in front of Mother, even if he was annoyed. He didn't seem to realise Rufe was making the offer out of generosity, and she couldn't bear to lose it.

'So what do you think?' Rufe asked David.

'When could we expect it to happen?'

'Within the next few months. The first lot are on their way down, and we can split it in two.'

David's lips tightened a fraction, but he didn't argue. 'Very well. I'll start fencing off another paddock right away.'

Joy dropped her eyes. After all, it was for the good of Redwoods.

Joy was sorry when Rufe announced the next day at breakfast that he needed to return to Sydney the following day.

'With Federation in full swing I'm really needed down there,' he told her.

'And I'm missing little Ben,' Kitty added. 'I know he's in good hands with both Alice Preston and Mrs. Frobisher there to fuss over him, but I've been away from him for longer than I like to leave him.'

'I'll miss you, all of you,' Joy told them. She turned to Emma. 'Do you have to go too? Couldn't you and Johnnie stay longer?'

Emma's face lit up. 'There's no real reason why not, if you really want me to.'

'Oh I do. We're just getting to know each other properly.'

'Yes, why don't you stay, Sis,' David chimed in. 'You're good company for each other, and you'll only be going back to stay with Mum and Dad, and Johnnie's probably spent too much time with them already.'

'I'd really love to stay. Thank you.'

'Then that's decided,' Rufe said.

Joy smiled happily. Not that she didn't love Grandma, but it would be good to have another woman closer to her own age in the house.

Chapter Five

David was taking a salt block to the horse paddock when he saw one of the horses lying on the ground, rolling from side to side. Alarmed, he hurried toward the gate. Then he noticed another horse down, while yet another was showing signs of distress, pawing the ground so hard it had scraped off the grass, its hoof sending spurts of dirt flying.

'What the hell's going on here?' he asked aloud, breaking into a run.

Dropping down beside the rolling horse he tried to hold it still, but, with sweat pouring from it, the horse pulled from his grasp. Jumping to his feet, he looked around the paddock. Two more horses were showing signs of discomfort, one lying on its back, and the other tossing its head up and down.

Hurrying to the one that was pawing the ground, he felt its pulse. Way too fast, and the skin felt hot to the touch. Then he leaned his head against its belly, listening for sounds from the intestines. Hardly a sound. This was not good. These horses were sick. What could have happened to them?

He whistled and shouted to Patrick, who came running. Between them, they managed to hold the rolling horse still enough for David to check its pulse, while Patrick spoke soothingly to it.

'Too fast,' David frowned, and put his ear against its belly.

'I can't hear any sound,' he told Patrick, shaking his head. 'That means colic. We need to get him up on his feet, and get him moving.'

Between them, they coaxed the horse to his feet, and Patrick began to lead him around while David checked the others that were distressed.

'Colic!' he called out, grim faced. 'They've all got colic. We've got to keep them all walking, and we'll have to give them all an oil and water mix. We'll need help, go and call some of the others to come.'

All that afternoon they walked the sick horses round and round. At intervals David forced a rubber syringe down each throat and squirted in a solution, the known treatment for colic

As evening drew close all but one horse had been returned to the paddock, the helpers had left, and the only horse still sick was the one that David had noticed first, the one that had been rolling badly. After checking his vital signs and feeling the belly again, David shook his head, frowning.

After administering a second dose they resumed the walking, taking it in turns now. But as time passed the horse became progressively weaker, its breathing shallower, and its temperature and pulse rate increased. Its walking slowed. Finally, in spite of all their efforts to keep it moving, it stopped, teetered, and dropped to the ground.

'Oh Jesus.' Patrick gasped as they both crouched down beside it.

David attempted to lift its head, but as he did it drew one final, wheezing breath, moved its head weakly, and then dropped back again, all life gone.

David sat back on his haunches. 'He's gone,' he said wearily.

'Jesus, I'm sorry.'

'We did all we could. No one could have done more.' He stood up. 'Come on mate, come up to the house. I think we both deserve a drink.'

As David rose he narrowed his eyes. 'I want to know what caused this. For six horses to go down like that, all at the same time, it has to be something they ate. Before we go, let's check the feed.'

He led the way into the store room where the hay was kept. Pushing open the unlocked door he went across to the closest bundle of hay, with Patrick following. He began picking up the stalks, a few at a time, scrutinising them before placing them on the floor alongside the stack. After removing the top layer he picked up a crushed weed lying in amongst the hay. He turned it over in his fingers, uttering an angry oath. He handed it to Patrick and rummaged further, finding several more plants.

'Ragwort! Bloody ragwort! How did that get in here? It could've killed the whole lot of them!'

'How could ragwort have got in amongst the hay?' Joy asked a little later, when they all gathered in the sitting room to discuss what had happened.

David shook his head. 'It's a mystery. There were bits of it right through the top half of what was left of the stack, but nothing further down. And nothing in any of the other bundles.'

'And was that the stack you took the feed from?'

'Yes. And neither Patrick nor I have any idea how it could possibly be there. We checked the rest, all the bundles, and found no more.'

'And we don't have ragwort growing on the property,' Patrick told them. 'I swear I know every inch of ground and there's none, I'd stake my life on it.'

'Could it possibly have come in on a delivery cart, or some such thing?' Emma asked.

David frowned. 'I suppose it's possible. But if so, how would it have found its way into the feed?'

No one had an answer for that, and in the end, after much discussion, it was decided it was impossible to fathom, but that in future each lot of feed must be checked before it was fed to the horses.

'Do you think the ragwort was deliberately put into the feed, David?' Bella asked.

'I've thought about it. It's possible, of course. But who could have done it without being seen?'

'Someone could easily slip into the store room without attracting attention. No one would think anything of it.'

'Not if it was someone who has a right to be here, but a stranger would be noticed.'

'Unless it was done at night,' Emma added.

Joy nodded. 'Yes. It could be done.'

'But who would have a reason? Most of the men have been here for years–none of them would do it.' David paused. 'First the fire, now this. Can there be someone who has a grudge against us?'

Joy spent a restless night, tossing and turning as she wished morning would come. What if Gay Lass, pregnant with her precious progeny, had eaten some of the poisonous plant? Or Dreamer, or any of the other thoroughbreds? She woke at daybreak and as soon as she'd fed and bathed Xandra, she hurried down to the horses, anxiety speeding her steps. David and Patrick were there before her, both with one horse, a little apart from the rest. The horse was Gay Lass! Patrick was standing by her head, holding it while she tried to the pull away, and David had his ear by her belly. With her heart beating wildly, Joy ran the rest of the way.

'What's the matter?' she cried, as she came through the gate.

David had a worried frown on his face.

'She must have eaten some of the ragwort. When we came in she was pawing the ground and tossing her head.'

'Oh my God! How bad is she?'

'It's hard to tell yet. Her pulse rate's up. The foal makes it a bit harder for me to listen for sounds, but there's not much, I'm afraid. I think we'd better get her moving, and get some oil into her.'

'Is that safe, in her condition?'

'Safer than not doing it. Let's get her back to the stable and get started. We don't want to waste any time.' He led the horse towards the gate, with the mare tossing her head and pulling on the lead, and Joy walked alongside, talking soothingly to her.

After the oil was administered, they took it in turns to walk Gay Lass round and round the yard. Most of the morning passed and then, finally, they were rewarded.

'Thank God,' Joy breathed, looking at the steaming mound of manure. 'Do you think she'll be all right now?'

'I think so.' David nodded, with some of the strain leaving his face.

'Are any of the other horses showing any signs of sickness?'

'No. Let's hope this is the end of it, and that we don't have any more trouble.'

They woke three days later to find horses wandering all over the property, with all the horse paddocks' gates left open, and no one could say who had opened them. It seemed like another baffling accident.

Chapter Six

Joy answered a knock at the door and smiled as she saw their visitor—a tall, well built man approaching late middle age, with even features and dark hair showing streaks of grey.

'Why, Mr. Osborne, this is a nice surprise. Do come in.' She opened the door wide. 'It's months since we've seen you.'

'Yes, I've been busy at the yard. Haven't had the time to get out and about much.'

'Well, it's good to see you. We're just about to have morning tea. Come and join us.'

'Thank you. I'm on my way into town, but I thought I'd just call in to say hello.' He followed her down the hall and into the sitting room.

Bella rose from her chair as they entered, holding out her hand.

'Mr. Osborne, how nice to see you.'

'A pleasure to be here again, Mrs.. Morgan.'

After they shook hands, Joy turned to Emma.

'Allow me to introduce you to my sister-in-law, Emma Hardy, David's sister.'

After the introductions, Bella poured the tea.

Osborne took the cup she offered him and sat back in his chair. 'Well now, this is very pleasant.' He sipped his tea. 'And how are the horses, Joy? Are your thoroughbreds coming along well?'

'Yes, they're doing well. But we had a nasty incident a couple of weeks ago, and we lost one of the Walers.'

'Dear me, whatever happened?'

'Ragwort got into the feed somehow, and we had several horses come down with colic.'

'That's terrible. How did it happen?'

'We don't know. It must have an accident, though how it got into the feed we've no idea. It's hard to believe anyone would do it with the intention of harming them. And then a few days later all the paddock gates were left open so the horses could get out, and no one knows how that happened, either.'

'Good heavens, surely no one would do those things on purpose, and accidents do happen.' He took a sip of tea, frowning. 'And you lost a Waler, you say?'

'Yes, we did. And Gay Lass, one of the thoroughbreds, was amongst those that were sick, and she's with foal. She seems all right now, but we can't be sure the foal won't be affected until it's born.' Joy's throat tightened. 'I just wish we could know for sure it was an accident. It's bad enough, the loss, but not knowing, that's the worst. First the fire, and now this, it's terribly unsettling.'

'I'm sure it must have been an accident,' Osborne soothed. 'No one would do such a thing.' He took another sip. 'And your poor mother, I suppose she's upset by all this?'

'Yes, I've just had a letter from her. She's terribly worried.'

'I'm sure it must have been an accident,' he repeated. 'Unless, of course, there's some madman on the loose.'

Bella interrupted them. 'That's not likely, is it? But let's not dwell on it now. We must hope there are no more such incidents.' She picked up a plate of cake from the table. 'Please try a piece of this cake, Mr. Osborne.'

'Thank you.'

'Excellent, as always.' He smiled, before turning his attention back to Joy. 'And how is your mother? Is she enjoying living down in Sydney?'

'Oh yes, she's very happy down there, although she still comes up here whenever she can. Of course she's much busier now she has little Benjamin, and she doesn't have a lot of time to spare.'

Mr. Osborne cleared his throat. 'No, of course not.' He turned to Emma. 'And is that your little boy I saw playing outside just now, Mrs. Hardy?'

'Yes, that's my son, Johnnie.'

'A fine little fellow. How old is he?'

'He's four years old now.'

'And is your husband here with you? '

'I'm afraid I lost my husband a few months ago.'

'Oh, I am sorry to hear that. Please accept my condolences. It must be a great comfort to you that you have your son.'

'Indeed it is.'

He sighed. 'I wasn't lucky enough to be blessed with children. I lost my wife some years ago and I've often thought how much I would love to have had a child. But it wasn't meant to be.'

'It's never too late,' Emma told him. 'Perhaps it'll happen in the future.'

'Oh no, a crusty old bachelor like me, I don't think anyone would want me now.'

'What nonsense, Mr. Osborne, you've plenty of time yet. Look at what happened to me,' Bella told him with a smile.

'Ah well, one never knows, I suppose.' He put down his empty cup, and stood. 'And now I must be on my way into town. Thank you for the tea, ladies.' He turned to Emma. 'It's been a pleasure to meet you, Mrs. Hardy. Will you be staying for long?'

'Yes, for a while, I expect.'

'Then I hope I'll have the pleasure of seeing you again. And of meeting Johnnie too, when I have a little more time.'

'I hope so too, Mr. Osborne.'

Emma was out in the garden with Johnnie a couple of days later, enjoying the sunshine, when she heard the sound of an approaching rider and was surprised to see Harry Osborne dismounting.

Catching sight of her he approached, carrying what appeared to be a long stick.

'Good morning, Mrs. Hardy,' he greeted her. 'I noticed your little boy playing at horses the other day when I was here, and I hope you don't mind but I made this for him.'

He held the stick out to her, and she saw it was not just a stick, but a toy horse, complete with a carved wooden head and small handles at the sides, just right for a child to hold on to. The body, slim enough to fit between a small boy's legs, was fashioned from a straight piece of tree branch, smoothed all around and fitted with wheels at the base.

Emma was both pleased and surprised.

'Why Mr. Osborne, how very thoughtful of you.' She turned the gift over in her hands, marvelling at the details of the horse's face and the flowing mane. 'It's beautifully done, did you do all the carving yourself?'

'Yes.'

'It must have taken you quite some time.'

'Just a couple of nights, that's all. I enjoyed doing it. '

'And do you do much carving?'

'Yes. I find it relaxing these days, after a day's work. Fills in the time too.'

Emma ran her finger over the horse's flaring nostrils. 'It's very lifelike. Where did you learn to do such fine work?'

'My father taught me when I was a boy. It's all a part of boat building, you know.'

'Of course.' She handed the horse back to him, smiling. 'Here, you give this to Johnnie. He's been eyeing it off ever since he saw it, and it's only right he should know it's from you.'

Osborne took it with a nod, and crouched down beside Johnnie. 'Here you are Johnnie. Let's get you seated on your new horse.'

Johnnie's face shone as he straddled it. 'What's his name?' he asked.

'Perhaps we could name him together. If you had a pony, what would you call him?'

'Trumper,' he answered promptly. He looked up at Emma. 'I'm going to get a pony, aren't I Mummy?'

'Yes, when you're a bit older.'

'When I'm six,' he said earnestly. 'And he's going to be called Trumper.'

'You haven't thanked Mr. Osborne, Johnnie. What do you say?'

'Thank you.' He looked up with shining eyes. 'And now I'm going for a ride. Giddyup, Trumper, giddyup.' Johnnie galloped away. 'He can go really fast,' he called. 'Watch me.'

'I'm watching,' Emma called out to him before turning to Osborne. 'Thank you, Mr. Osborne. That'll give him hours of pleasure.'

'Think nothing of it. I'm glad to see he likes it.' He paused for a moment. "Perhaps you would give me the pleasure of taking you and your little boy for a drive one day? He might be interested to come to the boat yard and see the boats being built.'

'Why, thank you, it's very kind of you. I'm sure he'd enjoy that.'

'Good. We have a boat being built now that'll be safe to inspect inside soon. He might enjoy seeing it.'

'I'm sure he would.'

'Good.' He doffed his hat. 'Then I'll be on my way now. I'll see you again soon.'

Joy emerged from the house at that moment and her eyes widened as she saw him walking away. She looked at Emma. 'Mr. Osborne. What was he doing here?'

'He came to bring Johnnie this horse he made for him.' She gestured towards Johnnie, who was now sitting down examining the horse's face intently, tracing its detail with his finger. 'Wasn't that kind of him?'

'It certainly was.'

'He seems very nice. You've known him for a long time, you said?'

'Yes, all my life really, and he's always been nice. In fact, when I was young, I used to think Mother might marry him. I once overheard her and Grandma talking and I know he asked her, but she told him she didn't want to marry again. He was pretty keen on her; he used to be around here a lot. Until, of course, she met Rufe again, and married him, and that was the end of that.'

'I see,' Emma continued, watching Johnnie with the horse. 'It's a wonder he hasn't found someone else by now.'

'I guess he's never found anyone else he liked enough.'

'Look at Trumper, Auntie Joy,' Johnnie called out. 'He's called Trumper and he can go fast.' He jumped up. 'Watch me, I'm riding Trumper and he's going to win a race.' Off he galloped again, looking back to make sure they were watching him. 'Giddyup, giddyup.'

'Well,' said Joy, smiling. 'It seems his present is a great hit with Johnnie.'

'Yes, it certainly is.'

A few days later Harry Osborne invited Emma and Johnnie to join him for a drive and a visit to his boatyard. When they returned Johnnie was clutching a small model boat, his face alight with pleasure as he pointed out all its features to Joy.

'And I saw two boats just being built, and there's one same as this.' He held his trophy up for her to inspect. ' Mr. Osborne said I can go and see them again when they're finished.'

'Well now, that's really good of him, isn't it?'

'Yes, and he gave me some sweets too.'

'It sounds as if you had a good day. Do you like Mr. Osborne?'

'Yes, he's nice.'

'That's good.' Joy patted his head. 'I think Xandra is awake now, if you want to see her.'

'Yes, I'll show her my new boat.'

As he ran off Joy turned to Emma. 'And how about you? Did you enjoy the day too?'

'Not as much as Johnnie, I'm afraid, but, yes, it was quite pleasant.'

The following week Harry Osborne called again with sweets for Johnnie, and somehow he managed to call in at least once a week from then on, often with some little trifle for Johnnie, and he went out of his way to arrange outings, always including the boy.

Joy was delighted to find that she and Emma were forming a close friendship. They found that they thought alike in many ways, and liked and disliked similar things. As each had grown up as only daughters in their respective families they had both missed out on having a sister to share things with, and Joy began to feel a friendship with Emma that she'd not experienced before. So, when she entered the sitting room one afternoon to find Emma sitting on the couch crying softly, she felt an immediate rush of anxiety for her friend.

'Emma!' She crossed the room to sit beside her. 'Whatever's the matter?'

'Oh nothing really.' Emma sniffed, looking up with reddened eyes. 'I'm just being silly.' She blew her nose, gave another sniff, and hiccupped. 'Oh dear, I'm sorry you found me like this, and it really is nothing. I'm just being weak and stupid.'

Joy put her arm around her shoulders. 'Do you want to talk about it?'

Emma swallowed. 'It really is just being pathetic. I know you can't turn back the clock, so it's no use crying over it. And I have to think of Johnnie.'

Joy took her hand. 'You've been so brave. You must feel lonely without Matthew, but you never complain. I don't think I could be so brave if I lost David. If you want to talk about it, go right ahead.'

Again Emma's eyes filled with tears. 'Oh Joy, we've become such good friends, perhaps...well...you and David are so happy, you'll probably understand. I do miss Matthew terribly, not the way he was at the last, I'm happy he's finished suffering, but the way it was before, when he was well. When I lie in bed at night, I miss having him there alongside me, to cuddle up to, to...' she hesitated, and a flush crept across her face, 'to love me...if you know what I mean.'

Her flush deepened and Joy squeezed her hand.

'Don't be embarrassed, I know what you mean. Women aren't supposed to care about such things, I know, but we do care, don't we? How can we not, if we love a man? And why shouldn't we take pleasure in love? Why should it only be men who are supposed to enjoy it? I know I enjoy our love-making and I can certainly understand how you must feel. I know if anything happened to David, God forbid, I'd be the same. It's only natural for you to feel like this.'

'It's such a relief to hear you say that.' Emma's face lost some of its distress. 'I've been thinking I must be some sort of depraved woman for having such thoughts.' She bit her lip. 'Is it wrong of me to wish for someone else to love me like that?'

'Of course not. It's perfectly natural. You mustn't think otherwise.'

Emma twisted her fingers together, and Joy waited for her to continue.

'There's something else,' she went on hesitantly. 'You see, it's Harry Osborne. He's much older than me, and I can't think of him in that way. In fact, if I think about him making love to me, it...well, it quite sickens me, to be honest.' She twisted the handkerchief in her fingers. 'But where am I going to find someone more attractive? A widow in my thirties with a young child? There are only married men or widowers left, and it seems that men always look for a woman younger than themselves.'

'Has he mentioned marriage?'

'Not directly, but he hints at it. When he asked me if I thought of marrying again, I put him off by telling him I couldn't even begin to think about it until after another year since I lost Matthew. That's bought me some time.' She sighed. 'But he's very good with Johnnie; I think he really likes him. And Johnnie needs a father.'

Joy felt a terrible sympathy for Emma, but there didn't seem to be an answer to her problem. Unless she met someone more to her liking, she would have to make a decision when the time came.

'Then I suppose you can only continue as you are, and hope that you'll make the right decision when the time comes. But you must think of yourself as well as Johnnie.'

'Yes, I suppose so. I suppose it would be worse if there was no one who wanted me.' Her face brightened, and she laid her hand on Joy's arm. 'It's been such a relief to talk to you about it.'

Joy hugged her. 'Well, look at it this way. If you decide to accept him, you and Johnnie would be well looked after. But if you don't, you'll both always have a home here, and I'd miss you so much if you leave, so I'll be selfish and say I hope you stay.'

'Thank you for that, and for listening to me. I feel much better now.' She stood. 'Let's go and have some tea. I happen to know Mary baked this morning. I wonder what kind of cake she made?'

'A cup of tea and a slice of cake. The panacea for all ills.' Joy smiled, as they headed towards the kitchen.

Chapter Seven

David noticed the postmark on the letter before he opened it. 'Well, well, here's a surprise,' he announced, before slitting the envelope and withdrawing the sheets inside.

'What is?' Joy asked, looking up as she fastened the last pin in Xandra's nappy. 'Who's it from?'

'From Mrs. Winston Paget-Smythe, of Talahousie Stud, Kentucky USA, according to the return address.'

'Oh my goodness! From Lily?'

'I assume so, but let me check.' Unfolding the pages he scanned the last page before looking up. 'Yes, it's from Lily.' He looked again at the envelope. 'It was addressed to me at Riverside and forwarded here.'

'Of course, she doesn't know you're here now, or even that we're married.' Joy watched impatiently as he read. 'Well, what does she say?'

'She's married and very happy. The Paget-Smythes own a large, well established thoroughbred stud in Kentucky, and they live there. They have their own house apart from his parent's main home.' He continued reading. 'She goes on to say that Talahousie Stud has bred dozens of winners, and has a champion stallion called Knightly standing there now.' He looked up suddenly with a smile. 'Well, it seems they want to offer me a job.'

Joy's eyes widened. 'What? She wants you to go over there?'

David laughed. 'Yes, she says...' he read aloud, 'I know you like working with your father but you would find it so exciting to be part of this big operation, it is really big time. I have been telling the family all about you and they are very impressed, and would love to have you working here. They would pay you handsomely. Please say you will come David. At least come over and have a look.' He looked up. 'Well, what do you think of that?'

'What a cheek. She slips off in the middle of the night and runs away to America with Paget-Smythe, leaving her baby behind, and then acts as if nothing's happened. And expects you to come and join her!'

'Yes, a bit casual, I must say.'

'Hmmph. She has some hope! What else does she say? Does she ask about Benjamin?'

'No. She's had a baby, a sweet little daughter, she says, named Caroline, after her husband's mother.'

'So she didn't need to leave Benjamin behind and run away.' Joy fumed. 'I always suspected it was because she didn't want Paget-Smythe to know she was pregnant that made her so insistent on leaving London before it became obvious.' She paused, her mind going back. 'I wonder who the real father is,' she mused. 'Mrs. Frobisher suggested it might have been one of the three army men who were at staying at Bournbridge Hall over Christmas, and she could be right. Lily certainly liked to be with them.'

David shrugged. 'It's unlikely we'll ever know now.'

'I suppose so. I did wonder if it could have been my Uncle Hector. I saw him going downstairs one night when Lily was missing from her bed, but she swore she hadn't been meeting him.'

'He'd be a good bit older than her, wouldn't he?'

'Yes, but he's quite good-looking, and they were all very dashing in their uniforms. Lily certainly thought so.'

'Well, unless she decides to reveal who it was, we'll never know. And it wouldn't do much good to rake it all up again. Everyone's happy with the way things are now. Benjamin's happily settled with Kitty and Rufe, and only those close to them know they've adopted him, and that he's not their own child who was born while they were in England. And hopefully that's how it stays.'

'Yes, you're right.' Joy brightened. 'So what else does Lily have to say?'

'Not a lot more. It's all about the stud and the horses.'

'Well, she won't be happy when she knows we're married, and you have our own stud, and that you won't be going to join her.'

David folded the letter and put it back in the envelope and slipped it into his pocket. 'No, he said thoughtfully, 'although I must say I'd like to see it someday. It sounds outstanding.' He grasped her hand, laughing. 'You'd better treat me well, now you know I've had an offer from America, or I might decide to pay her a visit, just to see what it's like.'

'What? And leave your darling daughter Xandra? She hasn't got a hope.'

As David went about his work over the next few days all thoughts of Lily and America were pushed from his mind by the arrival of a telegram from Rufe telling him to expect the imminent arrival of the horses he'd promised to send, and to alert him to the fact that amongst them was a stallion that needed strong handling, and extra secure housing.

He checked all the paddock fences once again to make sure everything was secure. Then he enlisted Patrick's help to erect higher, stronger fences, and a gate secured by heavy bolts around an enclosure they formed a little way from the main paddocks. Then they built a single stall inside it. Once finished, David went around testing it all for strength once more, and stood back with his hands on his hips surveying their work.

'Well, that should hold the bugger, no matter how big and strong he is.'

'I reckon! He'd have to be Hercules to break out of there. I wonder how come there's a stallion with them. I'd have expected them all to be geldings or mares.'

'Rufe just said in his telegram I might want to keep him.'

'Sounds like he could be something special, more than your usual brumby.'

'I guess we'll know when they arrive.'

'I guess so.'

They didn't have long to wait, for three days later, as the long afternoon was drawing to a close, a noise like a long and continuous roll of distant thunder, accompanied by shouts and the barking of dogs, alerted them to the arrival of the mob. At the head of the cavalcade came Josh Frazer, who had come from England with the horses, and stayed to work at Riverside. He was mounted on his own horse and leading another. Behind him came a string of some twenty or more horses of different colours and sizes, with outriders and their dogs keeping control.

Even as David registered that Joy, mounted on Blaze, was alongside him to greet them, it was the stallion led by Frazer that took his attention. A superb specimen of horseflesh, he stood slightly taller than Frazer's mount. At a glance David estimated the stallion at close to seventeen hands, with a powerful chest, deep girth, and strong hindquarters. With a coat of dark brown dappled with black, a flowing black mane and tail, and black-tipped muzzle, he was a horse that would always catch the eye. He looked calm enough now as he cantered at the head of the mob, but the swish of his tail as they slowed signalled he was alert and wary.

David waved to Frazer to follow him as he wheeled his horse around and led them to the new enclosure. Once the stallion was safely settled there he guided the men to the paddocks he'd prepared for the rest of the mob.

After all the horses were safely installed in their new home, most of the men who accompanied them opted to go into Bulahdelah and sample the refreshments on offer there at the Plough Inn. But Josh Frazer accepted David's offer to join them in the house. The talk centred on the new arrivals as Josh sat with David and Joy in the sitting room for a pre-dinner drink.

'Yes, they've all been broken in, at some time or another,' he replied to a question from Joy, 'but none of them have been ridden much, from what I can gather. You have to remember they've been running loose on the station up north, which is why they need to be ridden a fair bit now so they'll be manageable when they're passed on to the army.'

'The stallion is a magnificent horse, do you know if he's ever been ridden?' David asked.

'He's been broken in, of course, and I saw your father take him out for a gallop during the couple of days they were at Riverside on their way here, but he said it takes a strong rider to control him. I've been given a message to pass on to you, that he's a present from your father and your uncle to you both, to use in your own breeding if that's the way you want to go.'

'Please thank them for me, it's a very generous gift, and I appreciate it. He's a wonderful animal. I'll start by getting him used to being ridden, though. I don't like the idea of him being too wild when there are so many people nearby.'

Frazer nodded. 'Very wise.'

'Does he have a name?' Joy asked.

'Not that I'm aware of.'

'With his size and colouring he looks like thunder.' She turned to David. 'What do you think? Shall we call him Thunder?'

He smiled at her, seeing she was excited by the horse. 'If you like.'

'Then Thunder he is.'

'Yes, he's rather like a thunderbolt,' Frazer agreed. 'You'll find he can go like the wind. I envy you; I'd love to have him for mine.'

Joy's eyes shone. 'Oh, I can't wait to ride him. Maybe he'll even turn out to be fast enough to race.'

David's stomach flipped. 'Don't even think about getting on him. It would be too dangerous. He'd be far too strong and hard for you to handle.'

Her mutinous expression told him she wasn't happy with his rebuke.

'We'll see,' she retorted, lifting her chin. 'After all, he's a gift to both of us.' She paused. 'Of course I expect to wait until he's used to being ridden, I wouldn't try just yet,' she added in a conciliatory tone.

'Not then or ever, Joy.' David managed to keep his voice calm, in spite of the churning inside of him at the thought of her being thrown and trampled by the huge horse. 'He's the type that's dangerous if he thinks you can't control him. And he'd know.'

'I'm well aware of horse psychology, thank you,' she replied, rising from her chair. 'And now I must go and see how dinner is coming along.'

Taking a deep breath, David watched her leave the room, knowing he'd upset her, but determined not to give in to her on this point. It was far too dangerous.

Remembering their guest, he turned to him with a half-smile. 'Time for a second drink before dinner, I believe.'

The rest of the evening passed cordially enough, but that night, as they prepared for bed, they had their first real argument, all about Thunder, with neither wanting to yield. Of course, they reached a truce eventually, when David put out a tentative arm to touch her as they lay stiff and silent in bed.

She turned to him and whispered, 'Oh David, let's not quarrel.'

What a brute he was for upsetting her, especially in front of a guest! He took her in his arms, and they made glorious love. But, afterwards, he had the feeling something had changed; there was a slight shift–oh ever so slight–in the way their marriage was.

Chapter Eight

The delivery date to the army for the new horses was set at three months from the date of their arrival, and so the days became exceedingly busy on Redwoods, being devoted to making sure the new horses became used to being ridden, and learnt their manners before being sent overseas.

Joy insisted on spending her days with the men, riding almost all day, and taking her part in the feeding and grooming work as well, in spite of David's objections.

'You should be inside with Xandra. She's barely a year old, crawling all over the place, and even trying to walk. Your place is with her.'

Joy shook her head. 'We're equal partners, remember? And that means sharing the work as well the benefits. And it's only for three months, and Emma just loves looking after Xandra, when she can manage to get her away from Grandma or Mary. They all dote on her, you know that, even little Johnnie, so she's in no danger of being neglected.'

Joy didn't tell him she'd far rather be out here with the horses than inside with her daughter and the other women. And she didn't tell him when, only three weeks after the horses had arrived, her monthlies failed to arrive,, and she thought she might be pregnant again. After all, perhaps it might be a false alarm, better to wait until she was sure.

When the next month came, and she was sure, she decided that, as there were only a few weeks until the horses left, she would put off telling him until then.

After all, it wouldn't do any harm, and she was so enjoying being part of the effort going into preparing the horses. She loved nothing better than galloping around the countryside on whichever horse David decided on for the day, and if she had the fun of that, then she believed she should also help with the other jobs that needed doing too. She often fell into bed tired out, but it was a good tiredness, and she thought she'd never been happier.

It was the middle of the night when she felt the first pain. Perhaps she shouldn't have insisted on taking that second horse out for a gallop yesterday; she'd probably pulled a muscle or something. There was only a week to go before the horses left, and it was important they were all properly ready. She was anxious for more orders from the army; it was such a good source of income for Redwoods. She slipped out of bed, careful not to wake David, and padded down to the kitchen. She searched around until she found some aspirin. She drank a glass of water and took two of the tablets, and slipped back into bed.

By morning the pain was much worse, coming in waves. She felt wetness between her legs and looked, and there was blood on her night gown.

Cold fingers clutched her heart. Something was seriously wrong, and she couldn't hide it from David any longer.

He dressed hurriedly and went to rouse Bella.

When Bella came in she took one look at Joy's white, stricken face, and the blood, which was coming faster now, and sent him to call Emma, and to bring towels.

'What is this, Joy? It's more than just your normal monthlies, isn't it? Do you know what's happening?'

Joy tried to push down the terror threatening to overwhelm her. 'It's the baby,' she quavered. 'I'm frightened for the baby.'

Bella's eyes opened wide as comprehension dawned. 'Dear God,' she exclaimed. 'There's a baby. How far...'

'About two and a half months.'

'Does David know?'

'No, I...I haven't told him yet. I wanted to wait...'

'You wanted to wait until the horses were gone, didn't you?'

The grim look on her grandmother's face cut right into Joy's heart, and she realised the terrible thing she'd done. She had endangered her baby, and all because she wanted to indulge her own selfish pleasure. To be part of the excitement of working with the horses. She had no time to reply before David burst into the room with Emma, who carried a bundle of towels, and Bella quickly pulled up the sheet to cover her.

'What is it?' David asked. 'What's the matter?'

Bella remained silent.

Joy looked up into David's worried face and knew she had to tell him.

'I...I...there's a baby...' she faltered, and stopped as she saw the bewilderment in his eyes.

'What do you mean, a baby?' A cloud came over his face. 'You can't mean you're carrying a baby?'

Joy nodded, trying to hold back the tears threatening to choke her.

'How long?' he asked. 'How long have you known?'

'About...about six weeks...I suppose.'

David's eyes narrowed. 'And you chose not to tell me.' His voice was harsh. 'Because you knew I'd make you stop riding and working with the horses, wearing yourself out day after day like you did.'

At that moment pain tore through Joy again. She doubled over, a cry forced from her lips, and Emma took David by the arm and propelled him out through the door.

He shot her a look of such rage as he went that Joy didn't know how she could bear it, but then another pain seared through her, and she forgot everything else. She couldn't hold back the scream forced from her. Grandma pulled the bedclothes back, and she was barely conscious of what was happening, but she realised they had the towels under her, and she knew she was losing the baby. Then she was swamped by the agony.

When it was all over, they rolled Joy on her side, and back again, so they could change the sheets, and did their best to make her comfortable. Joy leant back against the pillows and let the tears flow.

They tried to comfort her, but she asked them to leave her be, and finally they drew the curtains and left her alone.

Then she suffered such agonies of guilt and remorse she didn't know how to bear it. What sort of a worthless creature was she, that she could put her own selfish desires above the welfare of her coming baby? The poor little baby that was now nothing, that never had a chance to see the world, even to draw breath. Was it a boy or a girl? She would never know. Perhaps a darling little boy, looking just like a miniature version of David. Or a fair-haired version of Xandra, a sister to be close to her, something Joy had never known herself, and perhaps now her daughter would never know, all because of her own selfishness.

It wasn't as if she didn't like babies, because she did. Oh yes, there were aspects of raising a baby she didn't like, such as dirty nappies, and the way they sicked up all the time. But she really did love them, and planned on having several. But maybe God would never forgive her for what she'd done to this little one. Maybe He'd think she was unfit to be a mother, which she was, and He would never let her have any more. This thought brought on a fresh bout of weeping. She turned on her side and curled up into a ball. How she could even go on living, she felt so bad.

All that day she lay there, and when anyone came into the room she turned her back on them and told them to go away and leave her. She refused all offers of food or drink.

The next morning Grandma came in with a cup of tea, put it down on the bedside table, went across to the window, and pulled back the curtains, letting in a flood of light. She came and sat on the bed alongside Joy, and reached out her hand and stroked her hair.

'Come on, darling girl. Turn over and drink this tea, it'll make you feel better.'

Joy turned over and looked into that familiar face, now full of concern, and the tears welled again. 'Oh Grandma, how could I have ever been so bad, so wicked, as to have killed my poor little baby?'

'There, there now,' Grandma soothed, brushing back the wisps of hair clinging to her face. 'Things are never as bad as they seem. Sit up now, and drink your tea.' She slipped her arm beneath Joy's shoulders and helped her up, and then retrieved two of the pillows that had fallen to the floor, and placed them behind her, and handed her the cup.

Joy gulped down the tea, surprised to find she was thirsty, while Grandma watched, nodding in approval.

'There, that's better.' She took the empty cup and placed it back on the table, then took Joy's hand in her own. 'Now, whatever you've done, or think you've done, it's all over now. You've been through a terrible experience, one of the worst for a woman, and one that many women have to go through. But it's over now, and you have to get well and think ahead. There'll be other babies, there's nothing surer than that, and in the meantime you've got Xandra, and she's wondering why she can't come in to see you.'

'But you don't know what I did,' Joy told her, her guilt twisting inside her like a knife. 'I purposely didn't tell anyone about the baby, even when I was sure, because I knew David would want me to stop riding, and being involved with the horses .And I wanted to keep on until they left.' She drew a deep breath. 'It was so bad of me, and now I've killed my own child. What sort of a monster does that make me?'

'You mustn't blame yourself for something that may well have happened even if you stayed inside all the time. Miscarriages are not rare, unfortunately. But you're young and healthy, and you'll have more children.'

'Perhaps. If God doesn't decide that I don't deserve any more. But David will never forgive me.'

'Nonsense. David's very worried about you. He's sent one of the men to fetch the doctor, and, of course, he wants to come in to see you. I've asked him to wait until you're ready. Now, I'm going to get you freshened up and looking more like yourself. You wouldn't want him to see you like this, now, would you?'

Panic rose inside Joy at the thought of facing her husband. 'I can't bear to see him at all. He hates me. I know he does.'

'Don't be foolish, Joy. You know that's not true.'

'It is. I saw the way he looked at me when he knew about the baby.'

'I can't keep him out. But I think you should freshen up before he comes in.'

Joy looked at the crumpled bed and ran her fingers through her hair, and bit her lip. 'All right, I suppose you're right.'

After she washed in the bowl of water Grandma brought, and she and Mary tidied things, and Grandma brushed her hair, Joy felt a little better. But she quaked inside at the thought of having to face David.

When he walked through the door his face was impassive, but the dark rings under his eyes suggested he hadn't slept well. He came and stood by the bed, looking down at her.

'How are you feeling this morning?' His voice was heavy.

Joy swallowed. 'A bit better, thank you.'

'I've sent for the doctor. He should be here soon.'

'I'm sorry to cause you all this trouble.'

'That's not what you should be sorry for.'

A band tightened around her chest, making it difficult to breathe. 'I'm sorry for...the other, too.'

'It's too late to be sorry now. You should've thought of the consequences of your actions earlier.'

'I know, David, I know. I just didn't think...I mean...'

'That's just it.' His voice hardened. 'Unless it's about Redwoods, you don't think, do you?'

Joy felt as if he'd punched her in the stomach. 'That's not true,' she whispered. 'I think about you and Xandra...'

'When it suits you.' He took a deep breath, and when he spoke again his voice lost its hard edge, but it still sounded angry. 'At any rate, the main thing now is for you to get better. I'll see you again after the doctor's been. I have work to do now.' His lips twisted. 'We can't have anything holding up getting the horses ready in time for the delivery. I'm sure you appreciate that.'

With those words he turned and left the room, and Joy thought she could never be happy again.

The doctor came later in the morning and after he examined her he drew up a chair and sat next to her. He was a comfortable looking man, well into middle age now with greying hair and creases at the corners of his eyes. Joy had known him since she was a child.

'Well now Joy,' he smiled kindly at her, 'you've been through a nasty experience, and one that could've had a much worse outcome for you. But you're young and healthy and you should recover completely. I want you to stay in bed and rest for a week, and then take things quietly for the next month. I'll leave some medicine for you. I want you to take it until it's all gone. If the bleeding hasn't stopped in two weeks' time, or if you don't begin to feel better soon, call me again and we'll do a further check. Understand?'

'Yes, Doctor.'

'Right. Now, I've spoken to your husband, and he tells me you've been riding a lot and working quite hard and...'

'Is that what caused it?'

'Not necessarily. There can be many causes and we certainly don't know why this happened to you. However, in the light of this, I think that with your next pregnancy you'll need to take suitable precautions. You'll need to take things easy, at least in the first three months. I'd like to see you in the very first stages and keep an eye on you. It's possible that you might need to curtail your activities somewhat.'

Relief filled Joy at his words. 'So you don't think this will stop me from having more children?'

'Good gracious me, no. You're young and healthy; I see no reason why you can't have quite a brood, if that's what you want.' A note of caution crept into his voice. 'Of course, we can never say for sure, sometimes Nature plays tricks. But I certainly wouldn't want you to worry about that. I'd say it's most unlikely.'

'Oh, thank you so much Doctor. You don't know what a relief that is to me.'

He patted her hand before he stood and picked up his bag. 'You just concentrate on getting well now, and then let Nature take its course. I can't foresee any problems. Just make sure you rest and take care of yourself for the next few weeks,' he told her before crossing to the door and leaving, closing the door behind him.

After he'd gone Joy leant back against her pillows with a sigh. She still felt quite weak and sick, but at least she was thankful to hear that she shouldn't have any trouble with having another baby. That's if God forgave her. And David. And it still didn't change the fact she'd behaved irresponsibly, and caused the death of her unborn child. And for that she wasn't sure she could forgive herself.

She closed her eyes for a moment, and she must have drifted off, because when she opened them again David was standing by her bed, looking down at her. She sat forward with a start.

'Oh, I didn't hear you come in.'

'I didn't mean to startle you,' he told her. His voice, though cool, was not angry like before. 'How are you feeling?'

'A bit weak, but I'll be all right. The doctor said so.'

'Yes, I've seen the doctor and he tells me he expects you to make a full recovery. However, that doesn't alter the fact that you could've died. And you've lost the baby.' He paused, frowning. 'Which I didn't know about. Why didn't you tell me, Joy?'

She wouldn't lie to him. She took a deep breath and told him the truth. 'I never thought it could hurt the baby,' she finished.

David took a handkerchief from his pocket. He wiped away the tears she didn't realise were running down her cheeks, and handed it to her. 'Here, blow your nose,' he told her, not unkindly.

She did, and looked up at him, feeling as shaky as one of Mary's jellies. 'I only wanted to help,' she added. 'I wanted to do my share of the work.'

His mouth set in a straight line. 'You wanted to be part of the excitement, I know that. But you have to remember you're not a man, you're a woman, and a mother. There are other things in your life than horses, and Redwoods. Like your children. And they should come first.'

'I'm sorry David, I am truly sorry, and next time I promise I'll be a perfect example of motherhood and take every care. Truly, I promise.'

He breathed deeply. 'Well, I suppose everyone makes a mistake sometimes, though hopefully not with such drastic results as this, so we'll say no more about it now. The important thing is for you to get well again.'

'Yes, I know.'

'Well, I'll leave you to rest now.' He bent and pecked a kiss on to her forehead before turning and leaving the room.

Chapter Nine

Joy sat on the verandah gazing into nothingness. Three weeks had passed, and she couldn't seem to pull herself out of the cloud of apathy that clung to her. Sunshine laced the air, bees buzzed lazily as they went about their search for nectar, and the melodious warble of a magpie came from a nearby tree. But she didn't notice.

On the floor beside her Johnnie was amusing Xandra by walking her teddy up and down, pretending it was talking to her. Each time he made it leap at her, and nuzzle its head into her belly, she shrieked with laughter and tried to catch it, but Johnnie pulled it away quickly. 'More Johnnie, more,' she cried.

It was a game they never seem to tire of, and Joy knew she should be feeling happy to see them playing so well together, but she could summon no enthusiasm for anything.

Guilt still weighed heavily on her and although Grandma, Mary and Emma all tried their best over the past weeks to cheer her up, she had no interest in anything. She spent most of her time with the children, but even when Xandra brought Dolly in for Mummy to play with, or climbed all over her, persuading her to play games, it failed to pull her out of her misery.

Often she would pick up her daughter and cuddle her, feeling almost suffocated with love for her, and hating herself for having killed Xandra's sibling. As she sat there now she wondered whether it had been a boy or a girl, dark or fair. Would it have been boisterous and playful, or quiet and studious? She would never know, and the realisation made the tears, always close to the surface, trickle down her cheeks.

She was only aware of them when Johnnie stopped their game, and came to stand by her, reaching up to touch her cheek with his fingers.

'Why are you sad, Auntie Joy?' he asked her.

Joy pulled herself together, and quickly brushed the tears aside, ashamed.

'Oh no, I'm not sad, Johnnie.'

'But you're crying.'

'No, no, I just got something in my eyes.' She rubbed her eyes and blinked, summoning a smile. 'See, it's all gone now.'

'That's all right then,' he told her, and went back to Xandra, who was calling him, cross at having their game interrupted.

Joy left her chair to stand by the verandah rail, watching idly as a kookaburra swooped down from a tree to pick up a worm its sharp eyes spied in a garden bed. Carrying its prey back to the tree, the bird perched on a bough and swung its head from side to side, bashing the worm against the limb several times before swallowing it. Once the sight would have entertained her, but today she was indifferent to the wildlife and everything else around her. When the door to the verandah opened, she didn't even bother to turn to see who it was.

'Joy.'

She spun around at the voice.

'Mother!' Joy's heart leapt, and she flew across the space. The next second she was in her mother's arms, sobbing.

Kitty hugged her, and held her close for a minute, before disentangling their arms and holding her at arm's length.

'There now, that's a nice way to greet me,' she chided soothingly.

'Oh Mother, I can't tell you how pleased I am to see you. If ever I've wanted you, it's now.'

Kitty eyes were full of concern. 'I know you've been through a terrible ordeal, darling, and I want to hear all about it. I suggest we go somewhere we can sit and talk. Do you feel up to a walk down to the river?'

'Yes.'

'Then I'll just call someone to mind the children...' she broke off as Emma appeared in the doorway.

'I'll take over here. You go and spend some time together,' Emma told them, stepping out on to the verandah.

Kitty took Joy by the arm and they walked down the steps and along the path to the river. There they walked along the bank until they came to the stump that had always been Kitty's special place.

Kitty sat on it, and Joy sank down on to the ground beside her, as they'd always done.

Kitty draped her arm around Joy's shoulder. 'To lose a child is one of the worst things a parent can go through, you must be feeling terribly bereft.'

The guilt rose up again, searing her throat. 'I do, I'd give anything for it not to have happened. But the worst thing is that it's my fault.'

'Do you want to tell me about it?'

'Yes.' Joy told her mother everything – how she decided to say nothing about the baby and why, not sparing herself and leaving nothing out. 'So you see, it's all my fault, I killed my own baby. I'm not fit to be a mother and it's no wonder David hates me.' She hung her head, swallowing at the lump threatening to choke her.

Kitty took her arm from around Joy's shoulder, and used both hands to turn her face towards her.

'Look at me, Joy,' she commanded.

Joy looked up. There was none of the shock and horror she expected to see in her mother's face, only compassion.

'My darling girl, firstly. David does not hate you. He loves you and always will, I dare say. He may consider you acted without enough thought, but he certainly doesn't hate you, and he's honest enough to accept that we all do things we're sorry for. It's happened, and nothing can change that, and you both have to accept it, and get on with your lives.' Pausing, she took her hands from around Joy's face and picked up her hand instead, and held it in her own while she continued talking.

'Now, you may have been partly responsible for what happened, or you may not. Miscarriages are not uncommon, you know. Nature often decides, for whatever reason, that this was not meant to be, and no one's to blame. But whether or not you contributed to it, it's not the end of the world, or of babies. You're young and healthy, and unless you let this get on top of you and give you the vapours or some other such thing that's a refuge for the weak women in the world, you and David will make more babies together. And you'll take normal care of yourself, and they'll be born strong and healthy, like your beautiful daughter.'

Joy drew a shuddering breath. 'Is that what you really believe? If it was someone else, not me, would you feel the same?'

'Absolutely,' Kitty answered firmly.

They sat there for a long time then, not talking much, enjoying the peace and beauty of the river. After a while Joy began to wonder what was happening on the rest of Redwoods. She knew the horses had been delivered to the army, and a new batch arrived from the outback station. Work had started all over again, but no one talked about it.

Kitty stayed for the rest of the week, and she and Joy took long walks together, and played with the children, and the women all took tea together, and talked. Of family, children, men and household matters. Joy's 'mishap' was referred to once, in sympathetic vein, and that was the end of it, no need to be discussed again.

At night David and Jack joined them for dinner, and they talked about family matters, horses, and the merits of various horse trainers, for it would soon be time for Dreamer to go into training.

Each day Joy felt better than the day before, and by the end of the week she declared herself fit again, and Kitty was able to leave, knowing her daughter was going to be all right.

But beneath the layer of wellness Joy drew around herself for the world to see, a terrible sadness lingered.

David moved back into their bed again, after the prescribed month the doctor advised, but he didn't turn to her, and she knew that deep down he still blamed her. Her own desire for love seemed to have deserted her also, and she wondered if things would ever be the same between them again.

Joy finished settling Xandra down for the night a few days later when she received a message from David to come down to the stables straight away. Gay Lass was in labour.

Urgency hurried her steps, and when she arrived a quick look told her labour was well under way. The birth sac was already showing as Gay Lass, lying on her side on a bed of straw, legs stiff and straight out in front of her, heaved and strained, her breath whistling through her nostrils. David leant against the wall of the stall with his arms folded, watching.

'She's coming along nicely,' he told her.

Joy knelt down next to the horse's head, and stroked it gently, her heart swelling. 'There, there, Lassie, you're doing very well. Good girl,' she encouraged her.

She stayed there with her for a while before rising and moving to stand beside David, butterflies fluttering inside her as she touched his arm.

'She's doing all right,' he told her, a grin splitting his face.

'It's exciting, isn't it? Our very first foal! The real start to our breeding program.'

Suddenly David's arms were around her, hugging her, and he buried his face in her hair, before tilting her face up to kiss her.

'A new life, a new start,' he told her, releasing her from his embrace so they could continue their vigil.

Lassie heaved some more and soon the foal's front legs and head appeared. Joy jumped forward, grasped the two legs and gave a firm pull. The little body slid further out. Then one final mighty push from Lassie, and the rest of the foal followed, where it lay in the straw. Reaching her head around, Lassie sniffed and licked the baby, and it responded by making clumsy attempts to move, lifting its nose to her muzzle.

After a few moments rest Lassie continued encouraging her baby with licks and nudges, and the foal responded, moving its ears, lifting its head, moving its legs, and then rolling on to its chest. Finally Lassie stood, and the foal also tried to stand, only to collapse back on to the floor. After a few more tries, and more encouraging licks from Lassie, it managed to stand and take its first wobbling, tentative steps, and before long it was suckling.

As she stood there with David's arm encircling her waist, watching mother and baby bonding, Joy felt the wonder of this new birth bringing a connection to life she thought she'd lost, and somehow it washed away the pain and anguish of her loss.

And much later that night they made love again, with tenderness and passion, and she knew everything was going be all right between them.

Chapter Ten

Although Joy was down at the stall at first light next morning, drawing her jacket around her in the chill morning air, David was there ahead of her, checking on mother and baby.

He looked up as she approached with a big smile on his face.

'Congratulations, you have a fine colt.'

'We have a fine colt, you mean,' Joy corrected him. 'He's the first to be born at Redwoods Stud, the start of our breeding program. It's so exciting.'

She hurried over to where Lassie stood with the foal beside her, his slight frame supported on long, spindly legs. 'Good girl,' she told her, rubbing Lassie behind the ears. 'Aren't you clever to produce such a beautiful boy?' She held out the carrot she'd brought with her, and Lassie took it and began munching.

'She looks to have recovered all right.' She turned her attention to the foal, holding out her hand for him to sniff, and stroking him softly on the back before examining him carefully all over. 'He looks in good shape, too.'

David came to stand beside her. 'Yes, mother and baby both doing well, as they say.' He paused. 'Have you thought about a name for him yet?'

'A racing name, you mean?'

'Yes. I'm supposing you intend to keep him and race him, not put him up for sale?'

'Of course.' She stroked his muzzle. 'You're going to be a champion, aren't you? You're going to win lots of races, and then go on to father a whole brood of champions.'

David laughed at her. 'Still the little optimist, I'm pleased to see. We have to get him safely to the racetrack first, don't forget.'

'I know.' Nothing could dampen her high spirits this morning. 'We will. Now—about a name? Let's see, his father is Starlight and his mother's Gay Lass. Hmm.' She turned over names in her head. 'Starbright...Gaylight...Gay Lad...Hmm...He's going to be a star, and he's born on Redwoods, so how about Red Star?'

'Sounds fine to me. And what about his stable name?'

Joy looked at the foal, now suckling energetically. 'He's pretty chipper for just a few hours old, so that's what we'll call him, Chipper.'

'Then Chipper he is,' David laughed. 'I'm taking them down to the small paddock now for a few hours. Want to come with us?'

'Yes, I'll lead Lassie, if you like.'

With the two horses safely installed in the paddock, Joy and David stood leaning on the outside rail, their breaths curling in the morning air. As the sun rose in the sky the early morning mist dispersed, chased away by the fingers of warmth, and the shadows from the sheltering trees lifted, revealing the vista of sweeping paddocks beyond. It was an oasis of peace at this early hour, and Joy breathed deeply in the sharp morning air. She reached her hand out to David. He laced their fingers together, and smiled down at her as they stood there, watching.

At first Chipper stayed close to his mother, following her wherever she moved to nibble the sweet tender grass, but after a while he took a few steps away from her, and began to take an interest in his surroundings, poking with his nose and sniffing at the ground. When a magpie suddenly swooped close to him, picking up a worm before flying off, he shied, and scampered back to his mother's side.

They both laughed, and David turned to her. 'I'm glad you've got Chipper to think about now, because it's time for Dreamer to go to the trainer.'

Joy felt a sudden dart of sadness at the thought of losing her, but it was soon replaced by excitement. 'I know, and while I'll miss her, I'm happy it's finally going to happen. The first of our horses to race.' She squeezed his hand. 'How exciting that's going to be!'

'It will be if she's a winner,' David answered, a note of caution in his voice.

'A lot will depend on the training. Who's she going to?'

'Jim Travers.'

'He has his fair share of winners. Let's hope she'll be one too.'

'Time will tell.'

Joy turned her attention back to the horses in front of her. 'And it'll be interesting to see how young Chipper turns out.'

'It's a bit too soon to tell, but if he lives up to his bloodlines, he should develop into a good sprinter. You'll have to decide if you want to mate Lassie with Starlight again next time, or look elsewhere.'

'We'll see how he progresses. There's plenty of time yet to decide.'

Jim Travers slid his hands slowly down Dreamer's legs, one at a time, and stood up and dusted his hands together, nodding as he stood back and ran his eyes over her once more. 'Yes, she's a nice little filly. She's muscling up well so we'll give her some work, and then we'll put her into a trial, and see how she's shaping up. First of all we have to get her used to running on a racetrack, and the general hustle and bustle of race days.'

Short and wiry, with a weather-beaten face that could have been anywhere between thirty and fifty, the trainer inspired Joy with confidence.

'How do you go about that?' she asked.

'She'll do plenty of work on the track itself, and we'll take her with us on race days when we have other horses running, to get her used to the atmosphere. She'll just stay in a stall, but she'll be taking it all in.'

'You'll keep us informed of her progress as she goes along, won't you?'

'Absolutely, Mrs. Cavanagh.'

Looking around, Travers turned to David. 'Nice spread you've got here. I see you have a fair mob spread around the paddocks. Any more thoroughbreds?'

'Yes, a couple. We've just recently had an addition, as a matter of fact. A colt, only a few weeks old.'

'Really?' Travers gave him a bright-eyed look. 'Mind if I take a look? You'll probably want to race him when he's ready.'

'Sure, come on.'

David led the way to the paddock where Gay Lass grazed with her foal alongside her.

'So what's his bloodlines?' Travers asked as he ran his hand down Chipper's neck and along his back.

David motioned to Joy, who rattled off Gay Lass's antecedents, and listed the races she'd won in England.

'That's most impressive,' Travers told them. 'But aren't you going to race her here?'

'I hadn't thought about it,' Joy told him. 'We want her for breeding.'

'Yes, I understand that. But if she wins a few races here, it's going to make her offspring more valuable.'

'I hadn't thought of that.' She turned to David. 'What do you think?'

'It makes sense, I suppose.'

'If she does well it would make for a better price for her progeny, that's for certain. Even if she races for only a season.'

'Do you think she could win again after having a foal?'

'Of course. We could put her back into training again as soon as the foal's weaned. Why don't we take her then and see how she goes?'

'All right.' Joy made up her mind. 'She can go for a season after Chipper's weaned, and we'll see if she can still win races.'

'Good decision. Any more possibilities?'

David shook his head. 'No.'

'Then I'll be on my way now with Joy's Dream, and I'll keep you in touch about her. And I'll collect Gay Lass in a few months, and we'll see then how the foal's coming along too.'

The next few weeks passed quickly for Joy. Xandra was walking now and liked to spend more time outside than in the house, so Joy devoted part of each day to taking her to different parts of Redwoods to familiarise her with the extent of her home. She always included a visit to Thunder's paddock, where they stood outside the fence while she called to him, offering him an apple or carrot through the rails. At first he ignored her, but eventually he trotted over and accepted the treat. Finally he allowed her to reach through and stroke his muzzle or rub his ears, and Joy knew he was getting to know and accept her. That was all she wanted – for the moment.

Emma and Johnnie usually came with them, with Xandra toddling along beside her bigger cousin, whom she adored. Sometimes their beloved Grandma came too, and they were happy family outings that became a regular part of their lives.

The children always wanted to go and visit the foal so, wherever else they went, they always ended up with a visit to see Lassie and Chipper. The foal was growing steadily and his energy seemed endless. Around the paddock he galloped, jumping and prancing, although he never left his mother's side for too long. The children never tired of watching him. When Harry Osborne called to take Emma and Johnnie out, Johnnie was quite put out if he had to miss his daily visit to the horses.

'Well, today's the day,' David told Joy a few days later at breakfast. 'Today I'm going to ride Thunder. Do you want to come and watch how we go?'

Joy caught her breath and her heart began to beat faster. 'Yes, of course. When?'

'Right after I do my rounds. Say about half an hour.'

'Then I'll see you down by his yard.'

Although she knew David had been making overtures to Thunder every day, offering him treats and talking to him, as she had herself, nevertheless Joy watched anxiously as he entered Thunder's yard a little later, closing the gate behind him. He carried a rope and halter in one hand and a bunch of sweet thistles in the other, and strode decisively towards the watchful horse, stopping a few feet before reaching him.

Holding out the thistles temptingly, he called softly to him. As he moved a few steps closer the wary horse shied and skittered away, keeping the distance between them. Patiently David offered the thistles again and again, until finally Thunder could resist the temptation no longer, and gingerly closed the gap between them. As he bent his head to the thistles, David slipped the noose over his head.

Thunder shied, pulling against the rope, but David held it firmly as the stallion reared and lunged. He played out the rope at first, and then shortened it as the horse stopped bucking but still pulled against the rope. Round and round the yard he walked the horse, talking to him all the time, and progressively shortening the rope until the horse finally settled. Then David offered the thistles again, and Thunder took them.

Leading the horse to the fence, he tied the rope firmly around a post before retrieving the saddle waiting there. Thunder offered no resistance to having the saddle placed on his back and the girth tightened. David untied the rope, and with one deft motion he was on his back. Joy's heart was in her mouth as she watched Thunder give a great display of trying to unseat David, but he dug his heels into the stallion's flank, keeping him on a short rein, and finally Thunder decided David was master, and came to a halt.

David walked the horse across to where Joy waited outside the gate, a big smile on his face. 'He just needed to know I'm in charge, and he's learnt the lesson. My God, but he's a strong bugger! It's just as well he's been broken in, or I'd never have been able to get near him today.'

Joy felt his excitement. 'Are you going for a ride now?'

'Sure. Open the gate for me. I want to see what he can do.'

No sooner were they through the gate than David gave the horse its head, whooping as they went flying down the track, horse and rider moving as one, hoofs pounding and muscles rippling.

Joy watched them until they disappeared from view, amazed at how quickly Thunder accelerated, and how fast he raced. Even as she admired them Joy felt a wave of jealousy. How she longed to be on Thunder's back. How wonderful it must be to feel that power beneath you–why, it would really be the closest thing to flying you could ever experience. Thunder could easily beat any horse he chose, if he continued like that.

That thought made her think again about the possibility of racing him. Just because he wasn't a thoroughbred was no reason why he couldn't win races. Would David consider the idea? He certainly brushed aside her suggestion when discussing the horse, but she would bide her time and see what happened. She hadn't put the idea out of her mind, even if David had, and if Thunder could win races it would be a big boost for Redwoods Stud.

David rode Thunder every day for the next few weeks. As Joy watched them she could see the stallion settling comfortably into being ridden, and finally David went back to riding his own horse, Roland, most of the time, taking Thunder out less frequently.

Joy still visited Thunder daily, going into his yard now to give him his daily treat and to talk to him, and often he came trotting across to the gate when he saw her coming. But it wasn't until she went to saddle up Blaze one morning, and discovered he'd thrown a shoe, that the idea came crowding back into her mind. It was the perfect excuse to take Thunder instead. She checked Blaze's hoof, and saw that, yes, there was slight damage where the nail had pulled out. Better to leave him for a day or two before shoeing him again.

Quickly she carried her saddle down to Thunder's yard and, placing it alongside the gate, she went inside and called to him. He trotted up, ears pricked, and she gave him the apple from her pocket.

'We're going for a ride today, boy. What do you think of that? David's busy on Roland, so you and I'll go for a gallop instead,' she told him, rubbing his ears.

He stood quietly while she saddled him, and made no protest when she swung herself up onto his back, holding the reins firmly. She eased him out through the gate and walked him down the track, waiting until they came to a long clear stretch before urging him forward and giving him his head. Away he went!

Joy laughed with the sheer exhilaration of it as the wind whipped past her ears, and the trees on the side of the track went by in a blur. They reached the front gate in what seemed to be mere seconds, and Joy eased him down to a trot as they ventured out on to the main road and headed for a little used road nearby, where she urged him on again. She felt the power beneath her unleashing, and could hardly believe Thunder's speed as his long powerful strides ate up the distance. Finally she eased him down, her pulses racing and her breath coming in gasps as she patted his neck.

'Good boy,' she told him, 'I knew we'd be all right...you and me.' Her words came in spurts as she tried to regain her breath, but Thunder trotted easily, hardly breaking a sweat after his exertion. Turning him around, they cantered back to Redwoods at a more sedate pace.

As they reached the stables Joy saw David and Patrick were waiting for her – David white-faced and visibly shaking. As she reined in and slid from the horse he came over, grabbed the reins from her and threw them to Patrick.

David grabbed her arm so hard she cried out. 'What do you think you've been doing, you little fool?' he asked, jerking her around to face him.

Joy twisted in his grip. 'Let go, you're hurting me,' she cried out, trying to free her arm from his grasp.

He held it even harder, squeezing, his eyes wide and his breathing heavy. 'You bloody little fool, you could've been killed.' His voice was hoarse. 'I told you never to ride that horse.'

'Let go of me,' Joy shouted, swiping at his arm with her free hand, while her heart beat a rapid tattoo in her chest.

David released her arm and she rubbed it furiously. 'You hurt me,' she accused him.

'That's nothing compared to what could have happened to you,' he shouted. 'I told you never to ride that horse,' he repeated. 'It's a wonder he didn't throw you and trample all over you.'

'For your information,' she raged at him, 'he was quite happy to have me ride him. He was docile as a lamb. I do know how to handle horses, you know.'

'He's no ordinary horse, he's a wild stallion, and you were just lucky you struck him on a good day. I've had visions of you lying dead and mangled, and God knows where. You didn't tell anyone where you were going, or what you were doing. The first thing I knew about it was when one of the lads told me you'd left Redwoods on that beast at a million miles an hour. And after I told you implicitly never to try to ride him.'

Even in her anger Joy knew he'd been worried about her safety, and she calmed down a little. 'Blaze had thrown a shoe,' she tried to explain, 'and I knew Thunder would be all right with me, he...'

'Did I, or did I not, tell you never to ride him?' he asked through gritted teeth.

Joy's anger flared again. 'This is the twentieth century, and you can't tell me what to do or not to do. You sound as if you're in the last century, when women had to do as they were told. I'm sorry if you were worried about me, but you needn't have bothered. I was quite safe.'

With that she turned and walked away, leaving him standing staring after her. When she reached the house she stalked into their room, threw herself down on the bed, and cried. After she shed her tears she got up and walked out of the house and down to the river, where she sat on Kitty's stump and gazed out at the river. But it didn't bring her any solace.

Joy didn't see David again for the rest of the day, and he didn't speak to her at dinner, which was a miserable affair, with Grandma, Grandpa and Emma trying to act normally, but not succeeding very well. And when she went to bed he didn't join her, but elected to go to the spare room instead. And Joy cried herself to sleep, and wished they never quarrelled, because she did love him so much.

'I'm sorry you were worried,' Joy told David next day, 'I'm sorry for being so thoughtless and not letting you know what I was doing. And when Blaze is shoed again I'll have no reason to ride any other horse.'

'Very well,' David replied coldly. 'I accept your apology.'

But she didn't say she was sorry for riding Thunder. David didn't mention Thunder. An uneasy truce began between them. Peace reigned once more, and things went back to being as they were before. Almost.

Chapter Eleven

'Well, just listen to this.' Joy looked up from the letter she was reading as she sat with Emma and her grandmother after their morning walk. 'It seems we're to have a visitor from overseas soon.'

'Is that from your grandfather?' Bella asked. 'Is he coming out here?'

'Not Grandfather, although I wish he would come. I miss him and I'd love to see him again. No, he says my uncle Hector is coming to Australia, and would like to spend some time here with us after he's been down in Sydney. He says Hector has written to me himself.'

Putting down the letter she reached over and sorted through the pile of post that still waited. 'Ah, here it is.' She opened it and read. 'Oh my goodness,' she exclaimed a moment later. 'He's retired from the army, what a surprise! He was wounded and spent some time at home recovering, and he says he's now fit and looking to take his life in a new direction. He's interested in the prospects that may present themselves in Australia, which he sees as a land of opportunities.' She looked up. 'Well, I must say I am surprised. I'd never imagined him as wanting to change his life in any way. I never really thought about it, but I just can't see him as anything else than an army officer.'

Bella smiled. 'Well, you never know what lies behind people's actions, and something must have prompted a desire for change in him. I know when I was younger I never considered coming to Australia, but life changes. He was wounded, you say?'

'Yes, but apparently he's quite recovered.'

'Is he your father's brother?' asked Emma.

'Yes. My father was the youngest, and Hector was the next one up, just a little older.'

'William's brother,' Bella mused. 'I wonder what he's like.'

'He was always very pleasant to me. He was home on leave when I was at Bournbridge Hall.'

'He must be a bit old to be thinking of starting a new life in a new country, surely?' asked Emma.

'He'd only be few years older than Joy's mother,' Bella said, 'which would make him in his forties, or possibly a little older. About the same age as I was when I came here.'

'And look at you now!' Joy laughed. 'How your life's changed since you came here.'

'Yes' Bella smiled reflectively. 'I came here as a rather sad widow, thinking my life was over. But then I met your grandfather, and I've never been happier.'

'Well then, there's no reason why Uncle Hector can't do the same, although I don't believe he's ever been married. And it's not as if he's always lived in England, he spent years in India with his regiment. I'll write to him today and tell him he's most welcome, and we'll all be delighted to see him. But I wonder why he's decided to leave the army?'

When David heard of her letter later that day, he suggested she telegraph Hector Barron, in case he was anxious to make arrangements. She received an immediate reply from her grandfather to say Hector was already on his way to Sydney, giving details of his arrival date and hotel booking. so Joy posted her letter to the hotel, to await his arrival.

Two weeks later when Joy received a second letter from Hector, telling her he had arrived safely and was delighted to receive her invitation. He intended to spend a week in Sydney, and then come to Redwoods. He proposed to travel by rail to Newcastle and coach to Bulahdelah, and gave the date of his arrival.

Joy and David were waiting in Bulahdelah to meet the coach, and Joy hardly recognised the man who stepped down as the uncle she'd known in England. Although his hair seemed more liberally streaked with grey at the temples than she remembered, he was much leaner than the last time she had seen him, and there was a spring to his step. No longer in uniform, his well-cut clothes set off his athletic figure, and his reddish complexion was tanned by the long sea voyage. Although there were deep creases around his eyes, they sparkled as he scanned the waiting group. He gave the impression of a man who enjoyed life.

Joy hurried forward to meet him, and his face lit up as he recognised her.

'Uncle Hector, how lovely to see you,' she told him, reaching up as he bent to kiss her on the cheek.

'Joy, my dear girl, aren't you a sight for sore eyes.' He smiled. 'Still as pretty as I remembered. And you're a married lady now, and a mother, too, so my father tells me.'

'Indeed I am.' Joy turned to David. 'And this is my husband, David Cavanagh.'

Hector offered his hand. 'I've heard a great deal about you from my father, and I'm honoured to meet you at last.'

'Welcome to Bulahdelah, Mr. Barron,' David said as they shook hands.

'Hector, please. After all, we're family now.'

'Hector it is, then, and I'm David. I'm sorry I missed meeting you in England, but you'd returned to your regiment by the time I arrived.'

'Yes, but I've heard all about your exploits while you were there, when you and Rufe exposed the impostor who tried to swindle Kitty and Joy out of Redwoods. You must tell me the full story before too long.'

'Time for that when you've settled in and looked around. Now, let's find your luggage.'

They retrieved his bags, climbed aboard the buggy and headed off.

Hector looked around with interest. 'I'm looking forward to seeing Redwoods, and the surrounding area.'

'Grandfather told me you're considering settling in Australia,' Joy remarked, as they left the village behind.

'Yes, there's nothing much for me back home that I care to do and, besides,' he laughed, 'I can't stand the weather. I've become acclimatised to the heat in India, and I'm afraid I don't care for England's bleak winters. So, being foot-loose and fancy-free as they say, I decided to come out here and see if I can find a niche for myself. And it's good of you to have me, to see firsthand what the country is all about.'

'We're delighted to have you,' Joy assured him.

'Do you have anything in mind?' asked David.

'Well, something in the country appeals. Sydney is a beautiful city, with its splendid harbor, and Rufe and Kitty are very hospitable and took me all around, but to me it looks a good place to visit, but not to live.'

'Country living is certainly much more pleasant.'

'On the trip up here I was positively awed by all the forests and waterways I saw. We crossed over the Hawkesbury River, and that's incredibly beautiful. But I notice there's farming along the way too, and I'm sure there must be other opportunities. However, I know Redwoods prospered from its timber, and I really want to consider all my options before I commit myself.'

'Very wise,' David agreed as they passed through the gate to Redwoods and approached the house.

Hector looked from side to side, taking in his surroundings. The shimmering heat of the afternoon was giving way to a pleasantly balmy dusk as the sun sank low in the sky. A gentle breeze from the river whispered through the tree tops, and overhead a flock of lorikeets flew their noisy way home. A kangaroo, startled by the sound of their arrival, looked up from nibbling the grass in the paddock alongside the track and sat watching them as they drew near.

David slowed the horses to a walk. 'You never know which way they're going to jump,' he explained, as the animal bounded away in the opposite direction. 'If they decide to come this way, and they tangle with the horses it can cause an accident.'

'Of course.' Hector twisted in the seat to watch, his eyes wide. 'What amazing animals, and so fast! Just look at him covering the ground.' He sat back as the 'roo disappeared into the trees on the distant side of the paddock. 'Do you have many of them here?' His face was alight with pleasure.

'Oh yes,' Joy replied as David flicked the horses into a trot again. 'You'll see them whenever you go around the estate, particularly in the early morning and late afternoon, like this.'

When they reached the house a welcoming party appeared on the verandah, consisting of Bella, with Xandra's hand clasped firmly in hers, Jack, Emma with little Johnnie, and Mary and Patrick hovering in the background.

After introductions were performed, with much hand shaking and cheek kissing, they all made their way inside, Mary bustling ahead to show Hector his room and bathroom, and Patrick in the rear carrying the bags.

Allowing Hector time to freshen up after his trip, the family arranged to meet later in the sitting room before dinner.

Chapter Twelve

Joy studied her uncle covertly while David busied himself with drinks and Bella was asking Hector about his time in Sydney. She remembered him as rather stiff and starchy, pleasant enough certainly, but very much the officer. Now he was relaxed, and chatting amiably with Grandma. What had brought about the change? Or had he always been like this, but was intimidated by his domineering mother's presence? Or perhaps because he had junior officers with him then, he needed to uphold his senior image? Whatever the reason, he seemed to present a very different image to the one she remembered from Bournbridge Hall, now looking every inch the casual and affable gentleman.

This train of thought led to thinking about Lily, and how she became pregnant during their time at Bournbridge Hall, which coincided with the visit of Hector and his fellow officers home on leave from India. Lily refused to reveal the name of the father, but Mrs. Frobisher, their companion and chaperone for the visit, believed it might have been one of the three officers because Lily had been so put out by their leaving. Could it have been Hector? Joy could not forget seeing him heading downstairs late one night when Lily was missing from her bed, although he seemed less likely than one of the younger men. Had Lily had seen this different side of him? In spite of Lily's vehement denials there had always been a lingering doubt in Joy's mind.

'Sorry I'm so late,' Emma said as she joined them. 'Johnnie just didn't want to go to bed.' She turned towards Hector, who had risen from his chair at her entry. 'He was upset because he couldn't stay up to talk to his Uncle Hector, as he has claimed you, I'm afraid, Mr. Barron.' She smiled as she took the vacant chair next to him.

Hector resumed his seat with an answering smile. 'I'm flattered, Mrs. Hardy, and the relationship's close enough for me to be perfectly happy, if he so wishes.'

'Indeed he does. I'm sorry but I had to promise him that I'll ask you if you'll come with us on our morning walk tomorrow to see the horses, if you don't have other plans. Otherwise he threatened to come out here in his nightclothes.'

Hector laughed. 'I'll be delighted to come. That's if you haven't made other arrangements for me?' he asked David.

'Only to show you around, and a walk to see the horses could encompass that, if you don't mind the company of the children.'

'I'm very fond of children, so if it's all right with you, we'll include the walk in our itinerary. I'd hate to disappoint Johnnie.'

'Thank you, Mr. Barron. He'll be so pleased, but I promise not to let him monopolise you while you're here. I know you've come to have a good look around, and there's much to see hereabouts.'

'I'm led to believe, through my discussions with Rufe while I was in Sydney, and what I've observed so far, that Australia is indeed a land of diverse opportunities, and I'm keen to see what the local area can offer.'

As the talk turned to discussion of the various places that would be of interest to their visitor, Joy noticed Hector's gaze was never away from Emma for long, and she, in turn, seemed animated when she spoke to him.

The next morning Hector and David led the party that walked down to visit the horses. Johnnie was happy to accept his usual place in the group, acting as Xandra's guide and protector, until they reached Chipper's paddock, where he abandoned her in order to stand beside Hector.

'Chipper's our new foal,' he told him proudly, 'and he's going to be a champion racehorse when he grows up. He'll prob'ly win heaps of races and get lots of silver cups an' all.' He looked up at Hector with a serious face. 'And when he's bigger I want to ride him, but he'll prob'ly have to go to the trainers. But I'm going to get a horse of my own when I'm six anyway.'

'Chipper's a very fine looking foal,' Hector replied, 'but it might be better to have a horse of your own that doesn't have to go away to be trained, don't you think?'

'Ye-es, I s'pose so.' He thought for a moment. 'But Chipper can still be my friend, even when he goes away to be trained, can't he?'

'Of course.'

'Then that's all right,' Johnnie replied. He looked up shyly. 'And can you be my friend as well as my uncle?'

Hector smiled down at the little boy, and took his hand. 'I'd like to be your friend very much.'

Over the next few days Joy noticed that whenever Hector wasn't out riding around the district with David he spent a great deal of time with Emma. He joined them for their morning walk as often as he could, strolling next to her, and contrived to sit by her when they congregated in the sitting room for their pre-dinner drink, going out of his way to engage her in conversation. Joy would have been delighted to think that romance might be blossoming for her friend, except for that disturbing vision of Hector disappearing down the stairs on the night she discovered Lily missing from her bed. Had he been on his way to meet her? Could her uncle be the sort of man who would seduce a young girl?

Two weeks after Hector's arrival Joy and Grandma both needed to go into Bulahdelah on some errands and so Emma and Hector took the children for their morning walk without them.

As they strolled towards the horse paddocks, fitting their pace to Xandra's short steps, Hector turned to Emma, a half smile on his face.

'You know, this is the first time we've been alone together.'

'Not really alone.' A faint pink flush coloured her cheeks as she made a slight gesture towards the children.

His eyes twinkled. 'Ah yes, the proprieties are satisfied. But alone enough for us to be able to talk.'

'And what would you like to talk about, now that we're alone?'

'What I really want is to learn all about you,' he replied, his eyes serious now. 'I know you've lost your husband, and you have a delightful little boy, but very little besides that.'

Emma felt a pull on her heart strings. 'There's not a lot to tell, apart from that. I lost Matthew after a long illness, and I left Melbourne then, and Johnnie and I went to live with my parents at Riverside, about forty miles south of here. We came here to visit my brother David, and Joy and I became so close that we've stayed ever since. And that's about it.'

'That's only the bare bones, but it's a start.' He touched her softly on the arm, and when she turned to look at him there was such compassion in his face that her step faltered.

He took her arm and threaded it through his so that her hand rested on his arm. 'I'm sorry you lost your husband. I can only imagine how hard it must have been for you, but I won't say more than that now, although the day might come when you want to tell me more about it.' He touched her hand with his own briefly. 'I can see that you've found the strength to move on with your life, and I imagine having a son to care for has been largely instrumental in giving you that strength.'

'Yes, he's the most important thing in my life now, and I suppose he kept me going through the times when I felt life had nothing left.' She gave a quick shake of her head, and quickened her step. 'But enough of that, it's behind me now. Bad times pass.'

'Yes, I understand that.'

When they reached the horse paddock Hector released Emma's arm. Several of the horses headed across the paddock towards them, including the foal and his mother. The children called out excitedly, and it seemed as if Chipper decided to put on a special display for them as, after coming to the fence as if to welcome them, he raced away and galloped to the far side of the paddock and back.

While the children were occupied with watching the horses, Emma turned to Hector.

'I don't want to pry, but I can't help wondering what made you decide to leave the army. I've assumed it was because of being wounded. Am I correct?'

'No, that had nothing to do with it. I had been considering my position before that happened.'

'Really? Is it something you want to talk about?'

'If you're sure you want to hear.'

'Yes, I do, if you want to tell me.'

Hector drew a deep breath. 'When I joined the army, I fully expected to be posted to India, as I was. After the Indian uprising in the fifties, our main mission there was to keep the peace. Oh, there was fighting enough, I saw plenty of that in the Tirah Valley. But we were fighting the wild tribesmen, fierce fighters who seemed to revel in war, who gave no quarter and expected none in return.'

'You weren't afraid to fight?'

'No, it was what I was there for, and necessary to keep the peace. These were insurgents determined to disrupt our peaceful reforms for the country, and we couldn't have that. But when the regiment was posted to South Africa it was different. We found ourselves fighting farmers, who were just trying to protect their land and their homes. I found myself loath to order my men to attack them, but of course I had no alternative.'

'No, of course not.'

'I've never told another person this...'

'If you'd rather not...'

'No. I'd like you to know. That's if you really are interested?'

'Yes, I am.'

'Well, it was almost a relief when I took the bullet in the shoulder. It almost seemed like Divine intervention, because it meant I no longer had to order actions that went against all my instincts.' He swallowed, looking stricken at his admission. 'But I promise you I never shirked my duty,' he added.

Emma could tell her response to his confession was important to him so she chose her words carefully.

'Joy told me her grandfather wrote that you were wounded while performing an act of bravery for which you were decorated, so that goes without saying. I understand your reactions perfectly. I would have felt the same myself. I'm sure you wouldn't have made such a decision lightly.'

'No, it took much soul-searching. But I'm happy I made that decision.'

'And happy that you decided to come to Australia?'

'Yes, even more so now, than when I arrived. I'm sure this is where my future lies.'

'Good, then all you have to do is find an occupation that suits you.'

'Perhaps not all.' He turned towards her. 'I understand that Johnnie is everything in life to you, but do you think there could ever be room for anyone else as well?'

Emma's heart skipped a beat.

She looked up at him, and liked what she saw–a well-built, suntanned man of middle age, with a keen, interesting face, slightly apprehensive now as he waited for her reply.

She smiled at him. 'I'm sure there could be, given a little time.'

Hector's face became almost boyish as he answered. 'Time I have plenty of. No need to rush into things.'

Then he bent and scooped Johnnie into his arms and lifted him high in the air, laughing as he sat him on his shoulders. 'How do you like the view from up there?' he asked, as Johnnie squealed with delight. 'You and I are going to be spending lots of time together, so we need to have some fun.'

Joy was troubled. She couldn't help but see the growing attraction between Emma and her uncle, and she should have been pleased for them. Normally she would have been, for she had grown extremely fond of her sister-in-law, and she loved seeing the glow in her eyes and how her face lit up in Hector's presence.

But she could not forget what happened to Lily.

So what was she to do? She liked what she'd seen of her uncle, but if he was really the sort of man who would seduce a young innocent girl, then he would certainly not be the man she wanted to see Emma married to. She finally decided she must speak to Emma.

Her chance came on a morning when they walked alone with Johnnie and Xandra, and the children were engrossed in watching the foal as they stood outside his paddock.

'Johnnie seems to have taken a great liking to Hector,' Joy began.

Emma smiled as she nodded. 'Oh yes, they're getting along famously. They seem to have fun together, and Hector is even happy to spend time answering his questions. He's very patient with him.'

Joy hesitated, and then rushed in. 'And how about you, Emma? How do you feel about him?'

Emma's cheeks coloured. 'I like him. I like him a lot.'

'And he likes you, doesn't he? I can see it when you're together.'

'Is it that obvious?'

'Yes, I'd say so.'

'Well, we're not rushing into anything. At the moment we're just good friends, but he has intimated that he'd like to be more.'

'And how about Harry Osborne?'

'Oh Joy, you know I've never felt anything special for him.'

'Yes, I know. But you haven't told him you don't want to see him anymore?'

'Well, not in so many words...no. There's nothing definite between Hector and me.'

Joy bit her lip. 'But there well may be, and so there's something I should probably tell you.' She frowned. 'It might well be nothing, but I don't know, and I don't know how to find out.'

Emma's brow furrowed. 'What is it?'

Joy drew in a deep breath, and haltingly related what happened. 'So you see,' she finished, 'I felt I had to tell you. Lily wouldn't say who the father is, and she ran off before we could press her anymore.'

Emma paled. 'I can't believe Hector would take advantage of a young girl like that. Why, Lily's young enough to be his daughter.'

'Exactly. And I can't believe it either, and yet...' Joy's voice trailed off.

'And yet he was there.'

They were both silent as they thought about it.

'I suppose we could write and ask Lily,' Joy suggested slowly. 'Perhaps if she knows why, she would tell us the truth.'

'I don't think so. And we'd never know whether to believe her or not.'

A knot of tension coiled inside joy. 'I'm sorry to cause you distress. Perhaps I shouldn't have said anything.'

Emma shook her head. 'No. You had to tell me. I'd do the same. But I don't know what to think. I suppose the only thing to do at this stage is for me to see how things go between us, being aware of what happened to Lily. And if things develop further between us, maybe I'll go to Sydney and talk to Mrs. Frobisher myself before making any commitment. Perhaps she saw something, or knows something she might not have wanted to reveal at the time.'

Joy nodded. 'I suppose that's possible.' She thought back, remembering how overwrought they had all been at the time. 'Yes, it's probably all we can do.' She sighed. 'And Emma...'

'Yes?'

'Perhaps you should still keep seeing Mr. Osborne. Just in case.'

Emma drew in a deep breath, her face sad. 'Yes, I suppose so...'

Chapter Thirteen

Joy wanted to take the letter from David and read it immediately for herself, instead of having to wait for him to impart its contents, but that was the way of things–in a husband and wife partnership, all communications were directed to the husband. When he told her the news she couldn't stop herself from dancing a little jig.

'Isn't it exciting?' she bubbled. 'We never thought Dreamer would have her first race in Sydney, at Randwick, one of the biggest courses in Australia.'

David smiled down at her, still holding the letter from Jim Travers. 'Yes, I must say it's exciting. He says that after she won her barrier trial in such convincing time he decided she should have her first proper outing in a race at Randwick, instead of Newcastle as originally planned.' He paused for a second. 'But we must remember she'll be meeting stiffer opposition, probably more seasoned gallopers, than if she raced in Newcastle.'

'Yes, I know. But Mr. Travers must think she's up to it, or he wouldn't have decided to nominate her for it. I must contact Mother and let her know we're coming. And she and Rufe will certainly want to be there to watch her first race.'

'I'm sure they will. And a trip to Sydney will be a holiday for us all.'

Joy loved Randwick racecourse. It reminded her of Ascot with its bustling crowds and the women decked out in all their finery. She felt the excitement in the air as they walked through the betting ring, where the bookmakers shouted the odds, pausing only long enough to take the money thrust at them by the punters.

Rufe had arranged tickets for them to go into the Members enclosure, where they would have the best view of the finishing post from the grandstand.

'It's not as grand as Ascot,' Joy told Emma as they settled themselves in their seats, 'but the atmosphere is still the same.'

'Oh, it's all so exciting,' Emma enthused, gazing around. 'What a lot of women there are here, and all so stylishly dressed. This is my first visit to the races, and I didn't realise it's such a social occasion. '

'It's the same the world over,' Rufe said as he handed a race book to each of the ladies. 'In here you'll find all the horses listed for each race, with the names of the jockeys and their recent form,' he told Emma, opening the book for her at the first race, before turning to Joy with a smile. 'But it's the third race we're interested in, isn't it?'

'Of course, that's Dreamer's race.' Joy opened her book and thumbed over the pages until she reached 'Race Three, The Juvenile Stakes'.

'Yes, here she is. Number ten.' Her heart beat faster as she read aloud. 'Joy's Dream...Owner, Redwoods Stud. Trainer, J Travers. Jockey, W Small.'

'How does that make you feel?' Grandpa asked, smiling.

'Wonderful, to see it all in print.'

Kitty reached across and touched her arm. 'Your first runner,' she said with a smile. 'Well done.' She turned to David. 'And you too David. You've both accomplished what you set out to do. This is the start of big things for you, I'm sure.'

As they offered their congratulations, Joy smiled at David, wanting to share the moment with him, hoping he felt the same pride as she did. His satisfied smile told her he understood.

'Now all we need is for her to win,' he told her.

David and Joy walked along the row of horse stalls until they came to the stall with the name 'Joy's Dream' above it. Dreamer was already there with Jim Travers and the strapper, and when she saw Joy approaching she stamped and tossed her head, pulling at the halter. As Joy lifted her arm to stroke her neck she felt Dreamer's velvet nose foraging in her hand.

'Oh no, you're not allowed to have treats before the race. Wait until you've won and then you can have anything you want.' Joy turned to Travers. 'How is she?'

'As well as she's ever been.'

'Do you think she can win?'

'If she runs as well today as she's been running in track work, she has a good chance.'

'She looks well,' David said, 'let's hope she lives up to her looks.'

'If I was a betting man, which I'm not,' came the reply, 'I'd have a few shillings on her today. I reckon you'll get a good price, being her first run, and I doubt anyone from the city saw her win her trial. With a bit o' luck the bookies haven't got wind of it. She should be a good each-way bet.'

Joy rested her face on Dreamer's neck and gave her a hug. 'I know you'll do your best,' she whispered as she tried to quell the fluttery feeling in the pit of her stomach. As they walked away she looked back, to see Dreamer standing placidly, her tail switching at the flies that settled on her rump.

It was all Joy could do to sit calmly through the next two races, but then it was time for the race. While the others went to check out the prices and place their bets, she hurried down to wait by the parade ring long before the horses were due, her hands pressed against the rail to still their trembling.

Jim Travers arrived soon after and joined her.

'Not long now,' he told her, but she was too nervous to do more than nod in reply.

David joined them a few moments later and pressed a ticket into her hand. 'I put a pound on her for you,' he whispered.

Joy's eyes widened. 'A pound,' she gasped, shocked out of her silence.

'Certainly. You think she can win, don't you?'

'Yes, but a pound...' her voice faltered as the horses began entering the parade ring. Suddenly Joy's Dream was there, her coat gleaming in the sun, her muscles working smoothly beneath the skin as she stepped calmly along with her strapper. Joy smiled up at David, drawing a deep breath. 'Of course I do,' she told him in a firm voice.

At that moment the jockeys began entering the ring and Joy saw one of them was wearing the colours she had chosen for their silks – deep pink, with pink and gold bands on the sleeves, and a gold cap. This must be Bill Small, Joy's Dream's jockey. As Travers raised a hand he headed towards them.

As they were introduced Joy thought he looked little more than a boy with his slight build and sandy hair, but David had told her he was a top rider and had ridden the horse in track work to familiarise himself with her.

'You know what to do,' Travers told him. 'Settle her down and try to have her in about third place as you come round the bend, then let her go. Being her first race you'll have to use your own judgment as to just when to do that.'

The jockey nodded. 'Sure, leave it to me, Mr. Travers. I've got high hopes for her.'

'Good. Come on then, let's get you aboard.'

Together they walked across to Joy's Dream, and the strapper held her steady while the trainer legged the jockey up. Then Travers returned to stand with them while the horses began leaving the mounting yard one by one, through the gate and on to the course, and cantered towards the starting line.

'Right, let's go and watch.' Travers said then, and led them to the Owners and Trainers section of the stand.

Taking their seats they watched the horses milling around behind the starting line until the starter called them into line. Joy held her breath as she watched Joy's Dream take her place without any fuss. It looked as if they were all ready for a start when one of the horses reared. His jockey backed him out of the line as he tried to steady the rearing animal, unsettling the horses next to him.

A voice came through the megaphone. 'Number one, Flicker, has reared in the line.'

'Flicker, that's the favourite,' David told her.

Joy bit her lip, watching to see if her horse had been upset. Fortunately she was four horses away, and was still standing quietly. Flicker's jockey led him up again, with an attendant on each side, and this time he behaved himself and stayed in line.

A great roar came from the crowd as the starter let them go. Joy was relieved to see Dreamer rocket away. The jockey had her well placed on the rails, settling about halfway back in the field as they galloped onto the far side of the course.

The horses were well bunched up now, and Joy heard Travers muttering as he watched through his glasses. 'Get her out now; don't get trapped on the rail.' And then a satisfied murmur of 'Good lad,' as Small shot through a split in the horses ahead as they were coming up towards the bend.

Dreamer moved to the outside of the pack after they swung around the bend. They were close enough now to hear the thunder of the thudding hoofs. Joy's heart pumped with excitement. Flicker was in the lead now, with two horses neck and neck behind him and the crowd roaring. Joy's eyes were fixed on Joy's Dream, who was gaining ground steadily on the outside.

'That's right,' she heard Travers call, 'push her all out.' Almost as if he could hear him the jockey urged her on, and she came flying down the outside, overtaking the other horses. Now it was just Flicker and Joy's Dream fighting it out. The crowd went wild, calling for Flicker, the favourite.

Joy jumped up from her seat. 'Joy's Dream,' she yelled, 'come on Dreamer. Come on Dreamer! Dreamer!' She jumped up and down in her excitement, and when they went past the post seemingly locked together, she wasn't sure which of the two had won.

There was a hush over the crowd as they waited for the judge's decision. It seemed to take forever but finally it was announced. 'Number ten, Joy's Dream, first. Number four, Flicker, second. Number seven, Jungle Juice, third.'

'She's won,' Joy cried as she swung around to David and hugged him tight, her pulses racing. 'Dreamer's won her first race.'

David laughed aloud and swung her up, clear off the ground, and kissed her soundly.

'Yes, we've done it! And what a win!'

He put Joy down and turned, grabbing Travers's out-thrust hand and shaking it heartily. 'What a win,' he repeated excitedly. 'She just flew down the outside!'

'Yep, when he asked her for it, she gave him everything. You've got a mighty smart horse there, Mr. Cavanagh.'

David turned to Joy and put his arm around her. 'It's actually Mrs. Cavanagh's horse, to be exact.'

'Oh no,' Joy protested. 'It belongs to Redwoods Stud, we're partners.'

'Well then, congratulations to you both. And now we'd better go down and lead the horse in.'

Hurrying down they reached the gate in time to meet Joy's Dream and her elated jockey coming back. Joy took the horse's head and led her back in, past a mostly silent crowd who had obviously put their money on the favourite and were wondering where this first time winner had come from.

Chapter Fourteen

Joy gasped as the bookmaker handed her fifty-one pound notes in return for her winning ticket. With this as well as the prize money, it had certainly been a good day financially.

When she went down to the horse stalls to make sure Dreamer had pulled up well after the race, Jim Travers was standing in earnest conversation with a short, dapper man who was scowling as he rocked back and forth on his heels while speaking. His voice carried and Joy could not help but overhear his words as she approached.

'I tell you Travers, it's the end for me,' he was saying, 'I just can't afford to keep her any more, much as I'd like to. Business is bad at the moment, and now the wife has to have this flippin' operation that's going to cost me an arm and a leg. I was a bloody fool to think I could find the money by punting, and now I'm in deeper than ever. No, Bonnie Doon has to go, and quickly. D'you reckon you can find me a buyer?'

Travers frowned. 'I'll try, but it's a shame you have to let her go. She has plenty of ability, but I'm afraid you won't get a good price if you're in a hurry.' He paused before continuing. 'However, if you're sure, I have a couple of owners who might be interested...' Travers broke off as he looked up and saw Joy. 'Leave it with me, I'll be in touch,' he said abruptly as he stepped forward to greet her.

'Ah, Mrs. Cavanagh, come to see your star, have you?' he asked Joy, all smiles as his companion walked off, obviously in no mood to stay and make polite conversation.

'Yes, is she all right?'

'Good as gold. Come and see for yourself.'

Travers led the way to Dreamer's stall. She was standing quietly inside, but tossed her head and neighed as they approached.

Joy examined her carefully, happy to see she had taken no harm from her big effort, then turned to Travers, stroking Dreamer's muzzle as she spoke.

'Well, it's been a big day. You've done a wonderful job with her, and I'm looking forward to Gay Lass going into training as soon as the foal is weaned. I hope she'll be able to perform as well as this.'

'Ah, looking forward to more winners, I see.'

'Indeed I am. Apart from being such a thrill for me personally, it's good business for the stud.'

'It is that. As Joy's Dream is still so young, I don't want to race her too much this season. We'll maybe give her a couple of more starts, see how she goes, and then spell her for a while.' He looked at Joy reflectively. 'Would you be interested in buying another filly? She's a three-year-old who's already won two races and shows a lot of promise. She has good bloodlines. She'll make a good brood mare when the time comes, and I think I can get her for you at a good price.'

Joy turned his words over in her mind. Was this the horse they had been discussing when she arrived? If so, the owner was anxious to sell and he would probably take what he could get for her. 'A three-year-old, you say. Would I have heard of her?'

'I'll tell you her name, but if you decide not to go ahead, can I ask you not to repeat it?'

'Of course.'

'She's called Bonnie Doon, and if you watch the racing results regularly you would have heard of her.'

So it was the same horse they'd been discussing! It would make good sense to have another horse that was already in training. Especially if she could be bought cheaply.

'Are you training her now?'

'Yes.'

'And you'd keep her on?'

'Yes. Would you like to see her?'

'Yes, I would.'

'Come on then. She's down in the far stalls.'

Joy gave Dreamer a final rub to the ears and fell in step with Travers as he moved off.

'She hasn't raced since last season,' he continued as they walked towards the far end of the row. 'I spelled her after her last win. She's back in training now, and I brought her along today to re-acquaint her with the bustle of race days. She's entered in a race next month.'

'And you think she has a chance?'

'I do.' They reached the furthest stall and Travers went in and untied the horse inside and led her out. 'Here she is.'

Joy ran her eyes over the filly and liked what she saw. A bay filly with a touch of white on her nose, she looked at Joy with bright, intelligent eyes as she tossed her head and stamped a hoof. She had a deep chest and solid hindquarters, and long straight legs.

Joy stepped up to her and patted her neck. Talking softly, she ran her hands along the bay's back, then down each leg, picking up each hoof one at a time to check it carefully, then stood back and appraised her again. She had the right confirmation to be a winner, and, perhaps more importantly, a good temperament to go with it. Joy walked right around her, taking note that Bonnie Doon stood quite calmly throughout the inspection. Then she stood back again. Did she have that certain quality that made a winner? Did she have the will to win, the competitive spirit that kept a horse striving to be first past the post? The heart that would make her give that extra push to win? Only watching her race could tell that.

'I'm offering her to you first,' Travers told her, 'because you came along just at that moment, and I think she'd suit you, but I do have another owner who's asked me to look out for a good buy for him. I'm pretty sure she's just what he's after, almost certain to win more races, and good lines for breeding. I'll be seeing him after the next race, when I'm saddling up his horse, so I need to know now what your thoughts are.'

'How much are they asking for her?'

He named a figure that was almost the same as what she had won today with the prize money and her winning bet, and which she knew was below market value. What would David think if she went ahead and bought her? Well, he might know more about bloodlines and such things but she knew horses. And she had learnt a lot about what goes into making a winner since those days at Ascot, when Grandfather had introduced her to the races, and she had a good feeling about Bonnie Doon. She made a sudden decision.

'I'll take her.'

David was furious with her. 'What do you mean, you've bought a horse?'

'Just that. I've bought a horse. A racehorse to be more precise. Bonnie Doon, a filly, three years old, who's already won two races and who's ready to win again. With good bloodlines and who'll make a first rate brood mare when the time comes, and will be an asset to the business. And she was going for a very good price.'

'You must be mad. We've had no discussions about buying another horse. We're breeders, not buyers. We need to plan these things.'

'But David, I had to make a snap decision. It was pure chance I happened to be there at just the moment she became available.' She told him about the conversation she had overheard. 'And Travers was going to see someone else, so I had to decide then and there. Besides, the money I won on Dreamer and the prize money will pay for her.'

'I see.' He drew himself up stiffly. 'Well, it's your money. And Redwoods is your property, after all. You can do what you like with it.'

'You know it's not like that at all. We're partners, remember? And I know she'll be an asset. Travers thinks she can win more races, and if she does it's more prestige for the stud, without having to wait for years. It's just good business.' Joy swallowed against a tremor of apprehension. 'I knew you'd be surprised, but I thought you'd be pleased.'

David scowled. 'Hmmph. Let's just hope she lives up to your expectations.'

And Joy knew it would be not only the horse that would be on trial when Bonnie Doon raced, but herself as well.

David refused to have anything to do with the matter, so later that afternoon Joy put her signature to the papers assigning Bonnie Doon to the Redwoods Stud, and confirmed she was happy with the future racing programme that Travers had mapped out for the filly. She was due to have her first start back from a spell in three weeks time.

'Now then,' Travers told her, 'there's also a race on that day that will suit Joy's Dream perfectly, so I think they'll both be racing on the same day. That'll be a bit of excitement for you, won't it?'

Joy was excited, but the atmosphere in the house over the next weeks dimmed her eagerness as David spent long hours working apart from her, and was studiously polite to her when they were together.

However, they all gathered again for the races at Randwick on the designated day. When Joy's Dream won her race they all shared in the triumph and David hugged her, his face glowing.

Joy was as tightly strung as a piano wire, with anticipation and anxiety, as the time for Bonnie Doon's race approached. She went off by herself and sat on a seat under the shade of a jacaranda tree, fanning herself and taking deep breaths to calm the fluttering inside her, lest she make a spectacle of herself by throwing up. When it was time to watch Bonnie Doon saddle up Joy couldn't find David anywhere. It took all her self-control to go to the parade ring, alone and pretend she wasn't worried.

When the Redwoods colours flashed past the post in first place she felt a rush of adrenalin and shouted in triumph, but when she turned to David, he had turned his back to her. As Joy stood watching him accept the plaudits from those around him she felt as if he'd slapped her. Kitty pulled her into the little knot gathered around, making her feel part of the group, and she accepted the congratulations showered on her, and was able to force herself to smile.

Rufe praised her for her acumen in buying a winner, and David put his arm around her shoulders then.

'Yes, she is a clever girl, isn't she?' he agreed.

And once more Joy felt like throwing up, but she took a deep breath, and accepted a glass of champagne instead, and the afternoon ended with them all drinking champagne, and toasting the future success of the Redwoods colours.

Chapter Fifteen

Emma was surprised when, after dinner was over and the children were all settled in bed, Hector sought her out and asked her to come for a ride around the city with him.

'I know it's late,' he told her, 'but it's been an exciting day and it seems a shame to end it. And how exciting to view Sydney at night.'

'Thank you, Hector, yes. I can't say I feel ready for bed yet and that would be very pleasant.'

A few moments later they were settled in the back of a hansom cab. As they reached the city centre Emma saw the streets were filled with those intent on enjoying the many pleasures on offer this warm Saturday night. Couples spilled from the trams and thronged the footpaths as they made their way to the restaurants and public houses that catered to the population on their Saturday night out. They heard voices raised in song as they passed many of the pubs, and in some the clientele had even spilled out on to the pavement.

Hector instructed the driver to drive slowly around the Queen Victoria Building as they passed, so Emma could enjoy its night-time beauty, glittering with lights.

'Where would you like to go next?' he asked her.

'Wherever you like. I'm not terribly familiar with Sydney.'

'Then let's head down to the quay.' He called up to the driver, perched high above and behind them. 'Down to the quay, then just keep driving around.' He leant back and continued. 'I learned my way around Sydney fairly well while I was staying here with Kitty and Rufe, but I'm afraid that, although I like to visit a big city, I'm really happier in the country. Which do you prefer?'

'I find much the same, now that I've spent so much time up at Bulahdelah. I lived in Melbourne during the years I was married. At first I loved it but, while I'd spent much of my childhood in the country and couldn't wait to live in the city, now I find I enjoy country life more.'

Hector reached for her hand and squeezed it gently. 'Perhaps you liked Melbourne at first because you were happy then, and when your husband became ill you could no longer take pleasure in it.'

Emma returned the pressure of his fingers, thinking how understanding he was.

'Yes, that's probably true. But I don't think I'd be happy to live permanently in a big city anymore.'

She left her hand in his, enjoying the feeling of it as he played idly with her fingers as he nodded.

'That's how I feel too. I've been looking at various options since I've been here, but I'm coming to the conclusion that I would rather find something in the country rather than the city.'

The cab reached Hyde Park and Hector called out to the driver to stop.

'Do you want to get out and walk for a bit?' he asked Emma.

'Yes.' She nodded.

He alighted first and helped her down from the cab then, tucking her hand in his arm, he told the cabbie to wait. They walked slowly along the foot path under the lights, in company with a few other couples strolling along the boulevard, watching the play of light and shadow as they passed under trees ruffled by a slight breeze.

'When you were in India, were you stationed in the city or the country?' Emma asked him curiously.

'A bit of both, really. Home was in the city, but we were away on patrol a lot, and it was then we went into the country areas, some of them quite remote.'

'Home?' she queried. 'Did you actually have a home there? Or do you refer to barracks as home?'

'I was in barracks for a while, but I missed the home comforts so I had an establishment of my own that I was able to spend much time in.'

'An establishment?'

'Yes. I had a villa, as did many of the officers, with my own household.'

'Your own household? Do you mean servants?'

'Yes.'

Emma realised she really knew little about his private life, apart from what she knew from Joy about the Barrons' lives in England, but of course Hector had spent many years away from that while he was stationed in India. Emma thought about it as they walked. 'You've never regretted not marrying?'

He hesitated for a moment. 'I realised that a soldier's life is not conducive to a happy marriage. It's hard on a woman. I decided I was better not to pursue marriage, and I've never had occasion to regret my decision.' He stopped and turned Emma towards him, searching her face. 'Not until recently,' he added, 'not until I met you.'

Emma's heart began to beat faster, but at that moment a brash young man with a flashily dressed girl on his arm bumped Hector as they passed.

'Don't block the footpath, mate!' he admonished them.

They resumed walking, with Emma wondering how to respond to his words.

A few paces further along they came to a path that led into a patch of deep shade, and Hector steered Emma down it. They were quite alone here, with only the moonlight to show the way, and he stopped and turned her towards him. His arms went around her and his lips came down, seeking hers. As they met, her arms crept around his neck, and she gave herself over to enjoying the sensations the kiss aroused in her. She felt her fervour rising as their kiss deepened, awakening long dormant desires inside her as she felt a wild stirring of a passion so strong it shocked her. Her heart was beating a wild tattoo and her pulses were racing as she clung to him, going deeper and deeper into the kiss.

Finally he released her and they moved apart, breathing heavily as they gazed at each other.

All of a sudden a picture of Lily's face swam into Emma's vision. The last time she saw her cousin she was a schoolgirl, and she knew that when she went to England Lily was an innocent young girl. Someone took advantage of her, seduced her, and then abandoned her. Could it have been Hector? As she looked at him now, his face soft and eager and his eyes shining with hope, she couldn't believe it possible. But one of the men there at the time had been responsible for Lily's pregnancy, and until it could be proved otherwise Hector must be considered as being on trial with the others. She took a deep shuddering breath and pushed away from him.

'We'd better get back,' she told him, swallowing hard at the look of bewilderment on his face. She almost ran back to the cab, and didn't speak until they were both seated and Hector had directed the driver to take them home.

He turned to her then, his face a picture of distress. 'I'm sorry,' he said, 'I didn't mean to upset you. I'm sorry I got carried away like that, forcing you...'

'No, no, it's nothing like that. It's not your fault. It's just that...oh dear...' She bit her lip, wondering what she could say. 'There's something I must resolve. Something important.'

'Is it something I've done to offend you? Apart from what I did just then?'

Emma shook her head wordlessly, taking a deep breath. 'It's...something I have to sort out.'

'I see.' His voice betrayed his concern. 'Will you be able to tell me when you've sorted it out? Or should I take this as meaning you wish to have nothing more to do with me?'

'No, please don't think that... I...I will let you know,' she stammered.

They drove the rest of the way in silence.

Emma had to find the truth. In some way she must try to find who had fathered Lily's child. But how?

The next day Hector announced he was going to Melbourne on business, and Emma's heart plummeted. Had she driven him away? The thought was reinforced when she heard Kitty ask him if he knew how long he was going for, and he replied he wasn't sure, it depended on the outcome of a certain project he had in mind, but he would keep in touch. Did it mean he was going to look at business opportunities down South, far removed from her? After a formal goodbye he was gone, and Emma wondered if she would ever see him again.

As she sat morosely in the garden with a cup of tea later in the morning, Joy came out to join her, carrying her own cup with her.

'You look rather down in the dumps this morning,' she told her. She set her cup down on the table beneath a large Tibouchina tree, which had shed its rich purple blossoms over the ground below. 'Mind if I join you?' Brushing the blossoms from the chair beside Emma she sat without waiting for a reply. 'What's the matter?'

'Oh nothing really. I've probably just ruined the rest of my life, that's all. And Johnnie's too.'

'Oh dear. Is it Hector? Have you had an argument?'

'No, not really. But I'm afraid I might have scared him off forever.'

'And now you're sorry?'

'I shouldn't have acted the way I did. I should have been more tactful.' Emma twisted her hands together. 'I think he thinks I don't want anything more to do with him.'

'And you do?'

'Well... yes...' She paused. 'I think I'm in love with him, and I'm afraid I've scared him away.'

Frowning, Joy put her cup down. 'Do you want to tell me about it?'

'Well, you know we went for a drive around Sydney last night?' Joy nodded. 'And after we'd driven round for a while, we got out and took a bit of a stroll, and when we reached a secluded spot, Hector kissed me.'

'And you didn't like it?'

'It wasn't that. In fact I quite enjoyed it.' She paused, remembering the effect it had on her. 'Yes,' she sighed, 'but then I spoilt it. I suddenly thought of Lily, and the horrible thought went through my mind that maybe Hector was the one who seduced her, and if he was I just couldn't have any sort of relationship with him, and I...I just pushed him away. I couldn't tell him what was the matter, could I? You can't just up and say to a man who's just kissed you, 'by the way, did you seduce my young cousin', can you now?'

'So what did you tell him?'

'Nothing. That's it. I just hurried back to the cab and we came home. On the way I told him I had to sort something out.'

'And that's all?'

'Yes.'

'And did he say anything to you before he went this morning?'

'No. Just goodbye.'

'He'll be back, after all, he only took a small bag with him, I noticed.'

'That might not be until we're back in Bulahdelah, and then maybe he won't go back there.'

'We'll worry about that when the time comes. In the meantime we have to try and find out who it was, one way or the other.' She stood up. 'Come on, let's go and find Mrs. Frobisher, and see if she remembers anything more.'

They found her supervising the three children as they played together in Benjamin's nursery, and stood watching their games for a few moments while passing pleasantries with Mrs. Frobisher.

In spite of her concern over her own affairs, Emma was pleased to see how well the children were getting along together. Johnnie was a year older than Benjamin, and Xandra was the baby, not yet three years old, but they all seemed to be happy together. Emma smiled as she saw that it seemed to be Xandra who dictated what they were doing, with the two boys following her orders. They were playing a child's version of charades, with each taking a turn in acting out their parts, while the other two guessed who or what they were.

Mrs. Frobisher was in high spirits, as she had given Rufe five shillings to place a bet on Joy's Dream, and received thirteen pounds in return. They discussed the races for a few minutes, and then Joy brought the talk around to Ascot and their visit to England. From there it was a simple matter to introduce Lily into the conversation.

Mrs. Frobisher shook her head. 'Oh that Lily,' she lamented. 'What a trial she was. She...' she pulled up short, glancing at Emma.

'It's all right,' Joy told her, 'Emma's her cousin, so she knows the story. You needn't be afraid to speak in front of her.'

'You mean, about young Benjamin?' she whispered.

'Yes, Mrs. Frobisher,' Emma told her, keeping her voice low, although it was unlikely any of the laughing, squealing children were listening to them. 'It's such a mystery, and while we don't discuss it outside the family it's important, for...relationship issues, that we try to find out who was responsible.'

Joy nodded. 'Yes, we've been wondering whether you can remember anything more now, thinking back, that might give us a clue.'

Mrs. Frobisher frowned, shaking her head. 'Not really, no.'

'Do you think it was one of the gentlemen who were staying there at the time, or perhaps one of the visitors, there were plenty of them I recall, or even one of the footmen?'

Mrs. Frobisher sniffed. 'I think you can rule out the footmen. Miss Lily started to give herself airs and graces soon after we arrived, staying in that grand hall and all. I believe she would've considered the footmen below her. Started to order me about something awful, she did, when Lady Barron designated me as her ladies' maid.' She sniffed again. 'Nasty temper, she had, too, when things didn't go her way.'

'I'm sure she was quite unpleasant to you at times,' Joy commiserated. 'But what about the gentlemen who visited?' Can you think of any of them who paid her extra attention?'

'No, not really, but I think it might have been one of the military gentlemen who were staying. She was ever so upset when she found they'd left and gone back to their regiment. I remember her saying she thought they'd just gone into the village for the day.'

'Well, if so, that would narrow it down,' Joy said, frowning. 'But which one?'

Mrs. Frobisher shifted uncomfortably.

'What is it, Mrs. Frobisher?' Joy asked. 'Have you remembered something else? It is important, you know.'

'Well, I don't think it was Captain Hastings,' she spoke slowly, 'because, you see, well, he was sort of interested in me.'

'Was he now?'

'Yes, sort of. Nothing improper, you know!'

'No, of course not. I'd never think such a thing of you. But it would help to know for sure. Did you ever go to meet him?'

'Just once or twice. When it was my day off. Just to take a walk and talk, you know.'

'Yes, of course. Well, that probably rules him out. Which leaves the other two.'

'Unless it was someone we don't know about,' Emma added. 'One of the visitors, or neighbours.'

'Yes.' Joy tapped her toe on the floor as she stood thinking. 'It could have been. I wonder why Lily decided to call him Benjamin?'

'Perhaps she just liked the name,' Mrs. Frobisher said. 'Maybe she read it in a book.'

'Perhaps,' Joy agreed. 'Or perhaps it has a significance. Perhaps it's someone we haven't thought of yet. Could it be the father's name? Or a family name?'

Emma sighed. 'So unless we find a man called Benjamin we're not much further forward.'

When the end of the week arrived and it was time for them to return to Bulahdelah, Emma had received no word from Hector.

Chapter Sixteen

As they all settled back into Redwoods again after the excitement of the Sydney visit life picked up in the usual way again, with David and Joy both busy with the horses.

It was time to begin weaning Chipper and this was a trying time for both the foal and his mother as they needed to be separated for a while each day in order for Chipper to stop relying on his mother's milk, and to learn to accept the fodder that was offered to him in its place. The length of hours apart was gradually increased day by day, but Chipper wanted to be with his mother, and Lassie wanted her foal, so both were suffering, and Joy devoted much of her day to the two horses as they learnt to accept the fact that life had changed.

Emma was left alone with the children for much of the time, and she replayed the scene with Hector and its aftermath through her mind again and again, and condemned herself for the way she handled it. She decided that if she did see Hector again she must find some way to resolve the mystery of Benjamin's parentage, or else learn to accept that they would never know, and take the man as she knew him.

It was soon after breakfast one morning a week later when Mary told her Mr. Osborne had called to see her. He was standing looking out the window of the drawing room as she entered, his hands clasped behind his back, and he turned at her entry and came towards her with a smile on his face.

'As it's such a lovely day, I've come to see if you and Johnnie will join me on an outing. I have to see about some timber up near Wootton, and I've taken the liberty of having my housekeeper pack enough lunch for us all. It's through some very pleasant scenery, and I'm sure Johnnie will enjoy seeing the logging railway up there in action. I think you would both enjoy it, and I would certainly enjoy your company.'

'That's very kind of you.' Emma hesitated, thinking of Hector, but, after all, she didn't know if she would ever see him again. 'Yes, thank you, we'd be pleased to come.' She glanced out the window. 'As you say, it is a lovely day. Please take a seat while I call Johnnie, and check it will be all right to leave Xandra with Mrs. Morgan.'

A short time later they were seated in Harry's trap heading towards Wootton, travelling along a well rutted side road, with Emma glad of the good springing in Harry's vehicle. Following the track, they wound slowly upwards through the Wang Wauk forest. Harry was right;, the scenery was spectacular, with trees and moss-covered boulders edging the track. Colourful lorikeets screeched overhead amongst the trees from time to time, breaking the silence, and the ever present galahs fluttered their way off the track ahead of them, just when it seemed the horse must step on them.

They were deep into the forest when Harry slowed the horse to a walk, pointing up into the trees to show them where a koala dozed in the fork of a gum tree, its baby clinging to its furry back. A little further on they crossed a creek with a bridge that rattled as they passed over it and, as they rounded a bend, a waterfall cascading down the side of the hill over rocky outcrops came into view, and Emma marvelled at the beauty of the forest, which was preserved as public land and untouched by the timber cutters, and was pleased they'd come.

Much further on, past the forest, they heard the sound of axes, faint at first but becoming louder as they reached a large clearing in the wooded land. Harry pulled the trap over, and they came to a stop. There was plenty of activity going on in front of them. At the far side of the clearing was a railway line, and a group of men heaved and shoved, shouting and calling to each other as they worked, loading timber logs on to the flat tops behind a steam engine that would take them down to the mill.

'This is as far as we go,' Harry said. 'I have some business to discuss, and while I do that I thought you and Johnnie might like to watch as they get the next load ready to take to the mill.'

Johnnie jumped to the ground as Harry stepped down and offered his hand to Emma. She was pleased to stretch her legs and enjoy the sunshine as they made their way across the open ground to stand and watch the men at their work for a few moments, until Harry left them to talk to the man supervising the loading.

Johnnie tugged at his mother's hand, pulling her across closer to the engine, where a man inside stoked the fire, sweat pouring off him as he piled wood onto the already fierce flames. Johnnie hopped from one foot to another with excitement until finally the train was ready to go. The door to the burner slammed shut and the stoker stood back, wiping his face with a grimy cloth, and reached up to pull on a wire hanging from the roof. There was a piercing whistle as the engine-driver released the brake and pulled a lever, and the train ground slowly forward.

Johnnie clapped his hands excitedly. As the last of the load pulled out of sight, Harry came back to join them.

'Did you enjoy seeing all that?' he asked Johnnie.

'Yes.' He nodded emphatically. 'It was beaut. I'm going to be an engine-driver when I'm growed-up,'

'Well, how about we go and have some lunch now, while you think about it?'

'Yes, I'm hungry. And thirsty too,' he added. 'It's hot being an engine-driver.'

'Very hot indeed. Then it's a good thing I've brought some lemonade, isn't it?'

Emma packed away the remnants of their lunch while Johnnie lay on his stomach watching a beetle making its slow way along a twig at the edge of the forest.

Emma had kept the conversation on an impersonal level during lunch by discussing the trip to Sydney and the excitement of Joy's Dream's win, but now she was running out of things to say.

Harry cleared his throat. 'Are enjoying our outing?' he asked her as she packed away the last of the things.

'Yes, indeed. It's been most pleasant.'

'And Johnnie seems to have enjoyed it.'

'Oh yes, he's had a wonderful time.' She laughed. 'I think it's made up his mind to be an engine-driver.'

'I would like to think we could have many more such outings. In fact, I hope we can spend much more time together than we've been spending recently.'

'Life seems to be so busy...' Emma faltered, closing the lid of the hamper.

He brushed away her words with a wave of his hand. 'Not too busy to spend some time with me, I hope?'

Emma swallowed. 'Joy relies on me to help her with the baby now that she has to spend so much time out with the horses, and it takes up a lot of my time.' Even to her ears it sounded a lame excuse.

'Surely with Mary and Mrs. Morgan in the house you can take time away when you want?' He paused. 'After all, they would have to manage without you should you decide to leave Redwoods, and they can't expect you to remain with them forever.' He looked at her meaningfully. 'You may decide you want a home of your own again.'

Emma's stomach clenched as she looked across at Johnnie. It was obvious he was enjoying the trip, and that he relished male company. He needed a father, someone of his own who could devote time to him every day. But as she looked at Harry she knew he could never evoke the passionate response from her that Hector's kiss had stirred in her. But perhaps she would never see Hector again.

'I haven't any such plans at the moment.'

He narrowed his eyes. 'You may have forgotten, but I once asked if you had thought of marrying again.'

'And I seem to recall I said there was no way I could even contemplate such an action before Matthew has been gone for at least two years.' She shook her head. 'It would be disrespectful to his memory.'

'And when will the two years be up?'

'In about another three months.'

'Then I suppose I must be patient.' He got to his feet, his face unreadable. 'And now I'll put these things back in the trap, and we must head towards home.'

Emma was in a quandary. Harry Osborne's words left her in no doubt as to his intentions. When it was two years from Matthew's death, he would ask her to marry him. What was she to say? She knew she didn't love him, but would that matter so much? She tried to push away the memory of Hector's kiss, and the rush of passion it had induced in her. He'd made her feel ardour she'd never expected to feel again. Could love come twice in her life? It seemed so.

But she'd pushed him away, and it seemed he'd taken it to mean she didn't care for him. As each day passed and no word came from him she became more and more convinced that she wouldn't hear from him again.

She tried to weigh up the pros and cons of marriage to Harry. She'd seen the way he looked at her when he thought she wasn't watching, his gaze raking her from head to toe, lust on his face. He would expect it to be a marriage in the fullest sense of the word; she had no illusions about that. In return, he would become the father Johnnie needed, with all the benefits that being the only child of a prosperous boat builder would bring. And she would become mistress of her own home again. Happy as she was living here with Joy, she did miss that. Could she endure the nights in Harry's bed in return for the benefits the marriage would bring? Many women would consider it a good bargain.

A few days later, Harry called again and Emma and Johnnie joined him on a trip to the Myall Lakes so Johnnie could see a black swan that had an unusually large bevy of tiny cygnets trailing behind her, and Emma was impressed by his thoughtfulness.

Another week passed with no word from Hector, but another outing with Harry, this time by boat down the Myall River, and Emma decided she would probably be foolish to refuse Harry's proposal when it came.

Chapter Seventeen

Emma heard a great clatter outside, and the next moment Johnnie rushed into the house, his eyes wide his and face flushed with excitement.

'Mummy, Mummy, come quick. Come outside and see!'

'Whatever's the matter?'

'Come and see!' Pulling Emma along with him, he hurried her through the front door and out on to the verandah.

In front of the house stood a carriage, the like of which she had never seen. Black and shiny, it had four wheels, upholstered seats, and brass carriage lights, but no horse to pull it. It emitted a loud and ominous chugging sound. At the very front, where the horse should have been, a large metal box-like contraption with brass edging rested on a platform. Instead of reins the driver, who wore a dust coat, goggles and a cap, rested his hands on a wheel mounted on a column in front of him. It was one of the new horseless carriages she'd read about in the newspaper. A motorcar.

Removing his goggles the driver waved to her and called out, his face split into a wide grin. What he said was drowned by the noise of the engine, but she felt her pulses quicken as she realised it was Hector.

He beckoned to her and she walked down the steps, her mind swirling with a thousand questions, but first and foremost was delight that he'd returned.

'Hop in,' he shouted above the noise. 'Johnnie too,' he added.

Johnnie clambered onto the running board and Emma gave him a push up before gingerly using the handrail to pull herself up onto the seat.

Hector reached across Johnnie to take her hand and squeeze it. 'Hello.' His questioning eyes searched her face. 'Are you all right?' As he spoke he took his foot from the pedal to lessen the clamour, whereupon the motor spluttered and came to a shuddering stop.

'Yes.' Her voice was loud in the sudden quiet.

'Good.' He grimaced. 'Damn thing's stopped. Want to come for a ride?'

'Yes. If it'll still go.'

'She will, don't worry. I've had plenty of practice at this over the last few weeks.'

Hector hopped out, brandishing an iron handle, and next moment he was at the front of the vehicle, and inserted the handle into a slot and cranked it with mighty swings. As the engine roared into life he leapt back into his seat and released the hand brake. The car jolted forward and they were away. Hector steered forward along the track with a smile on his face, completely oblivious of the small crowd of onlookers they were leaving behind.

Emma sat forward in her seat holding on to the hand rail, while Johnnie ran his fingers along the dashboard in front, turned around to feel the leather in the seats, and even bent down to feel the floor.

'What's it called?' he hollered above the noise of the motor.

'She's a Tarrant,' Hector shouted. 'She's one of the first motorcars in Australia. Do you like her?'

Johnnie nodded enthusiastically. 'Yes.'

'And how about you Emma, do you like her?'

'I think so. Ask me when we get back safely.'

Hector looked across at her, laughing, and then, as the car lurched through a dip, he looked back at the road and concentrated on his driving.

After driving down to the river and back, they pulled up again outside the house, where a crowd had gathered, and this time Hector turned the engine off.

'You have some admirers waiting, I see,' Emma told him, 'so I'll leave you to it.'

'But I will see you later?'

'Are you staying?'

'If you want me to. Do you?' His eyes seemed to be pleading.

'Yes.' She smiled at him before stepping down from the car. 'Come on, Johnnie,' she said as her son made no move to join her.

'Can't I stay here?' he pleaded.

Hector ruffled the boy's hair, smiling. 'He can stay if you don't mind.'

'If he won't be in the way?'

'Never.'

'Very well then, but don't be a nuisance,' she told the excited boy as she turned away and moved through the press of onlookers. It seemed that work on Redwoods had been suspended for the day, and word must have spread around Bulahdelah since Hector drove through its main street, as many of the townspeople were here, curious to see this new wonder they had only read about.

Evening was drawing in when Hector finally came inside, with Johnnie trailing after him. He'd spent the whole time answering questions for those who came to see this new wonder vehicle, extolling its features and lifting the bonnet to show off the motor. It had only been the fading light that persuaded the last reluctant visitors to leave.

When the children were fed and in bed, the family gathered in the drawing room so Hector could tell them how he came by the vehicle.

'I'd read about the Tarrant in the newspapers, like everyone else, and I was curious to see it,' he explained, 'so, as I'd planned to visit Melbourne for a look around, I made a sudden decision. After the excitement of the races,' he flashed a glance at Emma, 'it seemed like a good time to go. When I visited the Tarrant Engineering premises they were just putting the finishing touches to the vehicle, and after a talk with Harley Tarrant and a drive around Melbourne – w here it attracted a lot of attention, I must say – I decided to buy it.'

'Just like that?' Jack Morgan asked.

Hector laughed. 'Well, no, not really as simple as that, actually. There was a lot I wanted to know before I made the final decision, and after I'd spent time watching Harley Tarrant working on it, and bombarded him with questions, I could see it was not just some new-fangled idea that was going to be forgotten in a year or so, but a new way of transport.' His face shone with excitement. 'I really believe it's the way of the future, and the time will come when everyone will have one, like they have a horse today.'

'But you can't possibly think it will take the place of horses, surely?' asked Bella incredulously.

'Yes, Mrs. Morgan, I do. A motorcar doesn't have to be fed and watered, or groomed, or cleaned up after like a horse, and it runs on fuel. It won't be as difficult to keep in a city establishment as a horse and carriage. It won't take up as much room or need as much attention. When you drive it to where you want to go, you just get out and walk away, and leave it where it is until you want it again. But the big advantage is that it doesn't have to be rested like a horse, it just keeps on going, mile after mile, until you want to stop, and it can travel at up to forty miles an hour, hour after hour.'

'You talk as if you're selling them.' David laughed.

'Don't joke about that,' Hector told him. 'I have thought about it. Maybe it'd be a good business. Harley Tarrant has offered me a proposition to be involved with him in producing and marketing the vehicles.'

Emma's heart plummeted at his words. So he was thinking of moving to Melbourne.

Joy was watching Hector thoughtfully. 'It doesn't sound a silly idea to me, if you really believe in it. Although I can't see it ever taking over from horses, it sounds as if it could have a good future, particularly for long distances.'

'I'm sure of it, but I told Tarrant I'll have to give it a lot more thought before making a decision. I need to see just how reliable it is mechanically.'

'Have you driven it all the way from Melbourne?' Emma asked him.

'Yes, and it didn't give much trouble on the way. I had a crash course in mechanics before I took delivery of it, and I need to do much more driving before I finally decide. In fact, I'm going to take it for a spin tomorrow. Johnnie seemed to enjoy being in it today, so I wonder if you'd both like to accompany me? That's if you think you can put up with the noise,' he added.

Emma's heart leapt. 'I think I could, and I'm sure Johnnie would love it, so, yes, thank you, we'll be happy to come.'

'Good, that's settled then.'

The rest of the evening passed in general conversation, and when Emma went to bed she was in two states of mind. Part of the time she was sure Hector couldn't be especially interested in her if he was contemplating moving to Melbourne, well away from her, while at other times she thought that he wouldn't have driven his new motorcar all the way back up here if he didn't want to be with her. There had been no chance for them to talk privately tonight, and she looked forward to the next day.

The entire household gathered next morning to watch them leave. The lunch hamper Mary prepared was stowed in the back and Johnnie was already in the car when Emma walked down the steps to join them, a scarf tied over her hat to hold it firmly in place. Johnnie was sitting in the driver's seat making 'vroom, vroom' noises as he turned the steering wheel, while Hector stood alongside smiling indulgently, the starting handle held ready in his hand.

As Emma seated herself Hector gestured Johnnie to move over, leaving the driver's seat free. Going to the front of the car, he inserted the handle and gave it a mighty swing. The motor sat stolidly silent. Another swing, followed by another, and another. When the engine finally roared into life a cheer went up from the little crowd. Perspiration beaded his face as Hector rushed back to the driver's side, hopped up into his seat, flung the handle in the back, and pressed his foot on the pedal, keeping the motor revving. Leaning back in his seat he took a deep breath and mopped his face. He shot Emma a triumphant smile before releasing the handbrake and easing the motorcar forward.

Another cheer went up from the group as he turned the vehicle and drove sedately along the driveway. Emma and Johnnie both turned and waved goodbye, and Johnnie squirmed in his seat with excitement.

'We're going to head up north,' Hector yelled above the noise of the motor, as he drove through the gate and turned out on to the road, 'maybe even as far as Taree, if we can manage it.'

Emma nodded, knowing her words would be lost. Seconds later she grabbed her hat as the car accelerated and the wind tried to whip it from her head. She tied the scarf more firmly.

Passing through heavily timbered areas, the road rose and fell as it followed the slopes of the hills. Emma wondered if they would make it up the steep inclines but, although they had to slow down often, Hector adjusted the gear levers and, with a growl and a jerk, the engine saw them safely to the top each time.

Going down the other side of a hill was different. Now the car picked up speed, and Emma gripped the hand rail tightly. Johnnie laughed aloud, bouncing in his seat. At the bottom of each slope he turned to her, his eyes sparkling, and shouted something that was lost in the rush of the wind, but she could tell he was enjoying the thrills.

They passed through Coolongolook and continued a few miles further until they reached Nabiac. Emma was quite relieved when Hector pulled the car to the side of the road outside the inn, and took his foot off the pedal, whereupon the car idled for a moment before coughing and shuddering into silence.

He turned to her. 'Well, how are you enjoying it?' he asked, his face alight with exhilaration.

His excitement was contagious, and Emma forgot her moments of fright and smiled at him as she answered. 'It's wonderful. I can't believe we've come all this way over the hills in such a short time. And now I can see what you mean by not having a horse to worry about. We could get out now and just walk away, and this will just stay here without any problem.' She stopped, gestured at the curious onlookers approaching them and laughed. 'Except for them.'

Hector shrugged. 'You get used to it,' he replied, as people clustered around, all asking questions at once. He answered them as best he could, explaining in general terms how the vehicle operated, before clambering down and making his way into the inn. He emerged a few moments later with two glasses of lemonade.

'Thirsty work, this driving,' he told them with a smile as he handed them each a glass.

Emma took hers gratefully, realising she was parched.

'Are we going to do some more driving now?' Johnnie asked after they finished their drinks.

'We are indeed. We still have a long way to go.'

Hector cranked the motor, which sprang into life instantly this time, hopped back in and slowly eased the car forward, causing the crowd to move reluctantly aside. With a wave, he increased the speed, and they were on their way again.

After crossing more heavily timbered hills they emerged onto gentler land. Here were paddocks on either side, with cattle grazing contentedly in the green pastures, and homesteads, often with sheltering gum trees nearby, clearly visible from the road.

There was little traffic along the way, but the few horses they passed were usually pulled to the side of the road by their riders as they approached, where they stood watching them go by, although there were some who took fright and shied away from the noise. Hector always waved as they passed, and Johnnie was soon imitating him. Although she couldn't hear the words, Emma feared that some of the shouted responses were abuse hurled at this disturbance on their roads.

After travelling a few more miles through yet another timbered area they pulled off into a side road, where casuarinas grew alongside a creek, and drove slowly along until they reached a clearing. Here they stopped, and Emma climbed gratefully from the car as Hector collected the lunch hamper from the back.

There was no opportunity for any private conversation as they ate their lunch. It was not until they finished their meal and Johnnie left them to venture down to the bank of the creek to find stones to toss that Hector looked across at Emma with a frown creasing his brow.

'We haven't had a chance to talk alone since I've been back, and I've been waiting for the opportunity to apologise to you for my behaviour that night. I really am sorry I offended you in that way.'

'You didn't offend me.' She wondered how she could explain without discussing Lily. 'It was just that you took me by surprise, I suppose...' she paused. 'I just wasn't expecting it. It's been a long time...'

'I'm sorry, I should have been more sensitive. I should have realised you're still grieving for your husband. Please forgive me.'

'There's nothing to forgive. I shouldn't have acted in such a childish way.'

'No, the fault is mine. Can we possibly put it behind us and begin again. I do so want us to be friends.'

Emma swallowed. It wasn't really what she wanted, she'd hoped for more than just friendship. It was her own fault of course. She shouldn't have reacted so.

'Of course.'

'Friends then?' he asked with a hopeful smile, as Johnnie came racing back.

'Friends.'

'Good.' He beamed. 'Then do you think that you could put up with another drive tomorrow and join me again for another trip? I thought we could go down to Sugarloaf Point at Seal Rocks and see if we can climb up as far as the lighthouse and see the view from there. That's if you'd like to?'

Johnnie jumped up and down. 'Say yes Mummy, say yes.'

Emma smiled and said yes, they would be happy to come.

Chapter Eighteen

The next morning Emma was in her room tying the scarf over her hat when Joy put her head around the door.

'Mr Osborne's here to see you.' Her brows lifted. 'Were you expecting him?'

Emma felt a flutter of consternation. 'No. I hope he's not called expecting us to go somewhere with him.'

'That would be awkward. Better be tactful.'

Emma drew a breath as she untied the scarf and removed her hat, smoothing her hair. 'Yes, indeed.'

But her intention was thwarted as she moved to greet her visitor, for Johnnie came bouncing down the hall, ready for their outing to Seal Rocks with his cap firmly in place.

'Hello Mr. Osborne, we're going for a trip in Uncle Hector's motorcar,' he enthused.

Harry Osborne's face darkened. 'I take it that's the contraption I saw standing outside?'

'Yes it's a motorcar. You don't need a horse with it and it goes really fast, lots faster than a horse can go.'

Emma took a dismayed step towards him. 'Mr. Osborne...'

'Well, it was my intention to ask if you would care to accompany me on an outing, but I can't compete with that, can I?' He drew himself up, his eyes narrow slits as he turned towards the door. 'So I'll say good day.'

Emma put her hand on his arm to stay him, but he shook it roughly away and stormed out, slamming the door loudly behind him.

Biting her lip with dismay, Emma felt a fluttering inside her as she watched him stamp angrily away. Surely he was being unreasonable expecting her to save her time exclusively for him? She hadn't been expecting him to call and, after all, she'd given him no commitment. Sighing, she returned to her room and replaced the hat, tying the scarf firmly in place before making her way out on to the verandah.

Hector came whistling around the corner a moment later. 'All ready?'

'Yes.' She nodded her head absently as she watched Harry Osborne's trap careering away.

Hector seemed not to notice her preoccupation. He took her arm to escort her down the steps and into the waiting motorcar, while Johnnie raced ahead to jump into his seat in the middle. The car started after only two swings of the handle today. Hector smiled broadly as he jumped in and revved the motor before moving off and turning his vehicle with a nonchalant air, heading along the drive and out onto the road.

'All set?' he called above the noise of the motor.

'Yes,' Johnnie yelled back, jiggling in his seat.

Emma tried to push all thoughts of Harry Osborne from her mind as she nodded and sat back, determined to enjoy the day.

The road took them around the edge of the Myall Lakes as they headed towards the coast, and they were soon the passing through heavily wooded scrub and timber, with fern glades full of bungalow palms, staghorns, and cabbage-tree palms among the taller eucalypts and casuarinas, while occasional breaks in the trees allowed them glimpses of the lake beyond.

After what seemed like hours of driving, the road turned as they reached the end of the lake, so vast it seemed like an inland sea. It teemed with water birds diving to feed, or floating lazily on its broad bosom. A narrow track led away from the lake and they jolted their way along it until they reached a clearing, where Hector pulled to the side and switched off the motor.

'Well, here we are.'

From the clearing the ground rose steeply, and a narrow track led up to the lighthouse, perched high above them, and the roar of the ocean came clearly.

'So what's it to be first? Lunch or the climb?' Hector asked Emma.

'I think I could do with a walk, so how about we look first and then eat?'

'Suits me. Come along Johnnie,' he called as the boy wandered over to investigate an ant hill he had spied among the low bushes at the edge of the clearing.

After a steep climb they came over the brow of the hill were alongside the lighthouse, which stood on a small plateau on the top of a steep cliff. Hector stood beside Emma, with Johnnie's hand grasped firmly in his own. They peered over the edge to see the ocean crashing against the cliff below them, sending white spume flying up into the air as each wave hit.

After watching the awesome display for a few moments they crossed to stand where they could look down into the chasm. White water churned through the channel between the two cliffs, its foaming currents eddying and swirling. Emma's heart pitched nervously as she looked down into the maelstrom and she soon tugged them back to the safety of the lighthouse walls.

'So what do you think of it?' Hector asked her then.

'It's beautiful, but it's such a dangerous place.'

'It is. There have been quite a few ships wrecked here, which, of course, is why they built the lighthouse.' He turned his attention to Johnnie. 'I want you to remember this place Johnnie. You must always remember to take great care when you're near cliffs. You can see how easy it would be to fall if you were too close to the edge, can't you?'

Johnnie looked up, his eyes wide. 'Yes.'

'Bulahdelah Mountain is just as dangerous as this, with its high cliffs. You must never go there without a grownup.'

'I won't,' he promised earnestly.

'Good lad,' he told him, then turned to Emma. 'But it has its softer side as well. Come over to the other side and we'll have a look.'

They walked around the lighthouse until they could see down onto the beach.

'Can we go down to the beach too?' asked Johnnie.

'Of course.'

They returned to the car and carried their picnic lunch onto the beach. After they finished lunch Emma rolled up the legs of Johnnie's trousers so he could paddle in the water.

'I've made up my mind that I'll definitely stay in Australia permanently,' Hector told her as they stood by the edge of the water, watching. 'At the moment I'm not entirely sure where I'll settle for good. I'm extremely interested to pursue my involvement with Tarrant Engineering, but I haven't ruled out looking for a country property. Perhaps sheep or cattle.' He shrugged. 'One is almost spoilt for choice here.'

'I suppose it's a matter of knowing what you really want to do.'

'Yes, and at the moment I'm keeping an open mind on that. It's dependent on the outcome of so many matters.' His smiled at her. 'But no matter what, I'm glad we're friends.' He seemed about to say more but at that moment Johnnie came running from the water, clamouring for attention to his wet trouser legs. For once Emma was frustrated that her son was with them.

As they drove home, with the motor too noisy for talking, Emma wondered just what he had been going to say. Was he saying he cared about her, or that he wanted to be just friends and no more? Had she been mistaken in thinking his kiss was an expression of deeper feeling? All of a sudden Joy's story of Lily and her seduction came flooding back to her. Could he be the man who seduced and then abandoned her cousin? And had his kiss been merely the prelude to an attempt to seduce her?

Once back at Redwoods no opportunity presented itself for private conversation, and the thoughts whirling through her brain led to a sleepless night for Emma. When a telegraph came for Hector the following morning and he announced he must pay another visit to Sydney immediately, Emma was more confused than ever.

The following week Harry Osborne called again. This time he made no offer to take them on an outing, but rather accepted the invitation to join the ladies for morning tea. When they finished he asked Emma if she would accompany him on a stroll around the garden.

'I hope you and Johnnie enjoyed your outing with Barron in his noisy machine last week. Did you go far?'

'We went to Seal Point, to look at the view from the lighthouse. And then Johnnie paddled in the water at the beach nearby.'

'Ah. He would have been delighted to do that, I'm sure. And did you like going in that machine?'

'It's rather noisy, but, yes, it was an interesting experience.'

'I've read of them in the newspapers, of course, but I can't believe they're anything more than a novelty. Here today and gone tomorrow, I should think. Too noisy and smelly by far, to say nothing of them frightening the animals. I wouldn't be surprised to see them banned from the roads.'

'That may be so, but I suspect they could become popular because of the long distances they can travel without having to rest.'

'Perhaps. But I didn't come here to discuss the horseless carriage, as you may well guess.' He stopped walking, turning to look at her, and when Emma offered no reply he continued. 'You may remember that some time ago I asked you if you would consider marrying again, and you replied that it was too soon for such a consideration.'

Emma's heart thudded as she nodded wordlessly. This was not what she wanted to hear.

'Well, considerable time has passed. I think I have been patient. So now I am asking you to marry me.'

Emma looked at him and remembered Matthew, how much she'd loved him, and how wonderful it had been before he became ill. Then she relived the moments of that night in Sydney, and how Hector's kiss had made her feel – how she realised she could still love again, still feel passion, and hunger for intimacy. Even though she didn't know how Hector really felt about her, she realised she could never marry Harry Osborne. She could never settle for less than love. Not even to give Johnnie a father, and the other benefits such a marriage would give him – indeed would give them both.

Emma drew a deep breath. 'Mr. Osborne, I'm conscious of the honour you do me by your offer, and I thank you for it. But I'm afraid that on consideration I realise I will never marry again.'

He sucked in a sharp breath as his face tightened. His eyes were flinty pebbles as he drew himself up stiffly. 'I see.' His voice was cold as ice. 'Then if you have made your decision there's nothing more to be said.'

'I'm sorry Mr. Osborne, I...'

'There's nothing more to be said. Good day to you, madam.' He turned on his heel. Emma shivered as she watched him go. There was hatred in his parting look.

Chapter Nineteen

'There are some things I wish to discuss with my father, so I intend to go to Riverside for a few days,' David told Joy one day as they came in from tending the horses. 'I'll leave tomorrow.'

'Oh! Shall I come with you?'

'No, that's not necessary. I'll be tied up with my father most of the time. You'll be far happier back here with the horses.'

Joy bit her lip. 'I see. How long do you plan to be away?'

He shrugged. 'I'm not sure. A few days probably. Maybe a week.'

Then I'll go and pack for you.' She turned to move away.

'No, you needn't bother, I won't need much. I'll toss a few things in a bag. I can do it now.'

Joy felt tears prick her eyelids as she watched him head inside. What was happening to them? What was happening to their marriage, to the closeness they'd once shared? What had become of the happy, funny young man who had found so much to enjoy in life, had teased her, called her 'shrimp', and loved her so much? She still loved David as much as ever, but she wondered if he felt the same about her. Sometimes he seemed so distant. Their only discussions these days seemed to be about the horses or Xandra.

Watching him leave the next day, after giving her a perfunctory kiss on the cheek, she made up her mind that when he returned she'd make an extra effort to try and revive some of the closeness they shared in their early days together.

Joy was busy in the store preparing Chipper's feed three days later when she was surprised to see Jim Travers arrive at Redwoods.

'Morning, Mrs. Cavanagh,' he greeted her, tipping his hat. 'I got a message from Mr. Cavanagh that the young colt is weaned now, and it's time for Gay Lass to go into training.'

'Oh. Yes. It is, but I wasn't aware my husband had been in touch with you.'

'Yes, I've had a note from him saying to come and pick her up and get her underway. So that's why I'm here.'

'Well then, if that's the case, we'd better go and get her.'

Joy put down the bucket and picked up a couple of carrots before leading the way down to the horse paddocks. As they passed Thunder's paddock the stallion poked his nose through the fence and whinnied. Joy stopped and walked across to the gate, pulled one of the carrots from her pocket and passed it through the gate to him.

Travers stood by her appraising the horse with narrowed eyes as Thunder crunched his treat.

'That's a nice looking animal. Belongs to you, does he?'

Joy sensed thinly disguised excitement in the trainer's voice.

'Yes. To Redwoods, that is.'

'Of course. Going to race him, are you?'

'We have discussed it,' she told him carefully.

'What else would you do with him?'

'He really came to us for breeding our stock horses.'

'Where did he come from?'

'He was a gift from my stepfather.'

'But where did he come from?' he persisted. 'What's his bloodline?'

'He's not a thoroughbred. He was with a lot of horses that came down from a station up north.'

'Ah! Up north you say.' He nodded. 'Yes, I've seen it happen. Sometimes good horses escape from the owners of those outback properties, join up with the wild brumbies. Reckon the odd thoroughbred was mixed in with that lot, because he definitely comes from good stock.'

As they stood taking in Thunder's intelligent eyes and the sense of harnessed power that he radiated, Joy felt her pulses quickening. Here was confirmation of what she believed. Thunder should be racing.

'Have you ridden him?'

Joy squirmed as she remembered David's reaction to her one ride on him, but Travers had no need to know of that. 'Yes, and he goes like the wind,' she told him, excitement growing.

'Mind if I take him out?'

'He's not easy to handle.'

'Reckon I can handle him.'

A short time later, after bringing the gear from the stables, Joy watched Travers swing himself up into Thunder's saddle and set off at a smart trot.

When they returned much later Travers slid down from the horse with a wide smile on his face.

'Well missus, I reckon you've got a beauty here. He needs disciplining, and a firm hand, but he goes like a bat outa Hell. We've just got to train him and channel all that power so he produces his best on race day and he could be anything. Anything, I tell you!' Travers shifted from one foot to the other, his eyes gleaming. 'The Gold Cup wouldn't be beyond his reach! You must race him; it'd be a crying shame not to.'

Joy's heart pumped. How ironic if this should be their champion, a wild horse from the bush, instead of one of their carefully bred thoroughbreds. But he was a Redwoods horse, and any profit and glory would go to Redwoods, and that was what mattered.

'Then of course we must race him,' she told him with a catch in her voice. 'You must take him when you want to start his training and prepare him as you see fit.'

'Right now.' Travers beamed. 'We'll start right now. When he's ready we'll set him for a few minor races, take him along slowly. Keep him under wraps, you know, until we're ready. He's just bursting to race. I reckon he's close on three years old and he needs training right now, while he's young. Give him good habits right from the start.' Travers was bubbling over with excitement. 'If you can lend me a lad I'll take him back with Gay Lass today.'

A note of caution entered Joy's head. David had brushed aside the notion of racing Thunder, but if he heard what Travers said, he would be bound to change his mind. Of course he would. Oh, why did he have to be away, just when he was needed?

She took a deep breath. 'Well, my husband's not here right now, but he'll be back in a couple of days...'

'But you can authorise me to take him, can't you? You're partners in Redwoods. I'd like to start with him right away, and, besides, it'll save me another trip back up here.'

It made sense for him to take Thunder back with him, she could see that. Thunder had been a gift from Rufe to both of them, so she did have the right to give Travers permission to take him. If Travers was thinking of the Gold Cup, one of the most prestigious and wealthy races in the land, then he would want to start training for that as soon as possible and yes, of course David would want it too, if he was here.

'Yes of course you must take him back with you now. It's very exciting to think Thunder has such potential. It's certainly a dazzling thought that he might be good enough to qualify for the Gold Cup.'

'That's what I'm going to aim for. I think he has the ability, I've just got to make sure he uses it right. But that's up to me.' He paused, thinking. 'Now, about his name. Thunder suits him, but I think it could be a bit more interesting, like, maybe...Thunderbird....or, what about the same name as that bushranger you had up this way...Cap'n Thunderbolt, wasn't it? He certainly goes like a thunderbolt.'

'Thunderbolt?' Joy tried the name. 'Yes, I like that.'

'Then Thunderbolt is what he'll be when he starts to race.'

As Joy watched them leave a little later she buzzed with excitement. Instead of having one more horse in training there would now be two more. And if Thunderbolt lived up to his name then he might be the one to put Redwoods into the elite list of the leading studs.

'I can't believe you've done this, Joy.' David was white faced as he confronted her. 'Without any consultation with me you've decided Thunder should become a race horse.' His voice rose. 'He's not a thoroughbred, as you well know; he's just a brumby from up north. He's not up to the class of the horses he'd be facing if you go ahead with this ridiculous idea. Just because he can run fast doesn't mean he can win races.'

'Well, it's certainly a good start,' Joy responded hotly. 'It's usually why horses win, because they can run fast.'

'There's a lot more to winning races. As you should well know.'

Joy set her lips in a mutinous line as her throat tightened. 'Jim Travers thinks he has enough class to win big races. He even thinks he could be up to Gold Cup class.'

'Gold Cup my arse! If you want to enter him in that then you go ahead and make yourself a laughing stock. I don't want any part of it.'

'If you'd been here when Travers...'

'Well I wasn't here, was I? And you took advantage of it. You just went ahead and made this stupid decision on your own. You couldn't wait for me to come back to discuss it. Oh no, you made the decision all by yourself. Just as you've made so many decisions in the past.'

'What do you mean by that?'

'You made the decision to buy Bonnie Doon without consulting me.'

'And she went on to win. Was that a bad decision?'

'Perhaps not. But I would've liked to have a say in it. But no, you had to go ahead and do it all by yourself.'

'I did it for the good of the business – our business. And it was a good business decision.'

'And I suppose all the other times you've taken matters into your own hands have been good decisions?'

Joy felt a shiver of apprehension as she realised this was blowing up into a full-scale quarrel. One in which things could be said that would wound them both. She should turn and walk away. But something kept her there.

'What are you talking about?'

'Like when you decided to keep riding when you shouldn't have. And lost our child because of it.'

Joy felt the words like a blow to her stomach. She gazed at him in mute despair.

'Or when you decided you wanted to be married before the new house was finished. I've never been sure you didn't engineer the whole thing, become with child on purpose so we'd be forced to marry when we did.' He drew a deep shuddering breath then, and made an effort to compose himself. 'But it's the decisions about Redwoods—you always manage to have the say in those. You don't care about me. You only care about Redwoods. And why shouldn't you? After all, it's yours.'

Her chest tightened at his words. 'No, it's ours!' She put out her hand to touch his arm, but he pushed it away, his lip curling.

'No it's not, it's yours. It always has been. I'm only an adjunct because I'm useful to you, but you don't need me. You only need someone to help with the horses.'

'That's not true. I love you.' Joy spoke past the lump in her throat. 'We're partners, we always have been.'

He looked at her as if he was seeing her for the first time. 'No we're not, not really.' He shrugged. 'At any rate, I've had enough. I've decided to pay a visit to Lily and her husband in America. She's sent me another letter asking me, and I've decided to go.'

Joy felt her world crumbling around her. 'No! Don't go David. We'll tell Travers it was a mistake, that we don't want Thunder to race after all.'

'It's too late. I've been considering this for some time now. You don't need me here. I've made arrangements so that Josh Frazer can come to take my place. You'll have as good support as I can give you.'

Joy felt the blood draining from her body. 'So you'd already planned this? My telling Travers to train Thunder had nothing to do with it.'

He gave a bitter laugh. 'Oh yes, that was the final straw. If it hadn't been for that I might never have taken the last step. So I suppose I should thank you, you've made me realise it's the right thing to do. And I've wanted to look at their methods over there for some time now. I'm sure there'll be plenty I can learn from them.'

'Is there anything I can do to change your mind?'

'Nothing. My mind is made up. I'll be leaving later today. I'll stay at Riverside while I make final arrangements. Frazer will be here within the week. Perhaps you'll be good enough to have Mary prepare one of the cottages for him.'

'Is this what you went to Riverside for? To discuss going away, with your father?'

'Partly, yes.'

'And what did he think about it?'

'He agrees with me that it'll be good to investigate the expertise in other parts of the world.'

'Even if it means leaving your family behind?'

'That wasn't part of our discussion.'

'And what about me? And Xandra?'

'You'll be all right, and I will miss Xandra. However, I'm sure you'll look after her to the best of your ability when I'm not here, and you have plenty of help with your grandmother and my sister both here.'

'How long will you stay?' Joy asked him through stiff lips.

'I don't know. I'll write to you.'

'But you will be back?'

'I'll write to you.'

And when he rode away later that day the foremost thought in her mind was, What if he doesn't come back?

Josh Frazer arrived later that week and his arrival quenched the hope Joy had been nursing that David might change his mind and decide to return.

She'd never given much thought to Frazer before, although she knew he'd worked at the highly successful Stanley Stables in Newmarket and was regarded as an expert in his field. Now, as she greeted him cordially, she took stock of him, wondering as she held her hand out to him how he would feel about working for a woman. She guessed him to be in his early thirties, not especially tall but well built with broad shoulders. He had tawny hair, a tanned face and lines around the eyes that suggested he spent much time squinting against the sun. As he took her hand with a firm grasp, his rather ordinary face came alive with a wide smile that was reflected in his dark brown eyes, and he didn't look ordinary at all.

In spite of his pleasant manner she felt an entirely irrational burst of resentment that he should be here instead of David.

'Welcome to Redwoods, Mr. Frazer, I hope you'll enjoy your time here, and that you'll be comfortable in your cottage.' She forced her antipathy aside. 'It's probably not all that much different to what you've been used to at Riverside.'

'Thank you, Mrs. Cavanagh. One place is much the same as another to me, it's the people you work with that matter, and I'm sure we'll all get along fine. Please call me Josh. I've taken to your informality since I've been in Australia.'

Remembering the time she spent in England, and the formality she found there, Joy smiled.

'Yes Josh, we certainly lead a more relaxed way of life here than in England, I do remember. Now, if you'll come with me, I'll show you to your new home, and you can get settled in. I think you met Patrick when you were here before, didn't you?'

'Yes, and Jack too. And I know my way around a bit. Where the stables are and so on, so it's not all strange to me.'

'That's a good start then. Take your time settling in today, go for a wander around, and tomorrow we'll go out and look at the horses.'

As she walked back to the house after escorting him to his cottage, she thought he would probably fit in quite well, and she certainly needed the extra pair of hands. It wasn't his fault he was here in David's place.

Chapter Twenty

The next few weeks passed without event. Josh settled into his new appointment with ease, proving to be a more than adequate replacement for David with the horses. As the days passed Joy found her resentment towards him fading, and she began to appreciate his skill with handling the horses. She even found herself developing a liking for him. Johnnie obviously liked him, he'd taken to spending a great deal of time with him, following him around as he tended the horses. Josh seemed to not mind having him tagging along, and was patient with answering his questions.

But Joy's heart was empty. She missed David with a deep yearning, and as she wondered how long it would be until she heard from him, dread settled over her that he might decide to stay in America. Perhaps he was glad to be away from her and would never return. She waited for a letter with a mixture of hope and fear. To help pass the time she decided to make a proper study of the thoroughbred bloodlines, using David's thoroughbred record books.

When she mentioned this to Josh one day, as they were occupied with the horses, he asked if the books included the Australian records, and she told him they did.

'Of course, our official records cover a much shorter period than those in Britain and America.'

'Well, yes, they would be, wouldn't they? Do they go back a hundred years?'

'Records have been kept as far back as that, but most of the earlier horses were imported from overseas, like Hector and Northumberland, so you can't class them as Australian.'

'That's very interesting. Do you think I could have a look at the books sometime?'

'Yes, why not? If you want to come over some evening I'll show you.'

They pored over the books spread out over the dining room table together that night and Joy realised it was good to have an interested companion to discuss them with. She extended her invitation to him to come whenever he wanted. Soon they were spending two or three evenings each week studying the record books and discussing the bloodlines. It took her very little time to realise that his knowledge of breeding outside of Australia was enormous, and he was happy to share his knowledge with her. As the weeks passed they developed an easy familiarity with each other, and she no longer resented his presence. In fact she found herself looking forward to his company.

Finally she received the letter from David that she had been waiting for. After she read it, Joy retreated to her room, and sat in a chair by the window, staring unseeingly at the familiar landscape beyond. Her heart sat heavy in her chest, and she was unable to suppress the tears that trickled down her cheeks. The letter had been short and to the point. He arrived safely and was finding much to interest him in the running of Talahousie Stud. He hoped she and Xandra were in good health. He would be in touch again at a later date. It contained none of the words she wanted to hear–no declaration of his love, or words to show he missed her.

Emma had almost given up hope of seeing Hector again. Apart from a short note from him to tell her he had gone to Melbourne to pursue his interest in the Tarrant Engineering Company, there had been no word from him, and she was resigning herself to a future of spinsterhood. So it came as a wonderful surprise when she heard the sound of a motor, and the toot of a horn outside. She rushed to the door, pulled it open and saw Hector alighting from the front seat of a much larger motorcar, one that had a back seat, doors and a roof. Filled with elation she tried to compose herself as she came out on to the verandah to stand at the top of the steps with what she hoped was no more than a welcoming smile, although she felt like shouting with happiness.

Hector stopped at the bottom of the steps and looked up at her, a look of uncertainty on his face.

'Hello Emma. How are you?'

She bit her lip. He didn't look terribly happy to see her. Perhaps he'd come back only to see the others. Perhaps he'd hoped she wouldn't be here.

'I'm well, thank you Hector. And you?'

'I'm fine. Just fine.'

'I see you have a new motorcar.'

'Yes. It's bigger, carries passengers. I've been working with Harry Tarrant, and I had a bit of a hand in the design of this one. More room, you see. And a roof for the weather...' he broke off and took a deep breath. 'But I didn't come all this way to talk about motorcars.'

'What did you come back for?'

'Why, to see you, of course.' He looked suddenly flustered. 'I mean to say...that is, if you want to see me. Of course, if you don't want to see me I'd understand. Of course.'

Emma felt a sudden rush of joy as she smiled down at him.

'Of course I want to see you. Hadn't you better come up?'

His face split into a wide grin, and he bounded up the steps to stand before her looking like a little boy in a lolly shop as he gazed at her.

Emma was sure he was going to take her into his arms but at that moment the door behind her burst open and Johnnie came bounding through.

'Uncle Hector! Uncle Hector!' He wrapped his arms around Hector's legs, hugging.

Hector reached down and swung him up into the air, then held him at arm's length to look into his face. 'And how's my favourite boy?' he asked, before setting him down again. 'My word, I think you must have grown about three inches while I've been away.'

But Johnnie spied Hector's new acquisition and turned to face him, eyes wide. 'That's a new motorcar. It's very big. Can I go for a ride?'

'Of course...'

'Not just yet,' Emma told him firmly. 'Uncle Hector has just arrived and he has other things to do before taking you for a ride.'

Hector ruffled Johnnie's hair. 'Later,' he told him. 'I promise. Now I must go inside and say hello to everyone. Come along,' he held out his hand to Johnnie. 'We'll all go in together.' He smiled at Emma as he placed his hand at her back to guide her inside. 'And we must talk later, too,' he added, his eyes shining, 'now that I know you're happy to see me.'

It was much later, when dusk was drawing in–a shining, golden finale to the day as the setting sun slipped below the horizon, and a faint rosy blush tinged the sky–before everyone's questions had been answered, and their curiosity about the new car satisfied.

Hector asked Emma to take a walk with him. They strolled down towards the river, her hand tucked through his arm. Birds flew overhead, black against the fading sky as they made their way home before night fell. All at once, as if at a prearranged signal, a croaking chorus from the myriad of frogs that lived along the riverbank filled the air.

'It's so peaceful here after the rush and clatter of the big city,' Hector told Emma as they stood by the river's edge looking out across the still, dark water. 'I think I'd become quite frazzled if I had to live in a city permanently.'

'So you're not going to live in Melbourne permanently?' Emma asked, her heart soaring.

'No, definitely not.'

'But what about your business with Tarrant Engineering?'

'My involvement would be in Sydney, if I decide to go ahead with it, and I wouldn't need to be there full time. I could still divide my time between Sydney and the countryside, now that transport is no longer the problem it was before I had the car.'

'Yes, I can see that.'

'I've been doing a lot of thinking since I've been away.'

Wondering what he had been thinking about, she let go of his arm and turned to look at him, and suddenly his arms were around her, and he was looking into her face, his eyes searching.

'Emma, my darling sweet Emma, it's been agony to be away from you for so long, but I wanted to give you time. I know you're finding it difficult to come to terms with losing your husband, and I don't want to rush you, but I love you so much. So very, very much, and I have to know if you feel there's a chance you might return my feelings. Given time, of course. I know I'm older than you, and it's probably difficult for you to feel I could ever replace your younger husband but...'

Emma placed her fingers over his lips. 'Why don't you stop talking, and kiss me?'

He pulled her to him and his mouth came down on hers, hungrily, and her body responded to him instantly with a warm leaping deep inside her. And as she kissed him back, and he pressed her so close to him she could feel his manhood, she knew she wanted him, wanted him very much, and moved even closer. His hands slid down to undo her buttons and caress her breasts, and he bent his head so his lips could kiss the swelling mounds. She moaned with pleasure. It flashed through her mind that whatever he might have done she still wanted him. Desperately.

He led her through the now deepening night, through the trees, to the little glade where they often came with the children to play. When he removed his jacket, placed it over a floor of grass and ferns, and eased her down on to it, she smiled up at him, and welcomed him with her arms open wide.

Later, much later, he drew back, stood up, and held out his hands to her. When they were both standing he lifted her hand to his lips and kissed it.

'I've loved you ever since I first met you, my darling. Now I feel I can ask you the question that's been burning inside me since those first days. Will you marry me?'

Emma's heart soared. 'Yes.'

Any further words were cut short as he pulled her to him and whirled her round and round, laughing and whooping like a young boy.

'Well, congratulations and much happiness to you both,' Jack said later as he raised his champagne glass in salute to the happy couple.

They were all seated in the sitting room, Patrick and Josh included, where Joy had gathered them together as soon as the happy couple returned, flushed and excited, to announce their news.

'And yet another link between the Cavanaghs and the Barrons,' Bella added, when they finished the toast. 'There can't be many more of marriageable age left,' she joked.

'Not until the children grow up,' Joy said.

'Then I give you future generations,' Hector told them, raising his glass.

It was some time later when the talk turned again to horses, and Joy told them her news. Thunderbolt was having his first barrier trial in Newcastle soon, and she intended to go down to watch him.

Hector turned to Emma. 'Would you like to go too?' he asked. 'We could all drive down in the car, make it a real outing.'

'Yes, that would be splendid.'

'That's exciting for you, Mrs. Cavanagh,' Josh said. 'I never thought, the day I delivered him here, that he'd ever be actually racing.'

'Well, it's only a trial, but it's important. We'll be able to see if he's living up to his promise or not.'

'I always said he could go like a thunderbolt,' Josh laughed. 'Now we'll see if I was being prophetic.'

'Would you like to come too?' Joy asked him impulsively. 'That's if it would be all right with you?' she hastened to add, turning to Hector.

'Absolutely. Plenty of room in the new car.'

'In that case, thank you very much. I'd love to see him in his first race.'

So it was arranged that the four of them would go, and Johnnie would stay at home with Xandra, Mary and Bella.

Johnnie was disconsolate at being left behind while they all went to watch Thunderbolt run in his first trial. To make things worse, Xandra had a bit of a cold and Grandma Bella wouldn't let her come outside with him.

He knew he'd be feeling really happy if he wasn't so lonely, because Mummy had told him their good news. She and Uncle Hector were going to be married, and Uncle Hector would be his new father. He could even call him Daddy if he wanted to, Mummy said, instead of Uncle Hector, and he said yes he did want to. He really loved Uncle Hector. It would be wonderful to have a father of his own, like Xandra. He couldn't remember his father very much. He knew he'd been very sick, that's why he died, and he'd spent a lot of time in bed. That's how he remembered him mostly.

He wandered up to Chipper's paddock and called him over to the fence, waving a carrot to entice him. Chipper came trotting up and Johnnie held the carrot out to him on his outstretched palm, the way Auntie Joy had shown him. He watched Chipper chomp it up, and stayed talking to him and stroking his nose and rubbing his ears the way he liked. But eventually he got tired of that, and wandered over to the stables.

Patrick was busy shoeing one of the horses and Johnnie stayed a while, watching him and talking. Then he started back towards the house to see if Xandra was feeling better. He was about halfway there when he saw a horseman riding in. As he drew closer he saw it was Mr. Osborne. He waved to him and the horse changed direction and came towards him.

Mr Osborne reined in his horse alongside Johnnie.

'Hello Johnnie. What are you doing out here all on your own? Where's your little playmate?'

'Xandra's got a cold, and Grandma Bella won't let her come outside.' Johnnie squinted up at him. 'If you're going up to the house to see Mummy, she's not there.'

'Oh, has she gone out?'

'Yes, they all have.' He kicked the ground with his shoe. 'I couldn't go, so I'm here all alone for two whole days, and I've got no one to play with.'

'Well that's too bad. So she won't be home again tonight?'

'No. They've gone to watch Thunderbolt race, and they're going to stay in the hotel in Newcastle, and they won't be back 'til tomorrow. And it's lonely all by myself.'

'So your Aunt Joy has gone too?'

'Yes. And Uncle Hector and Josh too. They've all gone in Uncle Hector's new motorcar.'

'What! So your Uncle Hector's back again, is he?'

'Yes, and Mummy and him are going to be married.'

Mr Osborne pulled on the reins so fiercely then that his horse shied as it turned. Johnnie stepped back quickly out of the way. As they streaked away, not to the house but back the way he'd come, he was surprised to see Mr. Osborne slash the horse with the whip.

Chapter Twenty One

Thunderbolt won his trial in brilliant time, and Joy felt she would explode with excitement. Hector bought a bottle of champagne to celebrate, and they toasted Thunder and his success. After they had all calmed down from the excitement, Jim Travers professed himself 'very happy indeed' with the result, and told Joy the horse was definitely ready to race.

'Do you think he's up to Gold Cup standard?' Joy asked him, as the butterflies inside her gave way to jubilation.

Travers nodded emphatically. 'I do. Of course, he has to progress through the grades to qualify first. Whether he'll make it this season is not certain, but it's what we'll be aiming for.'

'So when, and where, do you think he'll have his first race?'

'I'll have to work out what's best, but there's a Maiden coming up at this course in two weeks' time that should suit. No need to go to Sydney until he's further up in the grades. I'll send you word as soon as I know for sure.'

They stayed to watch another trial, but all agreed there was not much interest when they didn't know the horses involved, so they left the course and made their way to the Grand Hotel in Newcastle where they'd booked rooms for the night.

The bellboy carried Joy's and Emma's bags to the room they were sharing, and once they'd unpacked their few overnight necessities they went down to meet the men.

Hector took Emma's hand. 'I've discovered there's a well recommended jeweller in the town. I'm anxious to see you wear my ring, so how do you feel about us going to have a look at what they have?'

'Would you mind if we leave you for a short while?' Emma asked Joy.

'No, of course not. Off you go.'

'We won't be too long,' she assured her.

'We might as well wait in the lounge, and share a late afternoon tea,' Joy told Josh as they left. They found a vacant table, and Joy ordered tea for them both.

'I imagine you're feeling very happy after Thunderbolt's performance today,' Josh said.

'Yes, very happy indeed. His performance justifies my belief in him.'

'Yes, I think he'll prove a remarkable horse. Because I delivered him to you, I feel almost as if I can share the pride in him, feel a sense of achievement that I was able to be the instrument that brought him into your life.' A half smile touched his mouth. 'Now that's being fanciful, isn't it?'

Joy felt a stab of surprise at his words. 'Well, yes, a little, perhaps. But it's nice to know you take such a personal interest in your work.'

'Perhaps not the work, but the people I work for.' His eyes scanned her face.

Joy swallowed, feeling something flutter inside her. Was he flirting with her? Surely not. 'Well, it's the horses that count, of course,' she said uncertainly. 'I only hope Thunderbolt can repeat today's performance when he's in an actual race.'

'I don't think there's much doubt about that, Mrs. Cavanagh.' He toyed with his spoon. 'There are a lot of you around, aren't there? Mrs. Cavanaghs, I mean. There's Mrs. Cavanagh at Riverside, and Mrs. Cavanagh, your mother. And you.' He smiled as he stopped fiddling with his spoon, and looked intently at her. 'The most important one, of course.'

'Well, I can't say I agree with that.' She shook her head, and wondered why his words made her heart race absurdly.

'It's true. To me, at any rate. I feel as if we've come to know each other while we've been studying the thoroughbred records together. I'd like to feel we've become friends.'

He smiled at her with such sincerity that she couldn't feel offended. And her feelings towards him had changed. She no longer resented his presence – in fact she had come to look forward to his company.

She nodded. 'I'm sure we have, and I must say you calling me 'Mrs. Cavanagh' now does seem excessively formal, but...'

'But it wouldn't seem quite right for me to call you Joy. At the moment that's a bit too informal.' He hesitated for a second. 'I've heard Mary call you Mrs. Joy, how about if I call you that?'

Joy laughed, although she wondered about 'at the moment'. What did that mean, exactly? But she let it pass. 'Well yes, Mary's known me ever since I was born, and I was always Joy to her, or Miss Joy if she was cross with me, but when I married she decided I couldn't be Mrs. C, because that's my Mother, so I became Mrs. Joy.'

'And so you shall be to me, if you approve.'

'Yes, I approve.' She smiled.

'Of course, you were Miss Barron when I first met you. I remember the first day I saw you at the stables looking over the horses with your grandfather. A pretty little Australian flower. I thought then you seemed too much of a young lady to be mixed up with horses.'

'I'm surprised you even noticed me then, let alone thought anything about me!'

'You're not the sort of young woman to go unnoticed. Then or now.'

'Oh!' A faint flush of warmth spread through her as she read the unmistakable admiration in his eyes.

'I have to say I think your husband is foolish to go off to America and leave you here alone.'

'I'm scarcely alone. I have my grandparents and my sister-in-law, and the two children, and now my Uncle Hector as well.'

'If you were mine I wouldn't leave you alone for an instant. I wouldn't want to be away from you, I'd want to spend every moment I could with you.'

Joy's stomach flipped. 'I understand that David wants to visit his cousin and learn what they're doing over there. They have a very big stud in Kentucky, and he was curious to see it for himself.'

'And how long does he plan to stay away?'

'He wasn't quite sure. It all depends on what happens while he's there.'

'He's taking a big risk, leaving you all alone for...'

'Here are Emma and Hector coming back!'

'Ah, what bad timing. But not to worry, I'm sure there'll be another occasion for us to resume our chat.' With that he pushed back his chair and stood to greet them.

Joy drew a deep breath. She'd felt the conversation getting into dangerous waters. Dangerous because she hadn't been angry at Josh's presumption. Rather, she'd felt the stirrings of excitement. And that way lay only trouble. Of course she would never do anything to flout her marriage vows; that went without saying. She loved David. But she was pleased to have the distraction of Emma's ring, which was duly admired, and then the excitement and pleasure of toasting the future happiness of the couple, all of which ended that conversation, which made Joy realise that Josh had more than an employee's interest in her.

Joy knew something must be wrong when Mary came bursting through the front door before they pulled up, closely followed by Bella. Both women stood waiting, their faces showing signs of distress.

'The children have gone missing,' Mary called out as Joy scrambled from the car and hurried up the steps, closely followed by the others.

'We've looked everywhere for them,' Bella added, her voice distraught, 'and they're nowhere to be found.'

Joy's heart faltered as she looked from one worried face to another.

'What's happened?'

Both women started to answer at once, but Hector silenced them with a sharp word.

'Stop! Now, who saw them last, and when?'

'After breakfast,' Bella said. 'They came outside to play. I looked out a bit later, and they were still here, and again not long after that.'

Mary took up the tale. 'I came out with some milk and biscuits for them about mid-morning and sat with them while they ate them and drank their milk. Then I went inside to the kitchen for a while.'

'And when I came out a bit later they were gone,' Bella concluded.

'Oh my God! Where have you looked for them?' Emma's voice shook as she asked the question.

'Everywhere,' Mary told them. 'We thought they were playing hidey, so we looked all through the house and down to the stables. We even called out to them that we had some sweets for them, thinking they were playing a game with us, and that would certainly bring them out. But no, they're just not here.'

'When Jack and Patrick came in for lunch, they organised the men to go out and search for them, and that's what's happening now,' Bella added.

A knot of fear twisted inside Joy. What if they had wandered away and gone down to the river and fallen in? They knew they were not to go there, had been warned of the dangers of drowning dozens of times, but perhaps they'd ignored the warnings. Or what if they'd wandered so far they'd become lost, and couldn't find their way back. The nearby forests were so extensive they could be lost for days.

Hector spoke now. 'I suggest you ladies all go inside while Josh and I join the searchers.'

'I'm just going to take off my hat and change my shoes, and I'm going out too,' Joy told him. 'I can't just sit here waiting.'

'I'm coming too,' Emma said.

'I'll bring in your luggage,' Mary told them, starting down the steps. 'In case you want to use the motorcar again.'

Bella bustled down with her. 'I'll help you.'

In spite of all the clearing taken place over the years, there were still large tracts of bush land and forest left on Redwoods, outside the perimeter of the homestead and gardens. The property was bounded on one side by bush that extended to the bottom of Bulahdelah Mountain, and on the other side, past the mill, the trees continued until they met the large tract of thick State forest that extended for several miles, with no fence to mark the exact boundary between the two. On one side ran the Myall River, close to which were several workers' cottages, and the top boundary, fully fenced, was marked by the public road and the Redwoods entrance.

As Joy started out to begin searching she could not imagine what had prompted the children to go further afield on their own. They knew they must stay close to the house unless they were with one of the adults. As she set off she avoided the paths that led to the river or the horse paddocks, and headed through the native bush down towards the river.

The ground was uneven here and she often had to push her way between the ferns and clumps of native grasses that grew prolifically beneath the trees. She wore sturdy boots and carried a stout stick, mindful of the danger of snakes in the thick undergrowth. If you inadvertently trod on one, perhaps coiled as it slept, or happened to confront one in a confined space, it could strike with lightning speed. A strike that was likely to be fatal unless immediate aid was at hand. Trying to push such thoughts from her mind she continued calling as she made her way down to the river. Here everything was calm and serene. The late afternoon sun glinted on the placid water. Not a soul was in sight. And certainly no small children.

Joy made her way along the bank, scanning the river and its surroundings. Her heart almost stopped when she saw what appeared to be a piece of clothing floating in the water downstream. Picking up her skirts she ran, her heart pounding, breath catching in her throat.

Drawing level with the article she saw it was cloth of some sort. But what! It was too far out to reach with the stick. A fallen branch lay on the ground beneath a nearby gum tree. She picked it up, then leant out over the water until she was able to snag the floating object. She dragged it towards her, her breath coming in ragged gasps. As it came closer she saw it was a sack. Pulling it into the bank she lifted it out with the limb. Water streamed from it as she dropped it in a sodden heap and prodded it, making sure it was empty.

Dropping onto a fallen tree trunk she sat with her head in her hands until her heart stopped racing, and her breath returned to normal. Then she straightened up and continued searching, but as night drew in with no traces of the children she made her way back to the house, dejected and fearful.

A knot of the workers and their families were clustered around the front of the house enjoying the hot tea and refreshments Bella and Mary were dispensing, all talking and comparing notes on where they had searched. Those on foot had scoured the property, and the beginning of the forest, while those on horseback had gone further afield. But with no success. It was dark now, so it was decided to resume searching again next morning.

It was a grim and worried group who sat at the table that night. Joy pushed her food around the plate without actually eating, and Emma did the same. The discussion was all about where the two children might have gone, what had prompted them to go wandering off, and what more could be done to find them.

After the meal Joy and Emma sat together on the sofa, and Emma was soon in tears.

'Where can they have gone? And whatever made them go off like this?'

Joy, managing to hold back her own tears with difficulty, shook her head. 'I can't imagine why they would wander off, but I blame myself. I should never have gone off like that and left them. Thunderbolt's trial wasn't as important as them. I should have been here with them. Xandra is scarcely more than a baby. I shouldn't have left her. David said I'm irresponsible, and he was right.'

'Oh no, I'm to blame,' Emma sobbed. 'I didn't have to go with you. You needed to go and watch the trial, but I didn't. I shouldn't have left them.' She drew a shuddering breath. 'Who knows what's happened to them? They could have fallen in the river and drowned. Or been bitten by a snake, or...or...'

'Neither of you is to blame.' Hector came to stand by them and he spoke firmly, taking Emma's hand as he sat down beside her. 'Nor anyone else. It's no one's fault. It's just happened. Children do these things. They've probably gone wandering off and found themselves lost. They'll have an uncomfortable night, and they'll be a bit cold and hungry, unless someone has already found them and taken them in for the night, in which case we'll know in the morning. But whatever's happened we will have them back. Because we'll keep searching until we find them.'

But neither of the mothers could be comforted. They couldn't be sure if they would see their children alive again, for it seemed Xandra and Johnnie had disappeared without a trace.

Chapter Twenty Two

After a restless night spent tossing and turning, Joy emerged from her room early next morning to find Emma already in the kitchen, waiting for the kettle to boil for an early morning cup of tea. They had barely exchanged morning greetings before Mary arrived carrying a piece of paper, folded and with 'Mrs. Hardy' printed on the front, which she held out to Emma with a shaking hand.

Only a few words were scrawled on it but they were enough to make Emma drop, half swooning, onto a nearby chair. Her scream brought Joy to her side.

'What is it?' She took the paper from Emma's hand. 'You will never see your son again alive,' she read. Her heart pounded. 'Where did you get this?' she asked Mary.

'It was pinned to the door when I arrived just now.'

'Who could have left it?'

'I don't know. I just came across from our house, and it was there on the door.'

'Did you see anyone about?'

'No.'

The sound of Emma's scream brought Hector racing into the kitchen, still hurriedly tugging on his jacket.

'What is it?' he demanded. 'What's the matter?'

With tears streaming down her face, Emma held out the note. After scanning it he pulled Emma up into his arms and held her tight, trying to soothe her.

'This might have been written by some crank,' he told her, as she sobbed against his shoulder. 'Someone who knows Johnnie's missing and wants to frighten you. There are people like that. I've seen it before.'

But his words did nothing to reassure Emma, who continued weeping.

Joy felt unable to move, and was having difficulty breathing. Steel bands tightened around her heart. Where was Xandra? What had happened to her? As she watched Hector trying to comfort Emma, she felt a sudden stab of anger, alongside the panic rising inside her. Why was David not with her at this moment, trying to comfort her?

When Mary put steaming cups of tea on the table Hector gently disentangled Emma from his arms and sat her down, then added extra sugar to her cup before holding it to her lips and urging her to drink. After managing a few sips her sobs slowly subsided, and he took a handkerchief from his pocket and wiped her cheeks, talking softly to her all the while. Finally she drew a shuddering breath, and sat staring vacantly ahead, mute and trembling.

It was at this moment that Josh came hurrying into the room. After being told of the latest development, he asked Hector if he could have a word with him.

'I think I might have some news,' he told him when they were alone, 'though I don't know how it relates to the note. I went into the bar in the Plough Inn last night, hoping I might pick up something, perhaps someone might have seen the little ones. Well, I didn't find out anything about them, but I did hear some gossip that was very interesting. I was talking to one of the blokes and he was telling me that Harry Osborne had been in the night before, with another man, and he was acting very strangely. He told me he couldn't help but overhear them talking. Osborne had more to drink than he should have and he started ranting and raving to this fellow about how badly he'd been treated by the 'bitches at Redwoods', and how he was going to get his revenge. And he reckoned it sounded as if the other one was egging him on.'

Hector frowned. 'The bitches at Redwoods? Who did he mean by that? And what was he talking about? Do you know?'

'Not really, but I gathered it had to do with both Kitty and Emma, from what I could understand. He was really in a state it seems. Complaining about them both leading him on and then ditching him when someone better came along. But another worrying thing is what he was heard to say about the fire.'

'The fire? The one that burnt down the house while they were away?'

'Unless there's been another fire I haven't heard about?'

'Not that I know of. What did he say about it?'

'This fellow couldn't remember the exact words, but it was along the lines of, 'they'll be sorry for the way they treated me. If they think having their house burnt down was the worst that could happen, I'll make it worse this time'.'

Hector whistled softly. 'That sounds as if he was behind the fire, don't you think?'

'I couldn't put any other interpretation on it.'

'I don't like to upset them anymore but I think we'd better ask the ladies if they know what it could be about. Come in with me, and we'll see if they can help make sense of it.'

Hector asked Josh to repeat his story, and then posed the question. 'Does anyone understand what he was talking about?'

The women looked at each other.

'He once asked Mother to marry him...' Joy began.

Bella interrupted her. 'He first asked her many years ago, and repeated it more than once over the years. She always told him she had no intention of ever marrying again.' She paused. 'Then she met Rufe again, and changed her mind about marriage.'

'Perhaps he resented that more than he showed,' Hector mused.

Emma cleared her throat. 'There's something else too,' she told them, a faint pink flush colouring her cheeks. 'He's called here fairly often since I've been here, and he actually asked me to marry him too.' She bit her lip. 'And I'm afraid I gave him she same answer as Kitty – that I didn't intend to marry again.' She held her hand out to Hector as she finished speaking and he took it, patting it gently.

Josh raised his brows. 'And then you changed your mind too,' he said wryly. 'He must have felt slighted.'

'Be that or not,' Bella interjected. 'What does it mean?'

'I very much fear,' Jack said slowly, taking his wife's hand, 'that he intends to do something to harm Emma, and probably Kitty as well, through Joy.'

'Xandra and Johnnie.' Joy gasped, the blood thundering in her ears. 'He's behind this. It's him who's left the note. He's done something to the children. '

Jack was at her side in an instant. 'Now my dear, we don't know that.'

Joy clutched his arm. 'But Grandpa, it can't be a coincidence.'

'It could be, but we need to pay Harry a visit.'

Hector nodded. 'Yes. We need to see what he has to say. Maybe you could ride into town again now Josh, and see if you can hear any more news? While you do, we'll organise the rest of the searchers, we need to keep on with it. I think they need to go further into the State forest; it's such a big area to cover. Then I'll start the motor, and we'll head down to his boatyard and find Osborne.'

'I'll organise the searchers,' Jack volunteered after Josh left. 'You get your motorcar ready, and whatever you think you might need. I think I should stay here with the ladies, in case I'm needed.'

Josh returned just as Hector finished topping up the radiator and was screwing the cap back on. He told him Harry Osborne had been seen earlier riding past the town with a young boy on his horse. No one had taken much notice, nor recognised the child, or knew where he'd been headed.

'Then we'd better begin searching,' Hector said grimly.

Harry Osborne pulled Johnnie by the hand, trailing him along behind him. They were following a track through the scrub that led to Bulahdelah Mountain, and he walked fast. Much too fast for Johnnie to keep up with him. He had to almost run to keep up, and after a while his breath came in gasps. He called out to Mr. Osborne to not go so fast, but he took no notice.

The ground started to rise and it was even harder going. Johnnie slipped and fell. He hurt his knee and cried out.

Osborne yanked his arm and pulled him up. 'Shut up!' he told him, holding his hand tighter than ever.

They were staring to climb now, and the going was becoming even harder. Johnnie held back the tears that threatened, as he tried to keep up. Why were they going up the mountain? Uncle Hector said it was dangerous. And why was Mr. Osborne being so mean to him? He was his friend.

They drove for some time without finding anyone who'd seen either Harry Osborne or the children. Hector eased the car to the side of the road and pulled on the brake. He left the motor idling as he scanned the surrounding countryside through his field glasses. Lowering them, he turned to Josh with a frown.

'There's a horse tied up amongst some trees over there.' He gestured towards the base of Bulahdelah Mountain. 'It's an out of the way place, and there doesn't seem to be anyone around.' He handed the glasses to Josh and eased the brake forward. 'We'd better go and take a look.'

Josh raised the glasses and looked in the direction Hector had indicated. 'Yes. There's nothing much to take anyone there – there's nothing but the mountain and scrub.'

They jolted over a rough road, then turned on to an even rougher narrow track, and pulled up close behind the horse, which was tied to a tree in a small clearing. The ground was flat and stony, with low saplings around the edge of the clearing, but the gradual incline behind it gave way to the steeper slope of the mountain. Trees and boulders obscured the view beyond the first few yards.

Leaving the car, they walked over to the horse.

'Hello fella, who do you belong to, hey?' Josh stroked its muzzle. 'I wonder if it is Osborne's horse?'

'I'll check the saddlebag,' Hector replied. Before he could do so, a faint shout came from the hillside above them, and a large rock came rattling down and hit the ground about fifty feet away. They both looked upward but could see nothing. All was quiet again.

'There's definitely someone up there. Let's go see.'

They walked along until they found an opening onto a track leading upwards, where they changed course and followed it, toiling up and around between the trees over rough and uneven ground. It grew narrower as it went higher and they were forced to go in single file.

Hector led the way. He spoke quietly over his shoulder to Josh. 'I can't see where this is heading for sure, but if my sense of direction hasn't failed me, I think it's towards the escarpment that overlooks Redwoods. I can't see signs that anyone has been along here recently, but it's not easy to tell on this hard ground.'

'This could be just an animal track,' Josh suggested.

'True. But that was a human voice we heard.'

They pushed on. It was hard going and after about a half hour they paused and rested on a fallen tree trunk to catch their breath. The quiet of the bush was all around them, the only sounds a stirring of leaves by the faint breeze, or the rustle of some small native creature in the leaf litter.

'Reckon we can't be too far from the top now,' Josh said softly.

Suddenly from not far above them came a cry. Hector raised his fingers to his lips as he stood. Josh followed, and soundlessly they pressed on, hurrying as fast as the rough terrain allowed. Sky was visible above them now, and before long the trees became sparser, and the ground levelled out.

They reached an open plateau at the top of the escarpment, and halted in the shelter of the trees. To one side the cliff face reared still higher, and large boulders dotted the open ground in front of it. Ahead the ground ended in a sheer drop to the valley below. Seated on one of the boulders, a few yards in from the edge, was Harry Osborne. Head bent, he traced figures on the ground in front of him with a stick. Johnnie crouched down alongside him. They heard him muttering but couldn't catch the words. As they watched Osborne raised his head, stabbing viciously at the ground with his stick.

'Bitches,' he cried. 'Filthy bitches!'

Johnnie tugged at his sleeve. 'Please Mr. Osborne; I want to go home now.'

Osborne ignored him. Resuming his mumbling he went back to drawing in the dirt.

Hector touched Josh's arm and motioned him back into the trees, where he put his mouth close to his ears. 'I'm going to skirt around and come at him from the back. Give me a couple of minutes, and then you come out and distract him, while I come in from behind. Try and grab Johnnie.'

Hector melted away through the trees. When he emerged further around, and began to creep stealthily towards Osborne's back, Josh showed himself.

'Well Mr. Osborne. Enjoying the view from up here I see.'

As Josh spoke, Hector jumped forward and put his arm around Osborne's neck. Before he could catch him securely Osborne twisted, jerking his head, and managed to slide from his grasp. In one quick movement he jumped up and grabbed Johnnie, who let out a startled scream, lifted him in his arms, and covered the short distance to the edge in a few strides. He stood there with Johnnie, only inches from the edge.

Johnnie clutched at his captor with both hands, his eyes wide with fear as he looked down at the void beyond.

'Stand back,' Osborne shouted, eyes darting wildly from one to the other. 'If you come any closer the boy goes over.'

'Now then, you wouldn't want to be hanged for murder, would you?' Hector said calmly. 'Come away from the edge and put him down.'

'You,' Osborne screamed, 'you were the cause of it all! You and your new-fangled contraption. Until you came along everything was going well. She was happy with me. But then you came along with your flashy horseless carriage. You lured her away.'

'No, that's not how it was,' Hector soothed. 'Now then, you don't want to be in trouble with the law, do you? Come over here, and we can talk about this sensibly.'

'No! Get away! Go away and leave us, or it'll be the end of the brat. I'll drop him over, and then we'll see how the Jezebel feels. That'll make her suffer. Then she can see what it feels like!'

'Now then Harry, let's talk about this sensibly. You...'

'No. I'm going to make her suffer for what she did to me.' Osborne's eyes blazed.

'You don't want to end up dancing at the end of a rope. No one's worth that.'

'Bastards,' he screamed, 'both of you! You're as much to blame as her.'

Spittle flew from his lips as he hurled a stream of obscenities. His eyes bulged. He flung Johnnie to the ground at his feet.

Josh darted in and hauled Johnnie to safety as, with a maniacal howl, Osborne lunged at Hector. Hector stumbled as the maddened Osborne tried to pull him to the edge of the escarpment, shoving with his hands as well as using his body weight. Regaining his balance, Hector grabbed at his assailant. Osborne swung a wild punch that caught Hector on the side of the face. The pain of the blow fuelled his anger. He retaliated with a blow to Osborne's chin. It connected with a sharp crack. Osborne staggered, letting out a roar.

Hector wrapped his arms around him in a bear hug, striving to subdue him. Osborne clawed at his face, tried to poke his fingers in the eyes. Hector released his grip, tried to pinion his arms. Osborne shoved him off, stepped back and threw another wild punch. Hector side-stepped, bunching his fist. He landed a punch to the jaw. Osborne staggered. Shook his head. Came at him again. Fists flailing. Harder. Faster. Roaring. Hector ducked. Grabbed him as he charged. Locked his arms around him.

Together they struggled back and forth, round and round, as Hector tried to subdue his assailant. Osborne tried to manoeuvre him ever closer to the cliff edge. They grappled only a hairs-breadth from the brink, arms locked around each other.

Osborne freed one arm and got his fingers to Hector's throat, squeezing viciously on his windpipe. Hector let go of him to pull the hand from his throat. As Osborne bunched his fist for another punch he took a step back, and his foot caught on a protruding rock.

A look of shock crossed Osborne's face in the seconds it took for him to fall backwards. A piercing scream filled the air as he went over the edge, and after that there was only silence.

Hector stood frozen for a second, then rushed to the edge and looked over. The scene was spread out before him as he looked down. The horses in the paddocks, the swans floating on the river, the smoke curling lazily from the kitchen chimney. It all looked so normal. Except for the dark patch lying motionless at the bottom of the escarpment.

Chapter Twenty Three

Joy and Emma sprang from their seats as they heard the car pull up outside. Had they found the children? Joy's heart thudded as they hurried out on to the verandah, and she craned to see if the children were inside. Hector was in the driving seat and when Josh opened the door Joy saw Johnnie huddled on his lap. But where was Xandra? Fear filled her, and her legs could went weak.

Emma shouted as she raced down the steps. Josh handed Johnnie out of the car and he rushed to his mother. She scooped him into her arms, hugging him. The little boy burst into tears and hid his face in her breast, his hands clutching her.

Joy watched in horror as she realised her daughter was not with them. As Hector turned off the motor and hopped from his seat to hurry around and join them, she held onto the rail to prevent herself from falling. Josh bounded up the stairs and took her hand in his, while Hector guided Emma and Johnnie up.

'Where's Xandra? What's happened to her?' Joy gasped, the words almost choking her.

'We haven't found her yet, but we will,' Josh promised.

'But you've found Johnnie. She must have been with him. Where did you find him?'

'He was with Harry Osborne, but Xandra wasn't with them.'

'Not with them? Where were they?'

'On Bulahdelah Mountain.'

Joy felt reality slipping away. The nightmare was worsening. Xandra was still missing. She stared blankly at Josh as she tried to make sense of his words.

'Bulahdelah Mountain? Why were they on Bulahdelah Mountain?'

Josh took her by the arm and led her inside. She went with him in a daze. He led her into the sitting room, guided her to a chair and sat her down. She stared straight ahead, her mind tripping over her thoughts.

'I think she needs a drop of brandy,' he told Bella and Mary, who followed them in.

Mary moved straight across to where the decanter and glasses stood, poured a measure of brandy into a glass and brought it back. Josh took it from her and put it to Joy's lips. Mary watched until Joy took the first sip, coughing a little. She poured a second glass and handed it to Bella, who was sitting stiff and tense. She took it with a grateful look.

'Perhaps we need to hear what's happened,' Bella said, after she swallowed a mouthful.

As she felt the liquid course hotly down inside her Joy tried to pull her wits back together. 'Yes. What did Mr. Osborne have to say? Was it really him who took them? And why didn't he tell you where Xandra is?'

'Osborne's had an accident. He wasn't able to tell us anything.'

'An accident? What kind of accident?'

'There's really not time to go into that. We need to get busy looking for Xandra.' He looked at the others. 'You all knew him. Is there some place where you think he might have left her?'

Joy felt the fear increase, coiling around her insides, squeezing, threatening to overpower her.

'The boatyard.' She pushed away the feeling of helplessness. 'And his house, alongside it.'

'But it's Sunday. The boatyard will be all locked up today,' Bella reminded them.

'Not to worry. Hector and I will check it out.' Josh turned towards the door.

Joy jumped up. 'I'm coming with you.'

'Come on then.'

He took her arm as they left the room, to find Hector just closing the door of Johnnie's room behind him. 'Johnnie's going to be all right,' he told them. 'Although I think it'll be some time before he feels he can trust anyone outside the family. But we've had a talk, and I explained to him that Osborne was sick in the head, and he seems to accept that.' His face was grim. 'Now we need to find Xandra.'

The drive seemed to take forever. Joy sat alongside Hector, the familiar landmarks sliding by without registering in her consciousness as she tried to fight off the fear gripping her, squeezing her innards into a tight knot. Her thoughts scattered like a squawk of frightened parrots. One moment she saw her daughter lying still and cold, abandoned to death in some remote spot. In the next, Xandra was awake and screaming, and yet again, alone. Cold. Hungry. Frightened.

Joy bit her lip and tried to think rationally. Perhaps her darling girl was already dead, but, if not, she would be terrified. And she needed to help find her. To do that she must keep calm and think. She clenched her fists tight and took several deep breaths. Think! She must think! If Harry Osborne had taken the children without anyone knowing, then it had to be for no good reason. Perhaps he had nursed a grievance over Emma's rejection of him. Perhaps he'd taken Johnnie to frighten her. But if so, what would he have done with Xandra? She must be at his house, or somewhere in the boatyard. Surely he would never harm her? No, she must push that thought from her mind. She must remain strong. David was not here. She must be strong enough for two.

Hector pulled the car up outside the entrance to the boatyard, and they clambered out. As expected, the gate was locked. It was a stout timber gate, set into a wooden fence that surrounded the yard, and ran down to the edge of the river.

'If you give me a leg-up I'll go over the top and open the gate,' Josh told Hector.

'Right-o.' Hector put his hands together and Josh used them as a step to heave himself over the fence.

There was the sound of a bolt being drawn, and next moment the gate swung inwards, and they were inside the yard. All was quiet. No work was being carried out today. The yard contained several small buildings and one large shed.

'You check out the big shed, Josh,' Hector directed. 'Joy and I will do these smaller ones.

Josh nodded and moved off, and Hector and Joy set about their search. The buildings were unlocked, and as they searched each one and found no trace that Xandra had ever been there, Joy's heart plummeted. When they came to the last building they found the door locked.

'I think this is the office,' Joy told Hector. 'I suppose that's why he locks it. Now what are we going to do?'

'Let's see.'

Hector put his shoulder to the door and pushed. At his third attempt the lock gave way and he stumbled into the room, with Joy close behind.

On the desk inside stood a plate containing a couple of biscuits, some leftover crumbs, and two glasses with traces of milk in the bottom.

Joy picked up a glass, her heart pumping. 'Milk! I can't imagine Osborne drinking milk.'

'And two glasses. And biscuits. I'd say they were here.'

As Joy looked around she spied something half hidden under a chair. With a cry she swooped and picked it up. 'A pink hair ribbon. This is hers, I'm sure.' She looked around wildly. 'Then where can she be?'

'Not in here,' Hector said grimly, opening the doors and checking inside the two cupboards in the room. He took her by the arm. 'Let's go.'

Joy clutched the ribbon as Hector led her outside. They hurried down to the big shed, reaching it as Josh was coming out.

'Nothing in there,' he told them. 'I looked behind every stack of timber, every box. Nothing.'

'We're fairly sure they've been here.' Hector filled him in on what they had found, then gestured down towards a partly built cutter by the water's edge. 'Let's check that out.'

After they had explored every possible space in the vessel with no trace of anything untoward a feeling of hopelessness wash over Joy.

'Where to now?' Hector asked.

'The house.'

Osborne's house was separated from his boatyard by a fence with a small connecting gate. When Hector turned the knob on the back door it opened, and they went inside. Silence hung over the house. In the kitchen they found the remnants of a meal on the table, and a few dirty dishes stacked by the kitchen sink. On checking the other rooms they found a large bed in what was obviously Osborne's room that had been left unmade, but all the other rooms were tidy, and there were no signs that anyone had been here apart from the owner.

As they left the house and walked back into the boatyard again Joy shook her head in despair. She stopped suddenly, dropping her face into her hands. She might never see her baby again, and it was her fault. She'd gone off and left her, and now Xandra was gone. A loud wail filled the air. Joy wondered where it was coming from, until she realised it was from herself. The floodgates had opened and the anguish was pouring out. Clenching her hands into balls she stuffed them into her mouth. As the howl turned to a whimper Josh moved quickly, and she felt his arms around her, strong and protective. She dropped her head onto his chest and sobbed.

Joy wasn't sure how long they stayed like that, with Josh's hand smoothing her hair and his soothing words soft in her ears, but finally she felt calmer and eased herself from his clasp.

He put his hand in his pocket, pulled out a folded handkerchief, and handed it to her.

'Here,' he said gently.

Trembling, she took it from him. 'Thanks.' She wiped her face and blew her nose. 'She's not here,' she whispered.

'We'll find her. We'll keep looking until we do.'

Joy took a deep, shuddering breath and nodded. It was all they could do.

When she looked for Hector she saw he had moved away and was poking about in the grass down by the river bank.

'Have you found something?' she called out.

'No. But let's wander around once more and call out to her in case she's somewhere we haven't looked, and hears us.'

They separated and wandered around the yard, calling her name. There was no response.

Josh left the main part of the yard and edged around the end of the fence alongside the river. He disappeared from view along the bank, and it was some moments later that Joy heard him call out to Hector to come and give him a hand.

Joy followed him. As they rounded the end of the fence she saw they were in a patch of scrub alongside the main yard that had not been cleared. Josh was further along the bank, pulling on a rope tied to a small cabin cruiser that was moored a little way downstream from the yard.

Hector joined him and together they tugged. The boat moved sluggishly towards the bank. When it came alongside Hector thrust the end of the rope into Joy's hand.

'Hold this,' he told her, and as she took it and watched the two men jump onto the vessel, her pulses beginning to hammer with a mixture of hope and fear. She held her breath as Josh ducked his head to enter the cabin, while Hector stood watching. When she heard a shout from inside the cabin, and Hector disappeared, her knees went weak. A few seconds later Hector reappeared.

'We've found her,' he called, and then he stood back as Josh emerged, carrying a small, still figure. A chill of fear ran through Joy. Xandra's eyes were closed, and her head lolled lifelessly.

Her blood went cold, but she managed to hold the rope to keep the boat steady. Hector jumped down, turned, and took the bundle from Josh. As he handed Xandra's body to her, his words were like manna from Heaven. 'She's all right. I think she's been drugged, but she's breathing normally.'

Taking Xandra from him Joy held the inert figure close, tears falling unheeded as she cradled the unresponsive head against her shoulder, resting her own cheek against her daughter's.

'My poor little baby,' she whispered. 'What has he done to you?'

'It doesn't look as though she's suffered any real harm,' Hector reassured her, 'but we need to get her home as quickly as possible. I'll go ahead and get the car started.'

As Hector strode off Josh held out his arms to Joy. 'Let me carry her to the car for you.' As Joy hesitated he added. 'She's too heavy for you, besides it'll be quicker.'

Joy nodded then, allowing him to take the child, and fell into step beside him as they headed back to the car. Hector had it idling when they reached it, and Joy slid into the seat and, reaching out, took Xandra on to her lap.

When they reached the house Josh was first out of the car, and opened the door for Joy.

'I'll carry her in for you.'

He took the still sleeping child, and carried her into the house. Joy hurried ahead to the bedroom, pulled back the bedclothes on Xandra's bed, and took her from Josh as he came in. She laid her down gently and covered her still motionless form.

'I'll stay here with her,' she told him. 'Will you please send someone for the doctor?'

As soon as he had gone Joy checked Xandra all over. She found no marks, nor any sign that she'd been hurt in any way. Xandra's forehead was warm, but not excessively so. If only she would wake up! But the child was still in a deep sleep, so she pulled up a chair and sat down to watch over her.

A short time later Josh entered the room, carrying a cup of tea.

'The doctor's on his way, and I thought you might like this.' Joy took the tea gratefully.

'Can I stay here with you for a while?' he asked.

Joy was surprised but she nodded. He pulled up a chair and sat close alongside her.

'Any change?'

'No.'

When she finished the tea Josh took the cup from her and placed it on the mantelpiece, then resumed his place on the chair beside her.

'You don't need to stay with me,' Joy told him. 'I'll be all right.'

'I know that, but I'd like to. That's if you don't mind.'

'No, of course not.'

After a few moments he reached across to take her hand.

Joy saw only concern and compassion in his face, and his eyes held tenderness and warmth, so she offered no resistance. It was comforting to feel his strong, capable touch. Taking a deep breath she relaxed a little and they sat like that, watching over Xandra together.

Some time later there was a knock on the door, and Mary opened it to announce the doctor had arrived. Josh rose unhurriedly, and stood back as the doctor came in, then slipped unobtrusively from the room.

As Joy pulled back the bedclothes for the doctor to examine her, Xandra stirred and murmured, 'Mummy'.

Joy's heart leaped. 'Yes darling. Mummy's here,' she soothed, stroking her forehead, willing her to wake up. But her eyes remained closed, and she fell back into deep sleep.

The doctor finished his examination, and declared the child had indeed been sedated, but he could detect nothing else wrong with her. Her pulse was strong and her breathing normal. He was sure that after she slept off the drug she would be fine, but he warned Joy to keep a good eye on her for a few days, and to call him at once if anything appeared to be amiss.

After he left Joy just sat, looking at her daughter. Xandra appeared to be sleeping easily now. Her daughter was safe. At last she could relax.

Leaving the room a little later she walked down the hall and looked into the sitting room, but there was no one there, so she wandered down to the kitchen. It too was empty. Making her way out on to the front verandah she saw Josh pacing beneath a tree in the garden, and went down the steps to join him.

He stopped pacing when he saw her and came to meet her.

'How is she?'

'Sleeping still, but the doctor says she's not been harmed in any way, and she should be quite all right after she wakes up.'

'Thank God for that. And Johnnie seems to have taken no lasting harm from his ordeal.'

Joy felt a mix of emotions welling up inside her. How easily it could have all ended in tragedy! If they had not found Osborne when they did...

Suddenly everything boiled up inside her as it all came flooding back. The fear of the last two days. Her resentment at David for not being here when she needed him. The loneliness of her life without him...

A choking sob caught in her throat.

In a stride Josh was with her, and it seemed the most natural thing in the world for him to take her into his arms and hold her close as great, wracking sobs forced their way up. She clung to him until finally the tears eased.

Josh tilted her head back and gently wiped away the tears on her cheeks with his fingers. Bending his head he kissed her lips tenderly. Then he lifted his head and looked at her with eyes that changed as she watched them, changed from compassionate to something more intense.

Joy drew in a sharp breath, feeling something flutter inside her. His head came down and his lips sought hers again, but this time it was not with tenderness, but with something much more powerful. As the kiss deepened she felt her body respond, not just her mouth but deep within her. A stirring of her passions that was as unexpected as it was frightening. She savoured it for a moment before pulling from his arms. He released her instantly. She turned and ran back to the house, her pulses hammering.

Chapter Twenty Four

Hector called the police after the doctor left, and the next morning the local police constable appeared. Gathering Hector, Josh, Joy and Emma together around the dining room table he told them he'd arranged for Osborne's body to be collected. Now he wanted to know the full story of what happened.

'I know the children went missing,' he told them, after settling himself at the head of the table with his notebook open in front of him. 'I was out looking for them myself.' He pursed his lips. 'But as for Mr. Osborne—well, he's a well known and respected businessman in these parts. I find it hard to believe him capable of what Mr. Barron has told me, that he actually kidnapped the children.'

He looked sternly at each of them in turn, and his gaze settled on Josh.

'Now, Mr. Frazer, please tell me what you know about this sad affair.'

Josh repeated his stories, both of the men who had informed him of the conversation he had overheard in the Plough Inn, and those who'd seen Osborne with a child on his horse that morning. And he corroborated Hector's account of what happened on the mountain.

After writing the names of the informants in his notebook, the constable looked at Joy.

'Mrs. Barron, you went with Mr. Barron and Mr. Frazer to Mr. Osborne's boatyard yesterday. Is that right?'

'Yes.'

'Will you please tell me what happened there?'

Joy told him what had taken place. How they found the biscuits and empty milk glasses, Xandra's hair ribbon, and finally Xandra herself.

'And you all agree with this?' the constable asked, looking around the table.

When they all affirmed the story he asked to speak with the children, both of whom had wakened refreshed after a night's sleep.

Emma and Joy left and returned with Johnnie and Xandra, both of whom seemed in surprisingly good spirits after their ordeals.

The constable was gentle in his questions to them but they both told the same story.

Osborne had persuaded them to go with him by promising them he was going to take them to see a litter of puppies, and that if they were good they would be able to choose one to keep. Their disappointment at missing out on this seemed to be greater than their concern at what had happened to them. Xandra had no memory of what had happened after they went with Osborne to his boatyard, and he had given them the biscuits and milk. Johnnie, although his memory was befuddled from the drug, remembered being pulled along up the mountain, and what had happened up there.

The constable wrote it all down in his notebook.

'Thank you for telling me your story,' he told them. 'You've both been very brave.'

'That's all right,' Johnnie told him seriously. 'Uncle Hector told us that Mr. Osborne was sick in the head otherwise he wouldn't have been so horrible. And we're sorry he fell over the cliff, but he shouldn't have been fighting anyway. And he should have known it's dangerous to go near the edge. Uncle Hector told me that when we went to Seal Rock.' His face brightened. 'But it's going to be all right because Uncle Hector knows where the litter of puppies is, and he's going to get one and bring it back for us. So we'll have a puppy after all.'

Closing his notebook, the constable thanked them, and left to make enquiries.

When he returned later in the day he informed them that both Josh's stories had been corroborated, and, after asking them to make sure they would be available for the inquest, he left.

Over the next week they were all relieved to see both Johnnie and Xandra seemed to have taken no lasting harm from their ordeals. True to his word, Hector brought them a puppy, which they decided to name Bouncer, because that's what he seemed to be fond of doing, and he became the focus of their attention to the exclusion of all else. Nevertheless Joy busied herself inside the house, fussing over them, because they needed all her attention after their ordeals. It had nothing to do with Josh, even if she didn't want to see him just yet.

Her feelings confused her. His kiss had stirred depths in her, depths that should only be stirred by the man she loved. And she loved David. She knew she did, even though she was angry with him for not being here when she'd needed him so badly. How dare he be in America enjoying himself, while she was going through the hell of not knowing if their daughter was alive or dead!

But she couldn't deny she'd enjoyed Josh kissing her. However that was as far as it was ever going to go. After all, they'd both been overwrought at the time.

When she could no longer avoid going down to the horses she made sure she was never alone with Josh. However, the day finally came when she received a message that he needed her help to deliver a foal for one of the stock mares who was having a hard time.

The two of them were alone in the stable with the horse. Finally the mare gave the last final push and, with Joy helping, the foal slithered out onto the floor.

'Well done, Mrs. Joy,' Josh praised her as they stood watching the mare smell and lick at her baby as she encouraged it to move.

Joy kept her gaze averted from him as she wiped her hands on a cloth.

'You could have done just as well. You didn't really need me.'

'Ah, but I did. I was thankful Gertie gave me the excuse to have you to myself for a bit. You can't avoid me forever, you know.'

The hot blood rushed to her cheeks. 'I don't know what you mean.'

'Of course you do. You felt it as much as me. I could tell.'

'I'm a happily married woman. I love my husband.'

'I'm sure you do, you're the dutiful little wife. But he's not here, is he?'

'He'll be back. He's only gone to see what's new in America.' She defended David hotly.

'If you were my wife I wouldn't leave you alone,' he said quietly. 'Not for a minute.'

She looked at him. His face was serious.

'You're far too precious to be left alone.' He took a step towards her. 'You're a woman who needs to be cared for, sheltered from harm, and loved.'

Drawing in her breath she stepped back, feeling slightly dizzy.

'You shouldn't talk to me like that,' she whispered.

A flicker of a smile lifted a corner of his mouth. 'You can always sack me.'

He stepped closer.

She bit her lip.

He took another step.

He was only inches from her.

He raised his hand, his fingers stroked her cheek.

'It will happen, you know,' he said softly. 'You're made for love. My love. You can't fight it forever.'

Joy gasped…and fled. Her flying feet led her down to the river, where she sat on Kitty's stump. This was madness. The feelings he roused in her were madness. It was only because she'd been so fraught during the children's disappearance, and he'd been kind to her. She would never betray her marriage vows. She must make him realise that.

Over the next few days Joy was politely distant to Josh as they went about their work. Sometimes she looked up to catch him watching her, and then he gave her a quiet little smile, and winked at her. She always looked away without acknowledging him, but it disturbed her. And when she lay in her lonely bed at night, she couldn't help imagining his arms around her.

Finally another letter arrived from David, and Joy tore it open with trembling fingers. Although couched in friendlier tones than the first, it told her only of what was happening at Talahousie Stud and little else besides. Apart from polite enquiries as to her health, and expressions of interest regarding Xandra, it contained nothing of a personal nature except to remark that he was sure she would be managing well without him, 'in your own inimitable manner', as he put it.

It was six months since David had gone, and still he gave no indication as to when he might return. Joy put the letter down with an aching chest, wondering how much longer long he would stay away. Perhaps he was pleased to be away from her. Perhaps Lily and her husband had offered him inducements to stay and he'd decided to accept. Perhaps he'd met someone else over there, someone who went along with his wishes and caused him no worry. Someone better than her.

But surely he would tell her if this was so. Or would he?

Making her way alone down to Chipper's paddock she went in, pulling the gate to behind her, and stood watching as he trotted up to her. She rubbed his ears, and when he whinnied and nudged her with his nose she laid her head against his face and let the tears fall.

'At least you still love me, don't you Chipper?' She snuffled as she stood back and fumbled in her pocket for a handkerchief.

'Why is it that women never have a handkerchief when they need it?' asked a voice at her side. 'Here, take this one.' Josh thrust it at her.

Taking it she wiped her eyes. 'Thank you.' She sniffed.

'Want to tell me what it's about?'

Joy shook her head, but the kindness in his voice brought on a fresh bout of weeping.

'I think you need more than a horse to comfort you,' Josh told her, pulling her into his arms.

She rested her head on his shoulder, feeling the rough cotton of his work shirt and smelling his smell – a mixture of horses, hay and fresh sweat.

'There, there now.' He stroked her back. 'Has something happened to one of the children?'

Joy shook her head.

'Have you had a falling-out with Emma over something?'
Again she shook her head.
'Your Grandma?'
'No.'
'Grandpa?'
'No.' She gave a tremulous laugh. 'And before you go through the list, I haven't fallen out with anyone.'
'Then it has to be something to do with that husband of yours.' He held her away from him. 'Am I right?'
'Yes,' she admitted, drawing a shuddering breath.
'Ah! Then there's only one cure for that.'

He drew her to him and his mouth came down on hers. His kiss caused the most delicious, fluttery sensations inside her. She couldn't help herself from returning the kiss, and the sensations became stronger. The heat filling her body caused a deep yearning inside her. She wanted love. She wanted him. Letting her body take over her senses, she swayed against him, feeling his body hard against her, her pulses hammering. When, much later, he lifted his mouth from hers and gently disentangled her arms, which she hadn't realised had encircled his neck, he took a step backwards, and her legs would have given way if he hadn't held her. Breathing heavily, his eyes, dark and molten, searched her face.

'My darling Mrs. Joy,' his voice was husky, 'the time is over for playing games. For both of us. What's between us is too strong. It's only my concern for your reputation that stops me from scooping you up in my arms right away, and carrying you off to my lair to have my wicked way with you.'

'You mustn't...I mustn't...' Joy gasped, trying to regain reality. 'This is madness. It can't happen...it mustn't happen.' Realising they were standing in plain view of anyone who happened to come along, with only Chipper's body to give them some sort of shelter, she stepped away from him.

He put out a hand to detain her.
'Come to me tonight.'
'No,' she shook her head. 'No, I can't. I won't.'
'I'll be waiting,' he told her softly.

With a sob in her throat she turned and ran, through the gate and along the track. As she reached the bend she turned to look back. He was standing motionless as she'd left him, watching her.

Joy's thoughts were in turmoil for the rest of the day, and when she went to bed that night she lay on her back staring into the darkness. Was he waiting for her? She re-lived their encounter, their kiss, and felt the longing all over again. She turned over, trying to will her eyes to close. It was no use. In her mind she saw his face, felt his mouth on hers, felt his body hard against hers, and passion stirred inside her once more.

Finally she couldn't lie there any longer, thinking about him. She needed to move around, anything to change the direction of her thoughts. Slipping on her wrapper she left the room and stole out on to the verandah, feeling the smooth boards through her thin satin slippers. Wondering if he was still awake, she leaned against the rail, her eyes making out the shapes of the trees by the thin light of the moon.

Hesitantly she put her foot on the first step. She was not going to him, of course not, but a short walk might help her to sleep. Carefully she picked her way down the steps and along the path. He would be asleep by now. Long ago. Somehow she found herself approaching his cottage. Well, she would just walk by. No harm in that. A pale light shone out. Stopping outside she stood staring at the flickering candle set in the window.

As she stood watching the door opened, and he stepped outside. He walked over to her and took her hand.

'I've been waiting for you.'

Chapter Twenty Five

Joy stirred languidly in the bed and stretched her arms above her head. She breathed deeply and let out a soft sigh. The faint light spilling from the lamp cast a soft glow over the room and, turning her head, she saw Josh's tawny head on the pillow alongside her. His arm rested lightly across her waist.

A smile curved her lips as she thought of the night before. Their first coming together had been hasty, their need for each other too strong to delay savouring the pleasure that was waiting. But after that first time he had taken her to new levels, seemingly intent only on giving her pleasure as he found ways to take her higher and higher and then, as she crested the wave each time, pausing as she was poised there until she cried out for release. But he made her wait, each time taking her still higher, until, finally, she surged over the peak into a crescendo of ecstasy. Only then did he take his own pleasure, crying out as he reached his release.

She drowsed again, and he next time she woke she sensed that first light was not far away. As she stirred he gripped her tightly.

'I have to go,' she told him.

'I wish you didn't. I hate to lose you.'

'I must.'

He sighed. 'I know.'

Raising himself on his elbow he looked down at her then leant over and kissed her gently.

'Thank you, Mrs. Joy.' He smiled.

She pulled his head down and kissed him again and then, as his arm released her, she slid from the bed. Hastily donning her garments and slippers she left him and sped back to the house, into her room, and into her own bed.

The next few weeks passed for Joy as if she was in a dream. She went about her duties as usual; she cared for Xandra, attended to her chores and ate and talked and acted as expected, but she lived only for the time she could spend with Josh. He was like a drug; she couldn't get enough of him. Every night she waited until the house was asleep, and then she left her own bed and went to him.

During the day she found reasons to spend more time with him than usual, relishing the fact they were working together, tending the horses together. When her treacherous mind told her it was just like it had been with David when they started out, working together, loving together, she pushed the thought away.

So the halcyon days passed, with Joy secure in her belief that no one knew of their liaison. She was jolted from her trance by the news that Kitty was coming for a visit.

Up until now she'd felt sure no one was aware of her nocturnal comings and goings. Her grandparents were sound sleepers, and Hector and Emma were so wrapped up in each other she was sure they noticed nothing else. In fact one night as she eased her bedroom door open she saw Hector going into Emma's room, and smiled as she waited to be sure he was safely inside before venturing forth. But with extra people in the house she would have to be more careful, especially with her mother here, who rarely missed anything that was happening.

'Do you think you're being wise, Joy?' Kitty asked her daughter as they walked down towards the river the morning after she arrived.

Joy caught her breath. 'What...what do you mean?'

'You know what I mean. Josh.'

Joy bit her lip. She hadn't left her own bed last night, so how could she know?

'I...I don't know what you mean,' she stammered.

'Come now, did you think no one knew about your night time visits to him?'

Joy's footsteps faltered as she went cold all over, and when she made no response her mother stopped walking and turned to face her.

'I'm not here to scold you, darling. You're a grown woman, and must make your own decisions. I realise it's very difficult for you with David away, and I can't say I agree with him spending all this time in America. But I am concerned. For you. For the future.' Kitty took her hand. 'What about when David comes back? What will happen then?'

Joy swallowed. 'I don't know.'

'Haven't you thought about it?'

Joy's lips twisted. 'No.'

'Then perhaps you should,' her mother said gently.

Tears sprang to Joy's eyes as her pent-up frustration bubbled over. 'How can I? How can I when I don't know when he's coming back – or even if he's coming back. He wasn't here when I needed him – when Xandra was missing, and I didn't know if she was alive or dead.' Her voice rose. 'Where was he then? Over in America. I had to go through that all on my own.' She dashed the tears away angrily. 'If it hadn't been for Hector and Josh she might be dead now. Her and Johnnie too. And a fat lot David would have cared what happened to us. He's too busy enjoying himself in America.'

The tears spilled over, and Kitty put her arms around her, drawing her close. 'There, there, darling. I can only imagine how terrible it was for you, and I'm immensely grateful that you had Josh to help and support you then, but...'

'I love him,' Joy interrupted, her voice passionate.

'Ah. I see.' Kitty held her away so she could see her face. 'And you don't love David anymore?'

'No. I mean...yes...I mean...' Stepping back, she heaved a deep sigh, stifling a sob. 'Oh...I don't know...' she searched her mother's face. 'Is it possible to love two men at the same time?'

This drew a slight smile from Kitty. 'Well...perhaps...under certain circumstances.'

Joy sniffed. 'I think this is one of them.'

'Perhaps. But David is your husband. He's the father of your daughter, and the man you committed yourself to. I think you'll find that when he returns he'll have had time to think, time to miss you and Xandra, and he'll probably just expect to get on with your life together without any hesitation.'

'He went off and left me – left us, without even asking me if I wanted to come with him, or even how I felt about him going.'

'And how had things been between you, before that?'

Joy hesitated before replying. 'Not all that good. Everything I did annoyed him, he was always finding fault with me.'

'And did you ever give him just cause to feel that way?'

Joy dropped her eyes. 'He thought so.'

'Oh, my dear, there are times in every marriage when things don't always go right, and even in these enlightened times a man will always believe it's not his fault. And the person he blames is usually his wife. But if a marriage is built on solid foundations it can survive these upsets, and even be stronger for it in the end.'

'I don't know...' Joy's voice faded away, and then she looked up. 'Josh thinks whatever I do is perfect,' she said defensively.

Kitty laughed gently. 'I'm sure he does, darling.' She sobered. 'Well, I'll say only one more thing. How do you think your life would be if you decide you want Josh instead of David? How would you go about it? Would you just ask David to leave? Do you think you could stay here then, and face the disgrace of everyone knowing, people talking about you, ostracizing you? For that's what would happen, you know. They would turn their backs on you in the street. You'd be branded a scarlet woman forever.'

'No one need know. Josh could stay in his house, and I'd stay in the big house. No one need ever know.'

Kitty shook her head. 'And what about David? Even if he agreed to just go away quietly, which I don't think he would. You couldn't keep such a thing secret.'

A sudden thought struck Joy. 'Anyway, how did you know about Josh?' she asked.

'Your grandmother wrote to me. She didn't think it was her place to speak to you, but she was worried.'

'But she was always asleep when I went out. How could she have known?'

'You can't keep these things secret for long. Someone will always find out.'

'Well then, I hope she knows about Hector and Emma as well. I'm not the only one who moves around at night.'

'Of course she does. As does Mary. But that's different, they're to be wed.'

Joy set her lips. 'Well, I know she wears his ring, but they don't seem in a hurry to marry. I haven't heard of any wedding plans.'

'Emma told me she tried to tell you of their plans, but she said you've been...preoccupied lately. You didn't take any notice of what she was trying to tell you.'

A sudden pang of anxiety struck Joy. 'But...she doesn't know, does she? About me...and Josh.'

'I'm afraid so. You really can't have secrets around here. Everyone knows everyone's business. Did you really think no one knows?'

Joy nodded as the words sank in, wondering how she could face Emma. After all, she was David's sister. As well as her closest friend. How must she feel?

Kitty reached out and put her hand on Joy's arm. 'Emma understands what it's like to be alone. She made excuses for you to me. She's cross with her brother for leaving you so long, and believes everything will be all right when he returns. She's a loyal friend.'

But Joy wondered where her loyalties would lie if she really chose a life with Josh, over David.

Kitty stayed a few more days before returning to her home with Rufe in Sydney. Although she never again referred directly to her involvement with Josh, Joy had the feeling she was being watched, and judged. She kept to her own bed during Kitty's visit, but as she lay in her own lonely bed she relived the nights she had spent with Josh, and as soon as her mother left she again crept from her bed to visit him.

But she no longer lived in the dream world she had inhabited before Kitty's visit. Although no one referred to their affair, Joy noticed that Josh's name was never mentioned in conversation with her, and this omission was in itself a tacit admission of their knowledge. Once again she began to worry about David's return, dreading it now, for it would mean she had to make a decision. She had no doubt of her love for Josh, but her mother's words were not easily forgotten.

All such thoughts were banished from her mind a few days later when a message came from Jim Travers that Thunderbolt would be running his first race in a handicap at Newcastle the following week. 'As it is his first start, he has been given a low weight, and I am confident he will run well,' the message concluded.

'Are you going to come and watch him again?' Joy asked Emma excitedly as she showed her the letter.

Emma's face lit up. 'Yes, of course. I wouldn't miss it for anything and I'm sure Hector will want to come too, so we'll go in the car again, shall we?'

'That would be wonderful.'

Emma looked down and fiddled with her ring, twisting it on her finger. 'I suppose you'd like Josh to come too?'

Joy swallowed. 'Well, yes. If...if Hector won't mind. I mean, I know he takes a great interest in Thunderbolt's progress.'

'Yes. Yes, of course. No, I'm sure Hector won't mind.'

'And he was there to see him win his trial.'

'Of course he was. No, that will be quite all right. Of course.'

Joy left it at that, but suddenly the day wasn't quite so exciting.

The day of the race dawned fine and warm, and it was with an air of excitement that the four of them piled into the car. The noise of the motor prevented all but the briefest conversation, and Joy, conscious of Josh alongside her in the confines of the back seat and wishing he could put his arm around her, nevertheless did her best to remain aloof from him.

The trip down to Newcastle was uneventful and they pulled into the Broadmeadows racecourse in plenty of time for the first race. Thunderbolt was entered in the third race, but he was already in his stall when they arrived, seeming quite unperturbed by the excitement in the air and the other horses nearby.

Jim Travers was in the stall with the horse, but he left him with the strapper and came to shake hands with each of them in turn.

'Well, Mrs. Cavanagh, this is a big day, eh? A lot rests on how he performs today.'

'Yes. And how do you think he'll go?'

'I expect him to finish well up with the leaders, and with a bit of luck in running he could come in first.'

'And if he does well?'

'Then we'll be on track to have a go at the Gold Cup.'

Joy moved towards the big black horse, with Travers behind her. Thunderbolt was standing calmly, only his watchful eyes betrayed his interest in the comings and goings around him. As she reached the rail at the front of his stall he stamped his front hoof on the ground, and then reached his head over towards her.

'Hello Thunder, how's my big boy?' She rubbed his ears. 'He hasn't forgotten me,' she told Travers over her shoulder.

'Not him. He doesn't miss a trick. Knows exactly what's happening round him.'

'He's very relaxed.'

'He saves his energy till he needs it. And he'll need it today; he's up against some stiff competition. But he'll give them a run for the money, you'll see.'

At his confident words a surge of adrenalin ran through Joy. She gave Thunderbolt a pat on the shoulder and some last words of encouragement before she stepped away. 'Then I'll see you before the race,' she told him.

Travers nodded. 'Righto, missus.'

Threading their way through the crowd, they found seats in the grandstand, and Joy tried to curb her impatience as she waited. After the second race she made her way down to the parade ring where she stood by the rail waiting for the horses, and was joined by Jim Travers. It seemed to take forever but finally the first horse appeared, led by the strapper and wearing the number one saddlecloth.

'Sea Breeze,' she muttered, reading from the race book.

'He's the main danger,' Travers told her. 'Won his last two starts.'

Joy scrutinised the horses as they entered the ring to parade in front of the crowd. 'Number two, Imperial Jester, number three, Humber, number four, High Hopes, number five, Applecross.'

Most walked quietly, but there were some, unsettled by the crowd pressed tight against the rail, who pulled against their leads, prancing, tossing their heads, and giving their strappers a hard time. Finally, at number eleven, Thunderbolt entered, walking sedately. He stood out because of his size and his coat of deepest brown dappled with black, gleaming in the sunshine, and his flowing black mane and tail.

After the jockeys mounted and the horses left the ring, Joy followed Travers through the crowd back to take her seat in the stand. Too excited to talk, Joy clutched her race book as she watched the horses milling around behind the starting line. Then, one by one, they took their places in the line.

'They're off.' The shout came simultaneously from a thousand throats as the horses jumped away, with Applecross leading the bunch.

Hector had his glasses trained on the horses as they went into the back straight. Joy stood and, after picking out the Redwoods' colours, glued her eyes onto Thunderbolt. Butterflies fluttered inside her. Thunderbolt was back midway in the pack, on the rail, with Humber now taking the lead. As they swept around the bend heading into the home straight Imperial Jester took over the lead, with Sea Breeze close behind. Thunderbolt was still midway in the field, one off the rail. As they raced towards the finishing line Sea Breeze inched closer to the leader and a great shout went up from the crowd.

Joy's heart beat madly as Thunderbolt was hooked to the outside and lengthened his stride. Jumping up and down in her excitement she shouted his name. 'Thunder! Thunder! Come on Thunder!'

A tumultuous roar went up from the crowd as Thunderbolt came sweeping down the outside, his long stride and cracking pace eating up the ground. While they were still a hundred yards from the post he flashed past the leaders and came away to win by two lengths.

Laughing as she jumped up and down, feeling her heart was ready to burst, Joy turned and hugged each of her companions in turn. When she turned to Travers he took her hand in both of his, wringing it, smiling broadly.

'Well missus, we're on our way to the Gold Cup,' he told her. 'If we can qualify,' he added, 'and we've only got three months left to do it in.'

A few days later another letter arrived from David. This one was couched in warmer terms than previously, and when she turned to the second page her eyes dropped to the bottom and she saw it was signed, 'your affectionate husband, David'.

As before, he described the happenings at the stud. As Winston's father was old and in ill-health, Winston had recently taken over complete control of the stud, although David's words suggested to Joy that Lily was the motivating force behind him. Winston's parents now spent their time in their second home at the Ohio River, where they were closer to their doctor in Louisville, as well as to the Churchill Downs racetrack, which Mr. Paget-Smythe still attended, with the rest of the family, whenever any of their horses were running.

Winston's sister Abby lived at Talahousie with her brother and family, and there were several coloured servants to run the house and stables, and to help with the horses.

David was enthusiastic about the horses, which were doing very well that season. In particular a stallion named Aristocrat, who had been winning consistently. 'In fact,' he continued, 'Lily is anxious to bring him to Sydney to contest the Gold Cup, as she believes he could beat any of the horses over there.'

Joy dropped the letter into her lap when she read this. Well, if Lily thought that, she was wrong. Thunderbolt was going to win the Gold Cup.

Chapter Twenty Six

Emma and Hector were married in St James Church in Morpeth, close to Emma's old family home at Riverside. The ceremony was attended by the bride's family and a few old friends from the surrounding area, and a small dinner at Riverside followed. Joy was Emma's matron-of-honour, and her only other attendant was Johnnie, torn between happiness at gaining a new father and self-conscious pride at being his mother's page boy.

When Emma had told her of their wedding plans one morning as they were taking the children for a walk, Joy stopped walking and threw her arms around her friend, hugging her.

'I'm so happy for you both. Tell me all about it.'

'Well, as I've been married before, and as you're the only family Hector has here, neither of us wants a big wedding. Uncle Rufe and Kitty will be coming up from Sydney, and there'll be my parents, of course, and a couple of old school friends from when I lived at Riverside as a girl. Apart from that, just you and your grandparents.' She paused briefly. 'Oh, and Mary and Patrick too.'

'And...Josh?' Joy asked.

Emma dropped her eyes. 'No. No, not Josh.' She looked up, her gaze direct. 'I'm sorry my brother won't be here to see me married for the second time, but I don't think it would be appropriate for Josh to accompany you.'

Joy felt as if she had been slapped. 'I see.' She swallowed. 'Well...yes...of course...it's not as if he's an old friend or...or anything. You don't know him all that well.'

'No, of course not. I knew you'd understand, and I'm sure he will too.'

'Of course he will.' Joy shifted from one foot to the other. 'Now, more importantly,' her voice was bright as she continued, 'I hope you're not thinking of leaving here after you're married.'

'We will want to find a place of our own, of course, and Hector has started looking around, but he hasn't found anything suitable yet.'

'Then please stay here until you find the right place.' Joy felt a moment of desolation at the thought of losing Emma, and clasped her hand. 'I'll hate it when you do leave. Please don't go until you must.'

Emma's face lit up and she smiled. 'If you're sure...'

'I'm absolutely sure.'

'Then of course we'll be happy to stay until we find something.'

'I hope Hector doesn't want to move to Sydney?'

'No. We both prefer the country and we'd like it to be somewhere near here, if possible.'

Joy drew a deep breath. 'Then all's well.'

She looked ahead to where Johnnie and Xandra, who had also stopped, were by the side of the track. Xandra was looking on while Johnnie was busily digging a hole with a stick. Catching her eye on him, Johnnie called out.

'We're looking for worms,' he told her, 'cause we're going fishing soon.'

The two women smiled at each other.

'How could we possibly separate them?' Emma asked.

Joy was helping Josh to prepare the feed for the horses in the store room a few days after the wedding when he put out his hand to stop her as she reached across him to pick up the tin of molasses.

'Leave that for now,' he told her. 'I want to talk to you. Come and sit over here for a moment.'

He led her over to sit on a bale of straw, and seated himself beside her. He leant over and kissed her gently, then picked up her hand and held it in his own.

'The time has come for us to talk seriously, my darling,' he began.

'What about?'

'About us.'

'What about us?' Joy asked him apprehensively.

'I want more than we have now—I want us to belong to each other, all the time. I love you with all my heart, and I don't want to have to hide it, like I do now.' His voice was urgent. 'I don't want us to have to creep around like fugitives. I want the world to know how much we love each other.' Pausing, he drew a deep breath. 'I want you to leave here and come away with me.'

Joy stiffened, feeling suddenly light-headed. 'But...I can't do that. I've got Xandra...and this.' She swept her free hand around. 'Redwoods...the stud...'

'Of course I mean you to bring Xandra. You don't think I'd want to part you from her, do you?'

'Well, no, but...'

'And as for the stud,' he continued quickly, 'I know I've never told you, but it's always been my intention to have a stud of my own. I only came to Australia for the experience. I've always planned to go back to England and begin on my own. I want you to come with me. We can do it together. It'll be just like it is now, but we won't have to hide how we feel about each other.'

'But...but you can't just start up a stud...with nothing. You have to have land, and...horses...and that takes...'

He put his fingers over her lips, shaking his head. 'Stop worrying about that, my sweet. My family has a property back home that would be ideal, or we could go to Ireland. You needn't worry about the money; my grandfather left me a more than modest inheritance.'

Joy gazed at him in silence as she digested his words. How wonderful it would be to be able to live openly together, to not have to worry all the time about being seen together. To be able to stay in bed together all night, instead of sneaking around in the dark like a criminal. She allowed herself a brief moment of bliss before reality stepped in.

'But I don't know if David would divorce me.'

'It wouldn't matter, my darling. We'd be away from here where no one would know us. If we had to live together without a marriage certificate we'd be the only ones who would know.' He paused for a moment before continuing. 'But perhaps if you write to him now, before he makes plans to come back, he might decide to stay in America. Then you could divorce him. Or even if you can't, we wouldn't have to worry about it.'

As Joy sat there turning all this over in her mind he seized her other hand.

'Don't you love me, Joy? Is that what's holding you back?'

She looked at him sitting there, his eyes pleading with her, and her heart lurched.

'Of course I love you.' She leant forward and kissed his lips.

He released her hands and pulled her to him, kissing her fervently, telling her that she was his entire world, that without her he would no longer want to go on living. And then as she returned his kisses she was sure, so sure, that she loved him desperately, and wanted to be with him more than anything else. He was all that mattered to her–except, of course, her daughter.

When they finally pulled apart, and realised the horses' feed was not yet ready, they went back to work, both firmly convinced that nothing could come between them.

That night, after their lovemaking, Josh told her about his home in Suffolk. It sounded idyllic, and would be perfect for horses. With the added advantage that it was not too far from Newmarket, with its racetrack and proliferation of horse trainers.

Suddenly a chill shot through Joy, and she sat bolt upright in bed. Suffolk! Oh, my God. That was not far from Buckinghamshire, the Barrons' home. She had forgotten about her grandparents!

'Oh.' She gasped.

Josh sat up alongside her. 'Whatever is the matter?'

'My grandparents. I quite forgot about them. They live in Buckinghamshire.'

'Well, that's far enough away that you're not likely to run into them. Besides, they're not going to know, unless you tell them.'

'Hector. Hector Barron is my uncle, although he asked me to stop calling him uncle when he came out here because it made him feel old. He'll write and tell my grandfather.'

'Then if it bothers you, we can go to Ireland instead, where nobody knows you.'

'But Grandfather will know.'

Josh said nothing for a few seconds. 'Then if that bothers you so much, you need to write to David immediately, and perhaps you should suggest it would be easier if he doesn't return. Then you'd be free before long, and we could be properly married.'

Joy chewed on her lip, and in spite of allowing herself to be pulled back down in the bed, she couldn't go to sleep. Until Josh, aware of her sleeplessness, took her in his arms again, and kissed her and caressed her until her passion rose, yet again, and drove all other thoughts from her mind.

When she crept back to her bed later she had forgotten all her doubts. She loved Josh. She wanted to be with him. She would write to David.

When Joy opened the door to Xandra's room the next morning she was surprised to see her lying listlessly in her bed. Usually, she sat up in bed playing with her toys until Joy, or Mary, came in to help her to dress. This morning, as soon as Xandra saw her, she started to cry.

'Mummy, my head hurts.'

Joy hurried to her, noticing she was flushed, and put her hand on her forehead. Yes, she was quite hot. 'Does it hurt anywhere else?'

'Yes, my throat's sore.'

'Open your mouth for me.'

As Xandra opened her mouth she suddenly coughed, a deep, hacking cough, and Joy felt her stomach lurch with anxiety. As the coughing continued Joy put an arm behind her and helped her to sit up until the spasm passed. Then she lowered her little frame back onto the bed and sat alongside her, taking her hand in her own. It was very hot.

At that moment Bella came through the open door.

'What's the matter with Xandra?' she asked.

Joy shook her head, frowning. 'I don't know, I just came in. She's very hot, and she has a terrible cough.'

'I know, I heard her from out in the hall. Let me have a look.'

Joy stood up and Bella took her place.

'There, there,' she soothed, wiping Xandra's running nose with a handkerchief before feeling her face. 'Yes, she's certainly running a temperature.'

She pulled back the bedclothes and raised Xandra's nightgown to inspect her stomach.

'Hmm, nothing there.' She tucked the bedclothes back and put her fingers up to the whimpering child's mouth, and rolled back first the bottom lip, then the top. 'Look at this, Joy. She has spots inside her lips.'

Joy looked, and saw the inside of her daughter's lips peppered with tiny, bright red spots.

'So what is it? Measles?'

'I'm afraid so.'

'Oh dear. She must have picked it up when we were down in Morpeth for the wedding. I'd better call the doctor.'

'Yes. I'm afraid you'd better.'

By the time the doctor arrived several hours later, Xandra's face was covered in spots. After examining her he confirmed the diagnosis as measles, looking grave.

'It's a serious disease, and I've seen several cases lately, unfortunately,' he told them. 'I'll leave some medicine that will help to ease the pain for her, and bring her temperature down, and another for her cough, but she needs to be looked after carefully.'

A knot of fear twisted inside Joy. 'How serious is it?' she asked him.

He pursed his lips. 'It can be very serious, so you must watch her. The rash will spread all over her body, but it's not the rash itself that's the danger. She must be kept away from other children until it completely disappears, as the disease is highly infectious. You can sponge her with cool water to try and bring her temperature down.'

'What else?'

'She probably won't want to eat, but make sure she has plenty to drink. Cold drinks will help to soothe her throat. It's best to keep the curtains drawn because her eyes will be sore. They're already quite red, as you can see. You must also take note if her ears seem to bother her. Call me immediately if that happens.'

After leaving the two bottles of medicine and promising to call again the next day the doctor left.

Joy sat by Xandra's bedside all day, administering the medicine to her every four hours and sponging her at frequent intervals. Xandra's breathing became more laboured, and she drifted into sleep from time to time, only to be woken by a fit of coughing.

During the afternoon she woke from one such sleep to toss fretfully from side to side.

'Daddy,' she called. 'I want Daddy.'

'Daddy's still away, darling, but I'm here.'

'I want Daddy.' She started to cry, her face screwed up and her nose running.

'There, there, darling. Mummy's here. I'll look after you.'

'I...' She hiccupped, 'I want Daddy.'

'Daddy's not here Xandra. He's still away. Remember, he went to America. But he'll be home soon, and you must get well so you can be here to meet him.'

Xandra didn't seem to have heard but she stopped crying. Joy spooned some more medicine into her mouth, and she drifted off to sleep again.

The next time she woke she called out for Johnnie, and once again Joy had to disappoint her, unable to risk Johnnie coming into the room for fear he would catch the measles too.

As the time slowly passed both Mary and Bella offered to take her place, but Joy refused to leave her daughter. All they could do to help was to bring her refreshments.

Towards evening, Patrick came into the room bringing one of the comfortable armchairs from the sitting room, and placed it by the bed. With a sigh Joy settled back, relaxing her tired body, and there she stayed all night, sleeping only fitfully between Xandra's coughing fits.

Chapter Twenty Seven

By the next morning the spots had crept down Xandra's neck and formed into a rash over her body. Her cough persisted, and she cried and said her eyes hurt, but what worried Joy most was that the fever seemed to be getting worse.

Mary showed Josh into the room during the morning. He tiptoed across the room and stood beside Joy's chair, looking down at Xandra's flushed face as she slept.

'How is she?' he asked, his voice anxious.

Joy turned in her chair, feeling tears close to the surface as she looked up and held out her hand to him.

'Oh Josh, she's not good. She's burning up with fever.' She took a shuddering breath. 'I don't know what else I can do for her, that's the hard part.'

He took her hand, squeezing it as he answered. 'Mary told me how you've been sitting up with her all night, giving her medicine and sponging her. You can't do any more. And children are resilient, aren't they? In a few days' time she'll be up and running around again.' After looking around at the open door, he leant over and kissed her cheek quickly. 'I wish I could stay with you, my darling,' he told her in a soft voice. 'I can't with things the way they are now, but that will all change before too long, and then I'll be able to be by your side whenever you need me. In the meantime, you must make sure you don't make yourself sick by worrying about her too much.'

Joy was startled at his words, realising guiltily that she had given him no thought since Xandra had been sick. She gave him a tremulous smile as she returned the pressure of his hand.

'I'm all right. I just need her to get well again.'

'I'm sure she will. It's you I'm worried about. Promise me you'll get some rest.' His eyes were full of concern.

'I will, as soon as I can.'

At that moment Xandra stirred and opened her eyes. She started to cough again and Joy hurriedly turned back to her. She put her arm beneath her shoulders to raise her into a sitting position, holding her there as the coughs racked her body. With her free hand she reached for the glass of soothing medicine and held it to Xandra's lips as the coughing eased.

'Try to drink some of this, my poor darling. It'll help the nasty cough.'

Xandra managed a sip before pushing the glass away and starting to cry. Joy eased her back onto the pillow, smoothing her hair away from her face.

'I'd better go,' Josh said.

She hardly noticed him leave the room.

When the doctor took Xandra's temperature later that afternoon he pursed his lips.

' One hundred and two degrees. The fever is worsening, but it's to be expected, and we can do no more than we are now. It must run its course. '

With instructions to continue with the medicine and the sponging, and to call him if the fever became worse, he advised her to get some rest, and left.

Joy finally yielded to her grandmother's pleas to follow the doctor's advice and relinquished her seat to Bella, and went to her room for a few hours sleep before returning to resume her all night sitting.

As she sat by her daughter through the long hours, keeping her lonely vigil, she realised that the person she wanted most to be with her at that moment was David.

By the afternoon of the third day the fever was worse. The doctor was called and when he took Xandra's temperature the thermometer read one hundred and four degrees. Shaking his head, he reiterated they could only wait and hope for the fever to peak, and then begin to fall.

That night Bella and Mary took turns at sitting with Joy as she watched over her daughter. Xandra was delirious, tossing from one side to the other, calling out in her sleep for Daddy, for Johnnie. And scratching at the rash, her little nails ripping the skin. She irritated it so much Joy had to bind flannel around her hands to stop her from tearing it.

As she sat watching her daughter, in between sponging and trying to spoon medicine between her lips, Joy felt a sense of helplessness tearing at her heart as she had never felt before. The doctor had said they must hope for the fever to break. But what if it didn't break? What then? Would Xandra last the night? Or would she be gone by morning, leaving only memories behind? Her sweet, adorable child. And she could do nothing to help her. She could scarcely breathe for the weight of her heart.

Through the slow night Joy watched, her eyes burning, hoping for the slightest change, some sign that Xandra was improving. But her little body continued to toss and turn. Her skin was still hot and dry to the touch, and her breath rattled in her chest. Joy rose and walked to the window, looking out into the garden where the trees were bleached of colour in the pale, cold moonlight. She shivered, wrapping her arms around herself. A sudden cry made her turn around.

Xandra had called out in her sleep, and was flailing her arms in the air. Joy rushed to her side and caught her arms in her hands, stilling them. Xandra stopped tossing and lay still and silent, and then Joy saw that her skin was no longer dry. Sweat oozed from her pores, pouring down her face. Grabbing the cloth from the bowl on the bedside table, Joy wiped it away, and laid her hand on her forehead. It was still hot, but not with the dry, searing intensity it had before. The fever was breaking.

With tears streaming down her face Joy touched her dozing grandmother on the shoulder. 'Grandma, look.'

Bella was awake in an instant, and up and out of the chair. 'What is it?'

Then, as she saw the sheen on Xandra's face, she leant and touched it, then turned and took Joy into her arms.

'My dear girl,' she breathed, stroking her hair. 'The fever's broken. She'll be all right now.'

'I know.' Joy sobbed, resting her head on her shoulder. 'Thank God. I thought I was going to lose her. I thought she was going to die.'

'There, there, now,' Bella soothed. 'She'll be all right now,' she repeated. 'She's not going to die. You just go ahead and have a good cry.'

When Joy raised her head a couple of moments later, she saw that Bella's face was wet too, and she gave a shaky laugh as she stepped back.

'Well now, a fine couple we are. Crying like babies.'

Bella smiled through her tears. 'With happiness. Nothing to be ashamed of.'

Joy leant over Xandra, who was breathing easier now, and felt her forehead again. 'She's not quite so hot, her temperature is dropping.' Seating herself, she smiled at Bella. 'You go off to bed now.'

'Call me if you need me,' Bella said as she reached the door.

'I will.'

Left alone, Joy settled back in her chair to watch over her daughter. She had no intention of falling asleep, but before long her head drooped, and she was soon sleeping as peacefully as her daughter.

The doctor called again the next day, and proclaimed himself happy with Xandra's progress. 'Mind you,' he warned, 'she's not entirely out of the woods. She needs to be carefully looked after for a while yet. Keep her in bed for another two days, and then make sure she doesn't over exert herself. We don't want her racing around all over the place.' He looked over at his patient, who was still lying listlessly in the bed. 'Not that she'll want to for a while yet, I don't think.'

'And how long before she's not contagious?'

'Oh, I don't think she is now, but to be on the safe side, wait until the rash is gone. It won't take long.' He picked up his bag. 'Now I must go and attend to a lady who is about to increase the population. Call me if you need me, but I think she'll continue to recover nicely.'

Joy saw him to the door, and was surprised to see him place his bag into a motorcar parked outside the front of the house. The next minute he swung the starting handle to start the motor, and when it roared into life he hopped into the driver's seat and, with a parting salute, drove off.

Johnnie had been moping about the house at a loose end, with Xandra sick and in isolation, and his mother and new father away on their honeymoon. So he was delighted when Joy told him the next day that all Xandra's rash was gone and he could go in to see her. It seemed to be the tonic that she needed, too. As soon as she saw her cousin she was out of bed and pulling out her toys from the toy cupboard, her lethargy all gone.

Joy had to shoo her back into bed, but she insisted on choosing her favourite toys to take back with her, so that she and Johnnie could play a game.

As Joy left them together, happily deciding whether to play 'Snakes and Ladders' or 'dominoes', she began to relax properly for the first time since Xandra had fallen ill, and made her way down to the kitchen to make herself a cup of tea.

Mary was already in there preparing a salad for lunch.

'These came for you while Xandra was sick,' she told her, handing her a small bundle of letters. 'You go and sit in the sitting room; I'll bring in your tea when it's ready.'

Thanking her, Joy made her way up the hall to the sitting room, checking the letters as she went. There was a postcard from Emma from Sydney, where the couple had stayed for a few days on their way down to Melbourne on a driving honeymoon.

'Married life is wonderful,' she read, smiling as she seated herself in a chair by the window in the cosy room. Joy was happy for them, but as she dropped the postcard onto her lap she stared out of the window, thinking of her own dilemma.

She was sure she loved Josh, and that she wanted them to be together as much as he did. But she had Xandra to think of as well as herself. She remembered how she had called out for her father when she'd been so ill. She had wanted David, not Josh. And Johnnie. How would she feel at being taken to live on the other side of the world, away from here and the people she loved? Was she still young enough to forget all about this life, and to be happy? Joy wasn't sure.

And then there was Redwoods, and the horses. Her dream had always been to breed a champion, and to make a success of Redwoods as a stud. She was hopeful that Thunderbolt would turn out to be that champion. Did she want to leave it all behind? Would she be as content helping Josh to realise his dream, in England?

Her mind turned to David. If he would agree to a divorce, she could have Josh and Redwoods as well. Xandra would not have to be torn from her home, her family. At this thought she felt the stab of her conscience. Was this being fair to David? But then, he'd been the one to go and leave her. He'd had no qualms about going to America without her, and without Xandra.

He hadn't been here when she needed him. And he seemed very happy over there. Perhaps he would be overjoyed to stay where he was, to forget all about her. She felt a slight pang at this thought, but pushed it quickly away. It was what she wanted.

Picking up the other letters, she saw that one was postmarked 'Newcastle'. It must be from Jim Travers. Tearing it open she scanned the message inside. It told her that Travers had arranged temporary stables down in Sydney until after the Gold Cup Carnival, in order to be able to more easily run Thunderbolt in the races he needed to qualify for entry into the Cup.

'He will be running in several races before the actual Gold Cup Carnival week. However, I understand that it may well not be possible for you to be down there to watch him run prior to Cup week, so I will send you a report of his placing each time he races. Here are the details of the races I have chosen.'

There followed a list of the races he had chosen for each horse.

Joy put the letter down with a trembling hand. At last she was on her way to fulfilling her dream. She was going to have a runner in the Gold Cup, one of the most prestigious races in Australia.

Chapter Twenty Eight

Joy had hardly seen Josh since Xandra had been taken ill, but she must see him now straight away, to tell him about the Gold Cup Carnival plans. He would be excited too. As she hurried to find him in the horse paddocks she realised that, of course it also meant that if David wouldn't agree to stay in America, she could certainly not go away with Josh until after Cup Week. But they could wait that long when so much was at stake. Besides, by the time she heard back from David, the Cup might well be over.

Josh's response to her news was less delighted than she would have wished. Although he told her he was happy for her, he seemed to be more interested in asking if she had written to David yet.

'No, not yet, I've really only just been able to take time for myself again.'

'I understand, but you will write to him, won't you, now that Xandra is so much better?'

'Yes, you know we agreed on it.'

'I've missed being able to be with you so much since Xandra has been sick.' He took hold of her hand. 'Come tonight.' His eyes burned as he looked at her. 'Please.'

Joy heart lurched. He loved her so much! 'Of course I will,' she replied, returning the pressure of his hand.

'And you will write the letter?'

'Yes.'

As she returned to the house Joy thought about how she was going to word the letter. How do you tell your husband you've found someone else? It was not something she looked forward to doing. How was David going to feel when he received it? His last letter to her had been more personal than previously, with enquiries about her welfare as well as indications that he was missing Xandra, at least, if not her. Would he decide to stay where he was, allowing her to divorce him? Or would the thought of losing his life here bring him hurrying home?

After checking that all was well with Xandra and Johnnie, she declined Bella's invitation to join her for more tea and instead went to sit at her desk. She drew a sheet of writing paper towards her, dipped her pen in the ink and started to write.

'Dear David,' she began. 'This is not an easy letter for me to write, but perhaps you will be pleased when you read it'.

No, that was not it. She put down the pen and screwed up the sheet, took a fresh sheet of paper and began again. 'Dear David, there is something I need to tell you.'

What was she going to tell him? That she had fallen in love with the man he'd sent to help her while he was away? Or was it best to say she had met someone else, without saying who? It was as she sat pondering this, pen in hand, that the sound of a motor outside heralded the newlywed's return from their honeymoon. She put down the pen and hurried to greet them. Arriving at the front door as they came up the steps Joy saw that Emma was radiant, and Hector had the satisfied look of a man who was content with life.

Before they could do no more than exchange greetings the door burst open behind them as Johnnie raced out and threw himself at his mother, hugging her legs.

'I missed you, Mummy,' he told her as she bent to kiss him.

'And I missed you too,' was all she had time to say before Johnnie turned his attention to Hector, who picked him up and hoisted him high in the air. He placed the squealing boy on his shoulders, and leading the way into the house.

Over lunch, where Johnnie insisted on sitting between his mother and his new father, Emma chattered about their trip, describing the places they had been and the new sights they had seen.

'It all sounds as if you had a wonderful time,' Joy smiled, pleased at their obvious happiness.

'Yes, we did. But the best thing happened right at the end. We have a surprise for you.' She looked across at Hector. 'Shall we tell her now, or should we make her wait?' she asked him, her voice excited.

He smiled indulgently at her. 'You know you're dying to tell her. I don't think you can wait any longer.'

Joy looked from one to the other, her curiosity piqued. Whatever it was, it was certainly something that pleased them both.

Emma's eyes sparkled. 'We've found the ideal new home for us.'

Joy felt a little sinking inside. She would miss them when they left, but she put a brave face on it.

'Well, that's wonderful,' she said, trying to sound cheerful. 'Whereabouts?'

Emma laughed. 'That's the best part. It's right next door!'

'What?' Joy could hardly believe what she was hearing. 'You mean...'

'Yes.' Emma laughed with delight. 'The property right next door, so we'll be neighbours. What do you think of that?'

'I think it's wonderful,' she enthused, 'but I didn't even know it was for sale.'

'Neither did we, until Hector started making enquiries about any properties for sale nearby.'

'So what are you going to do with it?' she asked Hector.

'All the good timber is gone, so I'm going to clear it and run cattle.'

Bella had been sitting quietly, listening to the younger ones talking, but now she smiled across at Hector. 'I'm sure that's a wise decision. I believe it's a good business to be in.' She toyed with her fork. 'And it will be so good for David having his sister living next door to him.' As she finished her words, she switched her gaze to Joy.

Joy saw the message in her eyes, as clear as if her grandmother had spoken it. A message. And a warning.

Waiting until she was sure everyone was asleep that night, Joy left her bed and made her way silently through the darkened house, down the steps and along the path to Josh's cottage. The light was in the window to welcome her, and Josh was waiting for her with the door wide open.

As soon as she was through the door he closed it behind them and clasped her in his arms, holding her close, kissing her and telling her how much he loved her. Then he lifted her from the floor and twirled her around, round and round, until she laughingly told him to stop before she became dizzy.

He put her down and kissed her again.

'You can't know how happy I am that you're here.' His voice was husky. 'I've missed you so much. I can't bear it when I'm away from you.'

'And I've missed you too,' she told him, her heart singing with happiness.

He took her face between his two hands and gazed deep into her eyes, then bent his head and kissed her again, long and gently. Then he scooped her up into his arms and carried her into the bedroom.

Much, much later, as she lay with her head on his shoulder and his arm around her, their needs for each other satisfied, he asked her if she had written the letter to David.

'I started it,' she told him, 'but then Emma and Hector arrived. And of course I had to hear all their news. But I'll finish it in the morning.'

'Promise me?'

'I promise,' she replied, running her fingers across his chest.

He caught her hand and brought it to his lips, kissing her fingertips. 'I can't stand this hole-and-corner life for much longer. I want you for my own.'

Joy bit her lip. 'I know. I want to be with you too. But it's not easy...'

'There will always be too many problems here.' He pulled her to him, fiercely. 'It's better if we go away, get away from all this. We could have a wonderful life in England. We'll start our own stud. We'll have horses racing at Newmarket, at Ascot. The very homes of thoroughbred racing. You'll love it. We'll be happier, away from here.'

Joy's breath caught in her chest. 'But...but I can't just up and go...' she stammered.

'Why not?'

'There's Xandra, and...'

'We'll take Xandra with us. I never intended anything else.'

'But the Gold Cup...'

He released his hold on her, sighing. 'Yes of course. The Gold Cup. All right, I know how much it means to you. We'll wait until after that to go.'

'As long as we're together, that's all that matters, whether it's here or England. Let me write to David. Let's see if he'll stay in America, so we can be divorced. Then you and I can marry, and we'll be happy here then.'

Josh set his jaw. 'Letters take too long. It'll take months to get his reply. Send him a cable. That way he can reply immediately.'

Joy drew a long breath. 'It's difficult to send this sort of news in a cable; it seems a bit...harsh.'

'It's harsh for me having to live in this situation. I can't go on like this, waiting and wondering.'

Joy licked her lips. 'All right, I'll send him a cable tomorrow. But whatever his answer, I wouldn't leave until after the Gold Cup.'

'I concede that. Unless David stays in America, we'll leave for England after the Gold Cup.' His eyes searched her face. 'Agreed?'

'Yes. Agreed.'

It took Joy a long time to compose the cable to David the next morning. She tried to explain how lonely she had been, how he was not there when she needed him, and how she never meant this to happen. It ended up being a very long cable. As she finished it and sat back with a sigh, there was a tap at the door. She slid the sheet of paper beneath the blotter on her desk.

'Come in.'

Emma came into the room. 'I'm sorry if I'm disturbing your work,' she apologised.

'Not at all.'

'Hector and I are going over to have another look at the house next door. He wants to make some alterations, so he wants to have a good look at it again now that it's empty. Would you like to come with us? I'd like your opinion on some of the furnishings.'

'Thank you, I'd love to come.'

Joy looked down at the desk. The cable would have to wait until the afternoon. There was no way she could go to the Post Office to send it when Emma was with her.

When Joy went into her office on returning from her visit, intent on retrieving the cable and taking it to the Post Office, she found a letter lying on her desk. The mail must have arrived while they were away. It was from David. This was strange; it wasn't very long since she received his last letter. Opening it, she found it was quite short. It told her that Lily and Winston had definitely decided to run their horse Aristocrat in the Gold Cup.

'So we will all be coming over with him and are due to arrive in Sydney a few days before the start of the Cup Carnival. They have made arrangements to stable the horse with a trainer in Sydney. By the time you receive this we will be on the high seas. There is quite a large party of us including Lily and Winston, Winston's sister Abby, and a strapper, and they have arranged to stay in Petty's Hotel in Sydney. As I will be helping with the horses I will stay with them until after Cup week. Lily is looking forward to seeing you all. And, of course, so am I. I am not sure if you will be in Sydney for Cup week. If not, I will leave for Bulahdelah as soon as possible after it is over. It has been a long time, and it will be good to be home again.'

Josh's face was grim when Joy finished reading the letter to him. 'So he plans on returning here as soon as Cup week is over. This changes things.' He frowned. 'We should leave immediately, so we're gone before he arrives.'

'No.' Joy shook her head vehemently. 'I will not leave before the Cup. That is definite.'

Josh closed his eyes and took a deep breath. 'And as he has already left, you can't contact him before he arrives. So when are you going to tell him about us?'

'I'll tell him when I see him. He doesn't plan on staying with Mother and Rufe, where I'll be, so that means I won't have to be with him in Sydney.'

'He'll probably expect you to share his room at Petty's Hotel when he finds you're in Sydney.'

'I won't do it.'

'Are you sure? Are you sure you still love me?'

'Yes.'

'Tell me.'

Her heart melted as she realised his anguish. 'I love you Josh.'

'And you will come away with me?'

She hesitated. 'If David doesn't agree to leave Redwoods, yes.'

Josh shook his head. 'He won't. I feel sure you will have to be the one to leave. We can't keep putting it off. You will come with me as soon as Gold Cup week is over?'

'Yes.' He looked so unhappy she put up her hand and stroked his cheek. 'I do want us to be together, you know.'

He pulled her to him and buried his face in her hair. 'It would break my heart to lose you. Promise me you'll tell him about us.'

'Yes. I'll tell him.'

One night a few weeks later, Josh greeted Joy with the words that he had news for her.

'I've made some arrangements for our future,' he told her. 'I've booked our passage to England on the Odessa. She sails from Sydney on the day after the Gold Cup. I've booked it as Mr. and Mrs. Frazer and daughter Xandra.'

Joy stared at him in disbelief.

'But we agreed that I would tell David about us when he arrives, and we'll see what he decides to do. What if he agrees to a divorce?'

'Then we'll go for a holiday, so you can meet my parents, and then we'll come back.'

'Oh, I see.' Joy could find no argument with that, and tried to adjust her thoughts to the fact that it was possible she might soon be leaving Redwoods.

The next few weeks passed quickly until it was time to leave for Sydney. Joy and Xandra travelled down in the car with Emma, Hector and Johnnie, their luggage piled into the car with them. Excitement for the Cup Carnival had been running high at Redwoods since the news Thunderbolt would be racing in the Gold Cup, and several of the staff made up a party to travel to Sydney, and Josh arranged to go with them.

Joy and Josh spent a tender night together on the eve of their departure. Josh told her he would be staying with the others at the Metropolitan Hotel, but he would seek her out at the races, and reminded her that the next night they spent together would be when they were on board the Odessa, bound for England.

Chapter Twenty Nine

Joy, Emma and Kitty gathered in the garden at the house in Summer Hill on the morning after their arrival in Sydney, taking morning tea and catching up on each other's news as they supervised the three children playing nearby.

Hector and Rufe had left much earlier to watch the early morning gallops and visit the stables. Joy would have preferred to go with them, but she knew she shouldn't rush away and leave the other ladies on their first day in Sydney, so she put off her visit to the stables until later in the day.

It was mid morning when Alice came out to tell Kitty that a lady had arrived to see Mr. Cavanagh. 'When I told her he was out, she asked for you. She said she knows all the family,' Alice added, 'so I've put her in the sitting room.'

'I wonder who it is? You'd better show her out here,' Kitty told her. 'Oh, and bring another cup and a fresh pot of tea, please, Alice.'

They all watched to see who would come through the door. There was a collective gasp as Alice ushered out a smartly dressed young woman, who stopped as soon as she was through the door and stood still.

'Well, this is a surprise,' she said, her gaze travelling to each of them in turn, her American accent sounding curiously out-of-place in the suburban Sydney garden. 'I come to see Father, and I find all my female relations instead.'

Kitty was the first to recover, and Joy admired her aplomb as she rose to greet her stepdaughter with a welcoming smile.

'Lily, my dear, what a wonderful surprise.' She advanced towards her with hands outstretched. 'Do come and join us for morning tea.'

Lily touched one of her hands briefly before allowing Kitty to lead her to the table.

Joy jumped up and pulled out an empty chair for her, taking in her elegant gown and stylish hat. She was definitely out to make an impression.

'Yes, come and sit here,' she told her, amidst a confused mix of emotions and memories. Here was her old school friend who became her step-sister, and had accompanied her on the visit to England when Joy had been presented at Court, and shared her London Season. But then came the disastrous revelation that Lily had engaged in a clandestine affair with an unknown man, resulting in her pregnancy.

As Lily sat next to her, Joy looked at the three children who'd stopped their game to look at the newcomer. One of them was Benjamin, the child Lily abandoned shortly after his birth, in order to marry Winston Paget-Smythe, and run away to America with him. She'd left Benjamin to be adopted and raised by Kitty and Rufe, leaving behind a note to tell them of her decision.

Lily took no notice of the children, but stooped to give Joy a peck on the cheek before sitting down.

'Hello Joy, it's good to see you again.' She nodded at Emma as she removed her gloves and laid them on the table. 'My goodness, Emma, I do declare I haven't seen you since I was a child,' she drawled.

'No, you're so grownup, I doubt I'd have recognised you,' Emma responded, smiling at her cousin.

'Would you like some tea?' Kitty asked, picking up the fresh pot Alice had left.

When Lily nodded with a murmured, 'Yes, please,' she poured, and passed the cup to Lily.

Joy noticed Lily's hand tremble slightly as she added milk and sugar to the cup and picked it up. She wasn't as self-assured as she wanted to appear.

At that moment Xandra came over and tugged at Joy's dress.

'Mummy, we want biscuits, please.'

'All right, Xandra.'

As Joy picked up a plate and put three biscuit on it to hand to her, she spoke to Lily.

'This is my daughter, Xandra.' She turned to Xandra. 'Say hello to your Aunt Lily, Xandra.'

Xandra smile shyly. 'Hello.'

'You haven't met our children, Lily,' Kitty intervened, her voice strained. 'I'm sure you'd like to meet them.'

Lily answered coolly. 'Of course.'

'Come here, boys,' Kitty called, and the two boys came running and stood alongside her chair. Kitty put her hand on Johnnie's head. 'This is Johnnie, Emma's son, and this,' she moved her hand to rest it on Benjamin's head, 'this is my son, Benjamin.'

Lily put her cup down unsteadily, her face pale. 'Hello, boys.'

'Hello,' they chorused. 'Can we go now?' Johnnie asked.

'Yes,' Kitty told him. 'Off you go. Xandra has some biscuits for you.'

There was silence at the table as they ran to join Xandra, intent on the biscuits.

'Benjamin has grown into a fine little boy, Lily,' Kitty told her gently.

Lily cleared her throat. 'I have a daughter, Caroline. She is a sweet little girl. I don't have a son.'

'Lily...' Kitty put out her hand but Lily drew back, shaking her head. 'Lily,' Kitty continued softly, 'you're amongst friends here, family, and we all know your story. You don't have to be afraid.'

'I don't want Winston to know,' she blurted out. 'He doesn't know, and I don't want him to ever find out. I didn't want him to come to Australia, but he insisted.'

'But Lily, it's not fair to Benjamin to not know who his father is.'

'He'll never know.' Lily spoke fiercely. 'I'm the only one who knows that, and I'll never tell anyone.'

'But Lily...'

'No. Never. And I want you all to promise me you'll never tell Winston about...about the child.' She glared around the table at them. 'Promise me, all of you.'

Kitty shook her head. 'Lily, we're not the only ones who know about Benjamin. You must realise that.'

'But promise you won't tell him,' she insisted. 'Winston believed it was you, Kitty, who was having a baby when we left London. He must never know.'

'Oh Lily! You told him that?'

'What else could I tell him?' She jerked her chin up. 'I was too young to have a baby. I was only a child myself. It would have ruined my life.'

'You weren't too young to have an affair, and to go to great lengths to hide it,' Joy told her.

'Just because you were little miss-goody-two-shoes...'

Kitty interrupted Lily. 'It won't help the situation to argue.' She put her hand on Joy's arm. 'It's all in the past now. We can't change anything.' She turned back to Lily. 'I think we can safely assure you that none of us is going to tell Winston.' She looked at both Joy and Emma. 'Am I right?' When they both nodded she turned back to Lily. 'Your secret is safe with us.'

Lily took a deep breath and leant back in her chair. 'Good, that's all I needed to know. Now, let's finish our tea, shall we? I have a million things to do before the races start tomorrow. I have a horse running in the Gold Cup on Tuesday, you know. Aristocrat.'

'Yes, I've heard,' Joy answered. 'So have I. Thunderbolt.'

'What, the brumby from the bush?' Lily laughed. 'David told me about him. Don't tell me he's running in the Cup?'

'Yes, he is. And the trainer thinks he has a good chance.'

'He hasn't got a chance against Aristocrat, I can tell you now. He's a champion. He's been winning all the big races in the States.'

Joy lifted her brows. 'Really? Well, we'll see on race day, won't we?'

That night, after the children were all in bed, Kitty asked Joy if she would come for a turn about the garden with her. It was still daylight, and after they walked around and admired the roses, and discussed Thunderbolt's chances in the Cup, they sat on a bench beneath a flowering Tibouchina tree, and Joy prepared herself to be questioned.

'What do you plan to do about Josh?' Kitty asked her.

'Mother, I love him.'

'I know that. What I want to know is what you plan to do about it, now that David is back.'

'Perhaps David will decide to go back to America,' she suggested hopefully.

'If he didn't want to come back here, I don't think he would have come with Lily and her husband.'

Joy swallowed. 'I'm going to ask him for a divorce.'

'I see. And if he refuses?'

'Josh is going back to England,' she said slowly. 'He's sailing the day after the Gold Cup.'

Kitty took a deep breath, her face grim. 'And you're planning to go with him, aren't you?'

'If I have to. But I'm hoping David will agree, and then Josh and I can stay here and marry.'

'They'll never accept him, you know.'

'You mean Emma and Hector? I'm sure they'll come round in the end when they see how happy we are together. They'll be happy for us.'

'And Emma will accept what you've done to her brother? I don't think so.' She drew a deep breath. 'But it isn't just them, although you will be losing a dear friend in Emma. It's everyone else. And people don't forget. The stigma will be with you for the rest of your life. And it will affect Xandra too, and any other children you and Josh might have.'

'Oh Mother, we're in the twentieth century now. Things are changing. We live in modern times.'

'Yes, and you're a modern woman. With a modern outlook on life. I know that. But divorce is still frowned upon. You and Josh would be branded, you'd be outcasts. Your children would be whispered about, teased at school.'

Joy felt the nervous flutter inside her tighten into a knot of tension.

'And if David doesn't agree,' Kitty continued, 'and you go with Josh, then what of Xandra? She paused. 'I presume you mean to take her with you?' When Joy nodded, she continued. 'How will she feel at being taken away from her home? From her real father? From Johnnie? Have you thought about her, Joy? What it will do to her?'

'She'll be happy with us. She's young enough to forget about all that.'

'Didn't you always wonder about your father when you were growing up? Wouldn't you have been happier to have known him?'

Joy felt her mother's words like a blow to the solar plexus, leaving her winded, remembering how she'd wondered about her own father. She could only stand and listen as her mother repeated all the arguments she'd already had with herself. When Kitty finished, Joy covered her face with her hands. She was no nearer an answer than before.

Joy felt a flutter of apprehension about the day ahead as she dressed with care the next morning. It was the first day of the Gold Cup Carnival and she looked forward to the racing. None of her horses were racing today, but she was more concerned about her personal problems. Would she see David? If so, would she see him alone? Would she have the opportunity to tell him about her and Josh today? Would she see Josh? Almost certainly, because he'd said he would see her at the races. What if he and David met? She felt hot at the thought. Worse still, what if they all met together? Her insides churned.

By the time they all arrived at Randwick racecourse Joy's nerves were jangling. As they threaded their way through the crowd on their way to the Member's grandstand Emma stopped suddenly with a little cry, and then hurried forward.

Joy saw Lily, looking every inch the smart young matron with a sable coat swinging from her shoulders and diamonds flashing at her ears and on her fingers, approaching from the opposite direction with her husband, Winston Paget-Smythe. David was behind them, walking beside a woman whose arm rested on his. On seeing his sister, David disengaged the hand from his arm, and stepped forward to meet her. As Emma and David greeted each other the two groups met. As people walked around them, they moved to one side, away from the main crowd.

Joy caught David's eye on her and, fighting the urge to turn and run, she waited for him to join her. They stood awkwardly regarding each other for what felt like minutes, but was probably only seconds, and then David raised his hat to her. Her body tensed.

'Hello Joy, how are you,' he asked, his voice uncertain as his eyes swept over her.

'I'm fine, thank you, and you?'

'Fine, yes.' He nodded. 'And how is Xandra?'

'She's quite well now, thank you, but she's been very ill with the measles.'

David flinched. 'Measles! That's bad, isn't it?'

'Yes, she was very ill.'

'I...I'm sorry I wasn't able to be here, to be with her.'

'I'm sure you are. I was sorry too. I hope you've enjoyed being in America?'

He drew a deep breath. 'It's been very informative.' He seemed about to say more when he remembered the others and swung around.

As David hurriedly began the introductions, Emma smiled at him.

'No, you have my name wrong,' she told him. 'Hector and I are married, so I'm a Barron now.'

'Well, well. Congratulations.' David grasped Hector's hand and shook it heartily. 'Another link between the two families, eh?' He turned then to the woman with Winston. 'None of you have met Mrs. Abby Fallon, Winston's sister. Mrs. Fallon's late husband was a partner in the Talahousie Stud.'

Ah, so that's where she fitted in. A widow with an interest in the business. And an interest in David too, from the way her eyes followed his every move. Probably about thirty, dressed all in cream, with even features and a soft pink mouth. Dark hair upswept beneath a wide brimmed hat, and a gown with a nipped-in waist that showed off her curvy figure. Very attractive.

As Rufe and Lily rejoined them, Joy saw Emma was watching Hector closely as David and Rufe greeted each other, and then David turned to Lily, hesitating, and back to Hector.

'I'm not sure if you've met my cousin Lily?' he asked him.

Hector glanced at Lily and shook his head. 'No, I don't think I've had that pleasure.'

'Why, Captain Barron,' Lily said. 'We have met before. At Bournbridge Hall, when I was there with Joy a few years ago.'

Hector looked bewildered for a few seconds, and then his face registered surprise. 'Were you Joy's young companion, Miss...er...Miss Cavanagh? Please forgive me for not recognising you.'

'That's quite all right, Captain Barron. I probably look different now.'

'You do indeed. I'm very pleased to make your acquaintance again.'

Joy and Emma exchanged glances, Emma raising her eyebrows, and Joy sensed they were thinking alike. From the totally unemotional way in which they greeted each other, Hector and Lily could not have been lovers.

Rufe glanced up at the grandstand. 'Perhaps we should take our seats now,' he suggested. 'I see the Stand is filling quickly.'

David seated himself next to Joy, and they sat silently until, finally, he cleared his throat and turned towards her. 'So, how is everything at Redwoods?' he asked her.

'Everything is going along quite well, thank you.'

'I hope Frazer has been proving satisfactory.'

Joy's throat tightened. 'Quite satisfactory.'

'He's not at the races?'

'He's probably here somewhere. He came down with some others from Redwoods.'

'Then I'll probably catch up with him sometime.'

'Yes, I suppose so.'

Joy could only hope he did not, but the possibility kept her anxious for the rest of the afternoon.

Chapter Thirty

Before the last race Joy and Kitty walked down together to stand by the ring. As they stood watching the horses come in one by one with their strappers and begin walking around Josh materialised by their side, doffing his hat to them.

'Good afternoon, ladies. I hope you're having a successful day.'

Kitty gave him a perfunctory greeting before turning her back to him and concentrating on the horses. He touched Joy's arm and moved away a couple of paces. She followed him, frowning, and shaking her head.

'We can't talk here,' she told him, the buzz of talk around them muffling her softly spoken words.

'Have you told him?'

'No, there's been no chance for a private word.'

'But you will tell him?' He put his hand on her arm, and she saw the anxiety in his eyes.

'Of course, but not here.'

'I saw him sitting by you. It's hard for me to see him with you like that.'

Joy stepped back and looked around anxiously. 'Please go. I don't want you to meet David.'

'All right, but we don't have much time left.'

'I know.'

Joy breathed a sigh of relief as he moved away, and she turned back to her mother, who made no reference to Josh's appearance but continued talking as if there had been no interruption.

'I like the look of number three.' Kitty checked her race book. 'Regal Ruler,' she continued, reading from the programme. 'I think I might have a little wager on him.'

Joy turned her attention again to the horses, trying to push thoughts of Josh to the back of her mind.

'Mm, I think I prefer Black Jester.' She checked her book. 'He's won at his last three starts. Oh, and his trainer is Jim Travers, so that settles it.' As she was about to close her book, Rufe and David came through the crowd to join them. 'Jim Travers has a horse racing in this,' she told them. 'Black Jester, and he's been running well.'

'Really.' David looked around. 'I must see if I can catch him. I'd like to have a word with him.'

A moment later Travers entered the ring and spoke to the strapper leading Black Jester around. Stepping back as he finished his conversation Travers stood looking around, waiting for the jockeys to begin appearing. His gaze rested on David and, as he recognised him, he touched his hat and began walking towards them, motioning to David to join him. David excused himself and went in through the open gateway.

As the two men stood talking there was a sudden commotion as a small dog suddenly shot through the crowd and tore into the ring. It raced around amongst the horses, barking, and causing them to shy and plunge, pulling on their leads. There was instant turmoil as the strappers tried to calm the frightened horses. Several onlookers ducked beneath the rails to chase after the dog, shouting and running after it as it continued barking while zigzagging amongst the strappers and the horses' legs.

As the dog changed tack and headed for the exit David jumped forward to head it off. At that instant one of the prancing horses escaped its handler and raced across the ring, its eyes rolling. David turned his attention from the dog to the careering horse, and the dog slipped by him and streaked out into the crowd. As David lunged to try and catch the horse's trailing lead it reared up on its back legs, its front hoofs pawing the air as it squealed with terror. Its offside hoof caught David a glancing blow to the head and he fell to the ground as the maddened horse continued on its way, finally managing to find the exit and bolt away down the race track.

With a scream, Joy rushed over to David, closely followed by Rufe, Kitty, and a crowd of onlookers. Kneeling down beside him Joy saw he was unconscious, and blood was trickling from the side of his head where the horse's hoof had struck him.

Pulling a handkerchief from her pocket Joy dabbed at the blood and then, putting an arm beneath his shoulders, made an attempt to raise him.

'No, don't move him,' a voice commanded as a man knelt down beside her. 'I'm a doctor, let me check him.'

Joy stood and moved aside, watching as the doctor bent to feel David's pulse, and then knelt down beside him and placed his ear against his chest. Nodding, he straightened up and lifted David's eyelid, then began feeling around his neck and shoulders. At that moment David moved his head and groaned. Standing, the doctor turned to Joy.

'I'm Dr Harding. Are you related to him?'

'Yes, I'm his wife, and he's David Cavanagh.'

'We need to get him to hospital, Mrs. Cavanagh, so I can examine him properly. I'll need to arrange an ambulance.'

David groaned again and opened his eyes, looked around, and made a feeble attempt to rise.

'Best stay where you are,' Dr Harding advised him, 'until an ambulance arrives.'

'Yes David,' Joy added. 'You need to stay still. You have to go to hospital.'

'I don't want to go to hospital,' he objected weakly. 'I want to go home with you, Joy.'

'But I'm staying with Mother and Rufe.'

'They won't mind having me as well.'

Hector stepped forward. 'I have a motorcar here. We can use that instead of an ambulance. It'll be quicker.'

'Then let's see if he can walk.'

Between them they helped David to his feet, where he stood swaying.

'I'm all right,' he told them unsteadily. 'I'm not going to hospital.'

'You need to be properly examined,' the doctor told him. 'You almost certainly have concussion, and maybe worse.'

'I'll go to Rufe's house. I won't go to hospital.'

Dr Harding shook his head. 'Well, I can't force you to go to hospital.' He turned to Joy. 'I'll come with you, if you like. I could examine him at home.'

'Yes, please do. I'd be most grateful.'

Rufe stepped forward. 'Hector, why don't you lead the way, while I help David?'

With that he took David's arm and the procession headed off with Hector leading the way. By the time they reached the car Hector had it already started. They bundled David into the back seat, and Joy climbed in beside him, while the doctor sat in the front with Hector.

David didn't speak, but slumped against Joy's shoulder, and she worried that he'd lapsed into unconsciousness again. Turning to look at him, she saw his face was deathly pale, and his breathing seemed ragged. The trip back to Summer Hill seemed to take forever, but finally they arrived.

As the two men half led, half carried David into the house, Joy was wondering where to put him. Mrs. Baker came bustling to meet them, her face full of concern. After Joy explained briefly what had happened she led them without hesitation to Joy's room and opened the door. The men followed and laid the patient on the double bed inside. Joy was at a loss what to do. While sharing a bed with David was the last thing she wanted, there were so many visitors in the house that there was not another bedroom free. He must stay here. Perhaps she could sleep on the couch in the sitting room.

With Joy watching anxiously, the doctor attended to the head wound, placing a dressing on it, before carrying out a fuller examination. Meanwhile David seemed to be slipping in and out of consciousness. At one stage he cried out and tried to sit, holding up his arms as if to ward off an attack, then fell back again, muttering. After finishing his examination the doctor replaced his stethoscope in his bag, and brought out a small bottle of white pills.

'When he comes to, I want you to give him two of these,' he told Joy, handing the bottle to her. 'If he wakes in the night and is disturbed, you may give him another.'

'How is he, doctor? Are his injuries serious?'

'It's too early to say. He has concussion, but with head injuries one can never be sure what other damage might have been done. We must wait and see. I'll be around to see him again first thing in the morning. In the meantime he must be kept quiet. No excitement.'

'Yes, I'll see to that. It's fortunate you were so close when it happened. Thank you very much for coming.'

'I'm pleased to have been of assistance. Good day to you now, Mrs. Cavanagh, I'll see you tomorrow.'

After showing the doctor out Joy went in search of Mrs. Baker. She enlisted her aid in helping to undress David and put on one of Rufe's nightshirts that the housekeeper had brought in with her and put him between the covers. He was of little help in the process, but he stirred enough to be able to swallow the pills. He then fell back against the pillows, where he lay, white and silent.

When Joy touched his face it was cold and clammy, and when she felt for his pulse it was irregular. Pulling a chair to the side of the bed she sat there until late into the night, her emotions in turmoil as she watched over him, fearful of the outcome of his injuries. What if the accident left him permanently damaged in some way? What would she do? David was her husband, as her mother had been so keen to point out to her, and Xandra's father. It would be her duty to stay with him if he was incapacitated.

Her mind went back to their early days together. They had been so much in love then. What had happened to that early rapture, their delight in each other? David had been such fun to be around then, what had changed him? Was it her? Or had their early life together been doomed to degenerate into dreariness, so dull it couldn't be sustained?

Then she thought of Josh. Her heart ached with love for him. She longed to feel his arms around her, his kisses on her lips. She must hope David's injuries were not severe, and they could still carry out their plans.

Later that night she slid into bed beside David, but her sleep was uneasy. When he woke during the night and cried out, Joy gave him another of the pills with a drink of water, and when he settled down again his breathing seemed easier. When she finally drifted off to sleep again it was with the hope that tomorrow would see enough improvement in his condition to be able to tell him about Josh.

Joy opened her eyes in the morning to find David awake and half propped up on his pillow, looking at her. His colour was better this morning, and he seemed alert, though puzzled.

'What happened?' he asked her, his voice hesitant. 'How did I get here?'

'You had an accident. Don't you remember? The horse...'

'Of course. The horse. I remember now. It reared up right in front of me when I went to grab it.'

'Yes, and it hit you on the head when it came down.'

His fingers went to the plaster on the side of his head. 'Ah,' he said, fingering it. 'That explains the headache.'

'You've got concussion,' Joy told him.

'This is Rufe's place, isn't it?'

'Yes.'

'How did I get here?'

'In Hector's motorcar. He and the doctor managed to get you back. You refused to go to the hospital.'

'Did I? Just as well. Now I'm back where I wanted to be...with you.'

Joy swallowed. This was not going to be easy.

'I'd better get dressed. The doctor will be here soon.' She hopped from the bed and scooped up her clothes. 'I'm going to the bathroom.'

He put out his hand. 'Joy. Wait a minute.'

'Later.' And with that she whisked through the door and almost ran to the bathroom, her heart pitter-pattering.

When she returned, fully dressed, it was to find Xandra waiting outside the bedroom door.

'I want to see Daddy,' she demanded.

'Just for a minute then. The doctor will be here to see him soon.'

'Why? Is he sick?'

'He had a bit of an accident, and he needs to be quiet for a while. So you mustn't be boisterous.'

'I won't,' she promised, reaching up for the doorknob.

Joy opened it for her, and right away her promise was forgotten as she bounded into the room and jumped onto the bed, bouncing all over her father.

'Daddy, Daddy,' she flung her arms around his neck, hugging him, showering him with kisses. 'I missed you Daddy. You been away too long.'

David hugged her to him, laughing. 'I know, I know. And I missed you too. I won't ever stay away so long again.'

'Promise!'

He twisted her nose gently. 'I promise, funny-face.'

'I'm not funny-face,' she told him indignantly.

Grinning, he kissed her again. 'No, you're beautiful. Just like Mummy.'

He looked across at Joy, and her heart sank. This was not going to be easy. Drawing a shaky breath, she moved to the side of the bed.

'Now come on Xandra, I told you not to be boisterous. It's time for breakfast, and the doctor will be here soon.'

'But I want to talk to Daddy; I've got lots to tell him. I want to tell him 'bout Mr. Osborne and Johnnie, and...'

'Later.' Joy told her firmly, lifting her off the bed. 'Time for your breakfast.'

'But I want...'

'Later, I said.' Joy carried Xandra to the door, opened it, and set her down in the hall. 'Off you go now. Find Johnnie and go down to the kitchen and see if Mary has your breakfast ready.'

Xandra pouted, but left obediently. As Joy was about to turn back into the room she was relieved to see Mrs. Baker open the front door and usher Dr Harding inside.

He strode purposefully down the hall.

'Good morning, Mrs. Cavanagh,' he greeted her. 'How is your husband this morning?'

'He seems much better.'

'Good, let's have a look. Perhaps you wouldn't mind waiting out here? I want to give him a thorough examination this morning.'

'Of course.'

He was in the room for some time before opening the door and inviting Joy in.

'I'm pleased to be able to put your mind at rest, and to report that although your husband has a concussion, for which I have prescribed a few days in bed, he's suffered no further apparent damage.'

'Thank goodness.' Joy took a deep breath. At least she could put that worry aside.

'I'd like him to come and see me in a week, so we can be quite sure, but I don't really anticipate any further problems,' he continued, before turning back to David.

'However,' he told him, 'remember what I said. Take it easy, and if you have any severe headache, contact me.'

David nodded. 'Thanks Doctor, I will.'

After seeing the doctor out, Joy was shocked when she came back into the room to see David out of bed, smiling happily as he dressed.

'What do you think you're doing? The doctor said to stay in bed for the next few days.'

'I feel fine except for a bit of a headache, and he's left me something for that.' He looked at her with a beseeching expression. 'Please don't be cross with me, Joy. I'm just so happy to be here with you.'

Joy stared at him in amazement. Was this the man who'd gone off to America without her? Who hadn't wanted her with him? She thought of her heartache then. How she would have loved to hear those words before he left. But now it was too late. She loved Josh.

'I want to talk to you,' he pleaded. 'Can we go into the sitting room? There's not likely to be anyone else there so early.'

Reluctantly she nodded, and he took her arm and guided her up the hall, into the sitting room, and down onto the couch. When she was seated he sat opposite her, pulling his chair up close so their knees were almost touching. Now they were here he looked a trifle nervous.

'Comfortable?' he asked her, running his fingers through his hair.

'Yes.'

He fidgeted with the buttons on his shirt. 'What did Xandra mean about Harry Osborne?' he asked.

Joy was surprised. 'Is that what you wanted to talk about?'

'No, no.' He shook his head. 'But I'm intrigued. What did he do that's so important to her? She couldn't wait to tell me.'

Joy took a deep breath and told him the story of the abduction and subsequent events, leaving nothing out.

When she had finished he took her hand in his, his face a study in remorse.

'Joy, I'm sorry you had to face all this by yourself. It was horrendous for you, and I can only blame myself for not being here with you.'

'If it hadn't been for Hector and Josh I don't know what I'd have done.'

'It sounds like they were both very heroic. I'm glad Frazer turned out to be so helpful.'

'Oh, he's been immensely helpful.' Joy swallowed. 'David, there's something I need to tell you...'

He interrupted her, his face serious. 'I have something to tell you, too. Perhaps you should hear me out first.' He took a deep breath. 'I had plenty of time to reflect while I was away, and I came to see that I was probably wrong about many things. Perhaps I was too sensitive to certain things. Like feeling I was living in your house, working your property.'

'David, it was never like that...'

Again he cut her off, shaking his head. 'I'd just like to tell you how I felt. Because of that, I became overly touchy about who should make decisions.' He gave a rueful smile. 'I thought you wanted to run everything your way. I suppose I thought you were bossing me around, and I didn't like it.' He shook his head. 'My god, if I thought you were bossy, I don't know what to say about Lily. The way she orders Winston around is shocking. And he doesn't seem to take umbrage. Just says, 'yes dear,' and does as he's told.'

Joy couldn't help smiling. 'Poor Winston.'

'What I'm trying to say is I was wrong. I realise that what you did was all for the business, and had nothing to do with how you regard me.'

'I always regarded us as partners.'

'I know, and things will be different from now on. Being away from you made me realise how much I love you. You'll find me a different person now.'

Joy took a deep breath. 'There's something I want to talk to you about,' she said slowly. 'Something I need to tell you...'

'I don't think so. Things are going to be different from now on.'

She bit her lip. 'When you were away, I felt very alone, and when Johnnie and Xandra were abducted, Hector and Josh were the only ones who were here to support me, and Josh...'

'Tell me later.' He pulled out his watch and looked at it. 'I must get back to the hotel. I need a change of clothes, and the others will be worried about me.' He was almost tripping over his words in his haste to speak. 'Besides, I came to help with the horses, and I mustn't let them down.'

Looking at him in dismay as he rose from his chair and held out his hand to her, Joy saw he was pale, and his face held a most peculiar look. He knows, she thought. Or at least he suspects. And he doesn't want to hear.

Chapter Thirty One

As they left the sitting room, Johnnie came running up to David, his eyes shining as he grabbed his hand. 'Uncle David, come outside. I want to show you something.'

David looked at Joy and shrugged. 'I suppose another few moments won't matter'. He allowed himself to be led outside, to where the Tarrant motorcar stood in all its glory.

'This is my father's motorcar,' Johnnie told him proudly. 'It's a beauty, isn't it?'

'It is indeed.'

'He'll take you for a ride if you ask him.'

'Then I'll certainly ask him.' David smiled down at the little boy. 'Perhaps we could both ask him, and then we can go together.'

'That would be good. And we could take Benji and Xandra too.' Johnnie looked up at him, eyes wide and trusting. 'When I didn't have a father I wished you could be my father as well as Xandra's, but now I'm lucky 'cause I've got both a father and an uncle.'

David ruffled his hair. 'You certainly have.' He smiled.

'So have I,' Benji chimed in, tugging at David's trousers for his attention.

'Of course,' David told him, 'we're all one big family now.'

Xandra came running up to join them, clamouring to be picked up, and David hoisted her in his arms. She fluttered her eyelashes against his cheek.

'This is a butterfly kiss, Daddy.' She giggled. 'Do you like butterfly kisses?'

'I love butterfly kisses. How about you?' He lowered his face and fluttered his eyelashes against her cheek.

'It tickles,' she chortled, pushing his face away.

David seemed to forget about going to help with the horses as he continued to play with the children. Joy's heart faltered as she watched them together. How could she tear them apart?

Memories of David's early kindness to Johnnie came to her, when Emma first brought him here to live, a lonely little boy who'd lost his father. David had tried hard to be a substitute, taking him about the property with him, talking with him, teaching him, endlessly patient and thoughtful. And then, unbidden, her mind conjured up his face as it had been when he held Xandra in his arms for the first time, when she was just a few minutes old. The wonder and awe and tenderness on his face. And the love that flowed between them then–the sense of wonder at who they had created together.

And looking at them together now she felt a slow stirring of that love. Oh, nothing like she felt for Josh. That was overwhelming, thrilling, exciting, irreplaceable. This was just a small, flickering flame. Different. Calmer. Less exciting. But it was love. Joy turned away. How could she love two men at once? She couldn't have them both.

After David left to return to his duties Kitty came out to join Joy, and they sat in the garden together, talking idly as they watched the children.

Finally, Kitty broached the subject that was on both their minds.

'So, what have you decided to do?'

Joy bit her lip. 'I don't know.'

Kitty looked at her thoughtfully for a moment, then reached across and took Joy's hand in her own.

'I know it's hard for you darling, I can tell that what you feel for Josh is very real. You love him, I do understand that, believe me. But sometimes love alone is not enough.'

Hearing the understanding and concern in her mother's voice seemed to stir up the conflicting emotions inside her, and Joy was unable to hold back the tears. They erupted from her with great sobs. Kitty turned and put her arms around her and pulled her close, and Joy laid her head on her shoulder and let the tears fall. Kitty let her cry until, finally, she drew back and wiped her eyes.

'My poor little girl,' Kitty said. 'I know how hard this is for you.' For a second Kitty's face took on a faraway look as she gazed back into her own past. Then it was gone, and Kitty continued. 'What you have to realise is that you're going to make a decision that will affect the rest of your life. And not only you, but others as well. I'm not going to preach to you, you know how I feel. It's up to you to decide. And you can make a decision knowing that whatever you choose, you don't have to be swayed by worries about security. Redwoods is yours. It will always be there for you, however you decide. You have the luxury of knowing you can do whatever you think is best for you and Xandra, knowing you will be financially secure. It's something previous generations of women didn't have. Our modern laws have at least freed women from that constraint.'

Joy sniffed. 'Yes, I know. But it doesn't make my decision any easier.'

Kitty patted her daughter's hand. 'No. Some things never change.'

'This message that has just come for you,' Mary said, handing Joy an envelope. 'It was hand-delivered and the boy didn't wait for an answer.'

Joy thanked her as she opened it. It was from Josh, saying he needed to see her and would wait for her at his hotel until she arrived.

When she reached the Metropolitan Hotel it was early afternoon, and the lobby was deserted. The receptionist came out from a back room when she rang the bell, called the bellboy and sent him up to advise Mr. Frazer of her arrival.

Josh came down promptly to greet her, and guided her to a corner table.

'I had to see you,' he told her, his face anxious. 'It's murder for me, wondering what's happening. I saw what happened at the racecourse, the accident with the horse, and I followed you all to Hector's car. Did you go to the hospital?'

With a jolt Joy realised he had no way of knowing David had been taken back to Rufe's home.

'No, David refused to go there, so we took him to Rufe's house, where the doctor could examine him. He came back again this morning, and David has a concussion, but he seems all right apart from that, and he's gone back to join Lily and Winston. He's helping them with the horses, you see.'

'Ah. So you were able to tell him about us, were you?' he asked eagerly.

'Well, no. I tried to tell him this morning, but what with one thing and another, I couldn't. I told him I wanted to talk to him, but, well, the children were there and he said we could talk later, and then he had to go.'

Josh drew a deep breath, frowning. 'So he still doesn't know.'

'No, but...'

He looked around as a man and woman came in from outside, ushering their two children ahead of them, and approached the desk. 'Look, we can't talk here. Come up to my room.'

'Oh, I don't think I should do that...' Joy faltered. 'What if we're seen together, going into your room?'

Josh looked around. The receptionist was busy with the new arrivals.

'There's no one here that knows us. Besides, what would it matter? We'll be leaving for England soon.'

Reluctantly she rose, and he hurried her up the stairs to his room.

Once inside he turned and took her in his arms.

'Oh my darling, I've missed you.'

For a moment she tried to resist him, but as his lips found hers she felt the magic begin again, and yielded to his kisses.

He took off her hat, placing it on a nearby chair, and eased her across the floor, never taking his lips from hers. When they were by the bed his hand slid inside her bodice and cupped her breast, squeezing gently.

As she felt her body respond to his caresses she suddenly saw David as he had been this morning with the children, and she flushed with shame.

'No!' With a supreme effort she tore herself from him, pulling her bodice back into place, her heart pounding. 'No Josh. I can't do this anymore.'

Josh stepped back, panting. 'What do you mean, you can't do it? You want me as much as I want you. Of course you do, I know.'

'I'm sorry. I'm truly sorry, but I just realise how wrong I've been. It's been wrong of me all this time. I've betrayed David. I've let myself fall in love with you, and I should have known better.'

'And you've just discovered that, have you?' His body grew rigid. 'When I'm head over heels in love with you. What about me? What about the plans we've made together?'

'They were your plans. Before you even met me. You can still start your stud without me.'

'It's not the stud I care about, it's you. I love you. I want you, now and always. You can't just turn away like this.'

Joy drew a deep shuddering, breath. 'I have to. I can't go away with you.' The pain of her words sliced through her heart. 'It would be wrong, for Xandra, for everyone.'

He stood back, his face white, his eyes blazing.

'So I mean nothing to you. You were just amusing yourself with me. Now that he's back, you've finished with me.'

Her throat tightened. 'No Josh. It's not like that. It's never been like that.'

'You don't love me, do you?'

'Yes, I do.'

'Then if you do, come away with me.'

'I can't.'

'So you won't be on the Odessa with me?' he asked slowly.

She swallowed. 'No.'

His fists clenched at his sides.

'Then damn you! Damn you to Hell and back. Now get out. Just go. Leave me alone.'

Joy picked up her hat and left the room, almost blinded by tears as she made her way down the stairs. As she reached the bottom she tried to brush the tears from her cheeks as she blundered out into the street. Not knowing what to do, she made her way to Hyde Park.

Here she wandered around for a while, oblivious to her surroundings. Then, unwilling to face anyone, she made her way to the ferry terminal and boarded the ferry for the trip across the harbor to Manly. Standing outside by the rail, hat in hand, she let the wind blow in her face, hoping it would blow her sadness away. The boat pitched and rolled as they passed by the entrance to the harbor, where the long swells rolled in from the Pacific Ocean, and the wind blew fiercely. But it suited her mood. When she disembarked she walked along the Corso, under the Norfolk pine trees, and out to the end of the pier, staring out across the water.

Mother had brought her here as a little girl, just the two of them. It brought back the memory of the regret she had then because she had no father in her life. Not that she'd been lonely, for there had always been Grandma and Grandpa, and Mary and Patrick. No, she had a happy childhood. But there had always been a hollow inside her, a place where Father should have been. And remembering that helped her resolve. She'd made the right decision. But how would she ever cope with losing Josh?

Chapter Thirty Two

The day of the Gold Cup dawned overcast and Joy felt the day matched her feelings, gray and dismal, as she walked into Randwick Racecourse. Instead of going with the others to find their seats she made her way instead to the horse stalls, and walked along the row until she came to Thunderbolt's stall.

He stood calmly inside, with his strapper sitting on an upturned bucket close by. In contrast, and much to Joy's surprise, Jim Travers was in the stall, moving from foot to foot while polishing a bridle vigorously. He dropped it when he saw Joy, and hurried from the stall, taking Joy's hand and shaking it energetically.

'G'day, Mrs. Cavanagh, g'day. Big day today, eh?'

Joy smiled at him. It was the first time she'd seen him so excited, and she realised it was a big thing for him to have a horse running in the Gold Cup.

'Good day, Mr. Travers. Yes, a big day indeed. And how is Thunderbolt?'

'Cool as a cucumber, missus. Knows what it's all about, mind you, but he enjoys race days. Can't wait to get out there and race.' He rubbed his hands together. 'This'll be his biggest test, but I think he's up to it.'

'Good.'

Joy felt her spirits lift as she walked across to pat Thunderbolt, who put his head over the rail at the front of the stall as she approached. He whinnied and tossed his head as she came near, then dropped it as she lifted her hand to rub his ears.

'Mr. Cavanagh was here earlier,' Travers told her as he watched. 'Seems as if it's his cousin that's brought the horse from America. That Aristocrat.'

'Yes, that's right. Lily believes it can beat Thunderbolt.' She turned back to the horse as he nudged her shoulder. 'But she hasn't seen you run, has she?' She stroked his nose. 'You'll show him, won't you?'

'Mmm.' Travers nose twitched. 'Seen Aristocrat run, have you?'

'No, I haven't. But I've seen Thunderbolt run. And I've studied Aristocrat's form and while he has been winning big races over there, his finishing times over this distance are less than what Thunderbolt has clocked.'

Travers nodded. 'Yes, I saw that too. This fella's got both speed and stamina. And a heart that's as big as the moon. He never gives up. And in the end that's what counts.'

'Yes. Whatever happens, we know he'll be doing his best.'

Travers was looking beyond Joy now and inclined his head. 'Ah, here comes your husband now. And looks like we've got a visitor coming to check us out.'

Joy turned and saw David approaching, with Lily by his side.

Lily quickened her pace and joined Joy ahead of David.

'Hmm.' She stood appraising Thunderbolt, acknowledging neither Joy nor Travers. 'Not too bad for a brumby from the bush, I suppose, but not a patch on Aristocrat.' She turned to Joy then, and gave her a perfunctory peck on the cheek. 'And how are you, sister dear?'

'Quite well, thank you Lily. And you?'

'Top of the world. But I'll be better when I'm holding the Gold Cup after the race.'

Joy stifled the angry retort that sprang to her lips. Instead she merely raised her brows as she replied. 'Perhaps you're assuming too much,' she said coolly. 'We shall have this conversation again after the race, I think.'

Lily shrugged as David reached them.

David introduced Jim Travers to Lily, and then turned to Joy.

'How are you today, Joy,' he asked, his eyes searching her face uncertainly.

'I'm fine. How are you? Have you been resting, as the doctor told you?'

'Oh yes. Lily's been making sure of that.'

'Good. And have you had any headaches?'

'For the first two days, but quite gone now.' He smiled down at her as he touched her arm, but she saw the hesitation in his eyes. 'I've been looking forward to being with you again. I hope you feel the same?'

Joy took a deep breath and forced herself to smile back. 'Of course.' She gestured towards Thunderbolt. 'And how do you think our horse is looking?'

'He's looking magnificent. I was here talking to Jim earlier, and I'm impressed by what he's told me about his performances. I must admit that you were right, and I was wrong. Let's hope he justifies your faith in him today.'

'I have no doubt...'

Lily interrupted her. 'Come on then, you two. If we're going to see any of the races, let's move along.'

After a farewell pat on Thunderbolt's shoulder, and a word to Travers that they would see him before the race, Joy turned and took David's arm for their walk back to the grandstand area.

When the bugle sounded to announce the imminent arrival of the horses in the parade ring before the start of the big race, Joy and David walked down together to stand by the rail, and were joined seconds later by Jim Travers.

As they stood waiting, making aimless conversation, Joy guessed they were both as tense as she was. It was one thing to believe your horse was capable of winning, but another to stand here knowing this was the moment of testing, when so many other factors could affect the outcome. A lot depended on how the race was run, the jockey's tactics, and whether the trainer had judged correctly to have the horse at his peak for this particular day.

Thunderbolt was number twelve on the card, and as Joy waited, taking stock of each horse as it entered the ring, her stomach turned nervous somersaults.

There was a ripple in the crowd as Aristocrat, the only overseas horse here, entered the ring. He was certainly an imposing animal. A chestnut, with a deep girth and strong hindquarters, he stepped out with his head held proudly. Joy clutched her race book tighter. Was Thunderbolt good enough to beat him, an acknowledged champion?

When all the runners were in the ring the jockeys began arriving, and Travers left them and went to have his last words with Billy Smart. Joy noticed Lily had gone in to stand by Aristocrat and was in deep conversation with his jockey.

'I see Lily is giving instructions to their jockey,' she said to David.

'Yes, she's very hands on. Likes to take control.'

'Then she hasn't changed much.'

As she watched them she saw them both look across at Thunderbolt, who stood calmly as Travers gave his last minute instructions to Billy Smart, and then resume their conversation.

'I don't recognise Aristocrat's jockey,' Joy said.

'No, he's not a local,' David replied. 'He came across with them.'

As the jockeys started mounting Travers legged Billy up and stood watching until he moved off towards the track, then he came to join them.

'Well, I've done all I can. Now it's up to the horse and the jockey.' He gave a quick jerk of his head. 'Come on, let's go take a seat.'

They walked with him to the owner's and trainer's stand opposite the winning post, and, as they took their seat alongside him, David reached for her hand and took it in his own, squeezing it.

'I can't remember ever feeling so nervous,' he confided in a soft voice, 'except, maybe when we were being married.' After a second's pause, he continued. 'And then, as now, because I was worried about you.'

Joy looked up at him, startled, and saw that he was smiling down at her, but with a look of concern in his eyes.

'About me? Why?'

'This means so much to you, doesn't it? It's more than just winning the Cup, amazing though that would be.'

'It's also about Thunderbolt...' she faltered.

'I know.' He bent and kissed her swiftly on the cheek, then sat back in his seat. 'Now, let's just wait for the race.'

They didn't have long to wait. As the starter let them go, a great roar went up from the crowd.

They're off!

The runners thundered past the stand for the first time, still bunched up together as they jockeyed for position. No shouting at each other from the jockeys here, where they all knew they could be heard by the public, but Joy knew it was different once they were out of earshot. Then words flew between them!

'And Jubilee leads, with Hustler second and Aristocrat in third place on the rails,' came the voice of the caller with the megaphone, who then rattled off the positions of the rest of the field, with Thunderbolt settling mid-field.

Joy's pulses were racing as she tried to figure out which horse was where as they became harder to watch as they went around the back of the course. David had his binoculars trained on the horses but, even without glasses, Joy could see there was a tight pack behind the leaders and the rest were tailed off.

'Hello, what's happening there,' David suddenly exclaimed.

Joy's heart leapt. 'What is it?'

'There's been some interference. It involves our horse. And Aristocrat.'

Travers jumped up from his seat. 'The dirty little bleeder's tried to spook him,' he bellowed.

Joy could pick out the jockey's colours now, and her heart plummeted as she saw that Thunderbolt had dropped right back to last.

Aristocrat had moved up into second place. As they swung around the bend and headed into the straight Aristocrat was inching forward. The crowd roared as he and Jubilee battled for the lead, with Nero a close third. They were still two hundred yards from the post when Thunderbolt began his run down the outside, and as his legs ate up the ground he passed horse after horse, ears flat against his head and tail streaming out behind him.

The crowd erupted.

Joy jumped up and down, screaming. 'Thunder, come on! Come on! Thunder! Thunderbolt!' Her voice rasped in her chest, but she kept on shouting as he passed Nero, then Jubilee and Aristocrat, and began drawing away from them. Still he kept going, and flashed past the post eight lengths ahead, with the crowd going wild. The local horse had easily beaten the import!

With her heart beating too wildly for her to speak Joy twisted to face David. He lifted her off the ground and swung her around, his face flushed and his eyes blazing.

'You've done it. You've won the Gold Cup.'

As he put Joy down, Jim Travers grabbed her and kissed her full on the mouth.

'Good on you, love.' He gasped for air before grabbing David's hand and pumping it up and down. 'The Gold bleedin' Cup. We've won the Gold Cup.'

And suddenly it seemed as if everyone was there congratulating them. Strangers came up to shake their hands. Rufe and Hector pushed through, making a path for their wives to follow, and hugged and kissed them both.

Then Jim Travers pulled Joy away and took her down to where the horses were coming back in, and pushed a way through for her, and they both took hold of Thunderbolt's bridle and led him in together, through the cheering crowd.

After the jockeys weighed in, and correct weight was declared, it was time for the presentation.

As Joy took the Gold Cup from the president of the Racing Club, for David had insisted she be the one to receive the trophy, she could barely hold back the tears of thankfulness.

It was only later, after they toasted the win with champagne, and received what seemed like hundreds of congratulations, that Joy realised Josh had not been amongst those who came to offer congratulations. She had seen him once, at a distance, but he turned away as he became aware of her glance, and disappeared amongst the crowd. It was a sad moment in the midst of all the gaiety, but she pushed it away, and turned to speak with yet another well-wisher.

When she slipped away later to check on Thunderbolt she found that the horse standing calmly in the stall, and Jim Travers whistling as he went about his chores.

'How has he pulled up?' she asked him, rubbing Thunderbolt's ears.

'Right as rain, missus,' he enthused. 'He could've gone round again, he wasn't even blowing. He's a wonder, he is.' He chortled. 'Mind you,' his face sobered, 'there was some dirty work went on 'round the back o' the course. Billy told me Aristocrat's jockey tried to unseat him. Pulled his foot half out of the stirrup. That's when he dropped back, well away from him. Billy knew he had a powerhouse under him, and when he asked him to go, well, we all saw what happened. He just left them standing.' He slapped the horse's rump. 'Didn't you, me bonny boy?'

A jovial group made their way back to Summer Hill after the races were over for the day. Rufe produced another bottle of champagne for them to celebrate with Alice and Mrs. Frobisher, who had remained at home to mind the children.

David made no attempt to leave and return to the hotel, and when at last Joy announced her attention to retire for the night he followed her into the bedroom.

'I don't think I'd be welcomed by Lily tonight after we trounced her so well,' he said, as he closed the door behind him. 'And as we'll all be returning to Bulahdelah in a few days, I'll collect my things tomorrow.' He moved across the room and put his arms around Joy. 'Besides, I want to spend the night with my lovely wife.' He kissed her gently. 'I do love you very much, you know. Being away from you made me realise just how much.'

'I see.' Joy swallowed at the nervous lump in her throat. 'Then I can't help wondering why you stayed away for so long?'

'I was a fool. I know that now. I've told you, things will be different from now on.' He put out his fingers and stroked her cheek. 'Come to bed now,' he repeated.

As they settled into bed and David turned to her they were awkward with each other, and their first coupling was tense and unsatisfying. But then Joy drifted off to sleep, and when they woke much later, and David turned to her again, she found herself remembering how much she'd always loved him, and she responded to his ardour, and this time she enjoyed herself very much.

When she woke again it was morning. She turned her head and saw David lying next to her, and studied his face as he slept. A wave of hot shame engulfed her as guilt gnawed her. What sort of a woman was she that she could go from one man's bed to another's so easily?

Later that morning Joy, Kitty, and Emma were taking morning tea together beneath the Tibouchina tree in the garden when Lily came bouncing out through the door.

'Well, well,' she drawled, 'all the ladies together. What a pleasant surprise.'

Kitty stood up and went to meet her.

'Do come and join us, Lily. We're having a relaxing morning after all the hustle and bustle yesterday.'

Lily took a seat and removed her gloves, laying them on the table as she spoke to Joy.

'It's you I've really come to see. I suppose you think your brumby is superior to my champion now, do you? Now that he's managed to beat him, once.' She tossed her head. 'Aristocrat hadn't recovered from the crossing. It sapped his energy, and he hadn't fully recovered. He's highly strung, like all thoroughbreds.' Her lip curled. 'Unlike brumbies. If you brought your mongrel horse to America to race, you'd find we'd have a different result. Under normal conditions it couldn't come close to Aristocrat.'

Joy felt the hot blood bubbling in her veins as she listened to Lily's scornful diatribe. She forced a tight smile to her face as she answered.

'Well now, I can understand how upset you are to lose, you've never been a good loser. That wouldn't be jealousy I hear speaking, would it?'

'Huh. I wouldn't be jealous of that flea-bag. And I certainly don't have to be jealous of you. You can't even hold your husband. He had to go to the other side of the world to find someone who appreciates him.'

Lily's sneering face swam closer, and then receded, as dizziness threatened to overcome Joy. 'What...what do you mean?'

'My sister-in-law Abby is a very captivating woman. You couldn't blame any man for losing his head over her, least of all David.'

Kitty's palm came down on the table with a thud.

'That will do, Lily,' she blazed, 'that's quite enough. You're in no position to be stirring up trouble. You forget that we all know you only too well. We all know your story, and it's none too pretty.'

Anger darkened Lily's face.

'You're all so self-satisfied, aren't you, in your own comfortable little worlds. I've seen enough of you, all of you.' She snatched her gloves and stood up, overturning her chair in her haste. 'You won't see me again. I'll leave you to stew in your own narrow little lives.' She headed for the door.

'Wait,' Kitty called. 'There's something I want to know before you go. Who is Benjamin's father?'

'I'll never tell you that.' She spat her words. 'That's my secret and I'll take it to the grave with me. It's one thing you'll never have.' With that she flounced through the door, slamming it behind her.

There was silence after she left, but as Joy recovered her composure she was conscious of being freed from a great weight. Was Lily's innuendo true? Had David and Abby had an affair? She remembered how Abby gazed adoringly at David. Yes, she felt sure they had. And if so, her guilt was bearable.

Later that day Joy made her way alone to Darling Harbour. Yes, there was the Odessa, making ready to sail. A crowd was gathered on the wharf alongside, farewelling friends, and streamers stretched between the onlookers and the ship. It was almost departure time, but the gangplank was still in place. She knew she only had to walk up it and she would be welcomed. Her chest ached with longing, but she stayed where she was – close enough to watch, but too far away to be noticed from on board. She stood there until the ship's whistle gave a long drawn-out toot, and the Odessa moved away from the wharf. Tears blurred her eyes. The crowd drifted away but she remained, a forlorn figure in the deepening dusk, until the ship was out of sight. Drawing a deep sigh she turned and caught a cab back to Summer Hill.

David was waiting for her. And that night, after the children had been put to bed, he took her arm and they went for a stroll around the garden. Under the Tibouchina tree he stopped and took her hand, turning her to face him.

'It's all right, isn't it?' he asked her, his eyes anxious. 'I mean...us...we're all right?'

Joy looked at him, seeing the changing emotions flitting across his face – eagerness, hope, doubt… and...yes...love.

She drew a deep breath. 'Yes,' she told him, 'we're all right.'

And as he laughed and let out an exuberant whoop and twirled her round and round before sweeping her into his arms and smothering her with kisses she knew he was still the same man she'd married.

Epilogue

Six months later

It was a golden morning with the sun warming the air and a faint breeze stirring the trees when Joy and Kitty sat outside on the verandah at Redwoods. Her mother was here to visit, and Joy had suggested bringing their morning tea outside, where they could watch Xandra at play in the garden below.

Kitty turned to Joy as they sat enjoying their tea. 'I haven't asked you before because I wanted to give you time to settle together again,' she began, touching Joy's arm gently, 'but how are things between you and David now? You certainly seem to be happy, but I mean really?' She paused. 'I know you realise it's only because I care about you that I feel I can ask, and if you don't want to answer you can tell me to mind my own business.'

Joy hesitated and turned to look at Kitty before replying. She saw only concern and love in her mother's face. 'I wouldn't do that, and I understand why you ask. And yes, we are happy together. I think we both realise now that we have to work at making our marriage happy. It doesn't just happen automatically because you fall in love and marry.'

'That's very true and, you know, I do understand about you and Josh. I blame David for going off and leaving you like that, but I had the feeling things weren't good between you even before then.' She paused to sip her tea before continuing. 'Josh is a very attractive man, and it must have been hard for you to give him up.'

It was a relief to be able to talk about it.

'It wasn't just that he was attractive,' she answered slowly. 'He made me feel alive and deeply loved...and...special, I suppose. I know it probably sounds silly, but I truly loved him, and I missed him terribly when he went.' She drew a deep breath as she remembered the pain. 'Yet I still loved David at the same time. Does that sound ridiculous?'

Kitty shook her head. 'No, not at all. I think we're all capable of loving more than once. It just happened that for you it occurred at a time when both men were important in your life, although apart at the time. I don't doubt for a moment that your feelings for both were...are...love.'

Joy sat silent as she thought about it. The pain of losing Josh had diminished now, and when thoughts of him came stealing into her mind she pushed them firmly away. She wondered if she would forget him in time. Could anyone ever forget such an intense love? And did she really want to forget completely? Perhaps when she was an old lady, she would want to take out his memory and warm herself by conjuring up the months of their love, and passion, and their delight in each other.

Resolutely she switched her mind, and turned to Kitty with a small sigh.

'Josh will always have a piece of my heart,' she said honestly, 'but here with David is where my life belongs. With David and Xandra, and Redwoods and,' she smiled as she patted her stomach, 'with Xandra's brother or sister.'

Kitty's face lit up. 'Oh Joy, how wonderful. When?'

'In seven months time. And the amazing thing is that Emma's having a baby too. My goodness, what a brood that's going to make, running around together.'

'More Barrons and Cavanaghs!' Kitty laughed. 'It almost seems as if the two clans are destined to be together.'

'Ah yes. The Barrons and the Cavanaghs,' Joy mused. 'I wonder what lies in the future for our brood, Emma's and mine?'

'And Benjamin.' Kitty spread her hands with a smile. 'Who can tell?'

'Indeed. Will they want to stay here and carry on what we've begun, or will they want to spread their wings and fly away? Who knows what changes this new century will bring for our children? Only time will tell.'

At that moment, they saw David approaching from the stables. Xandra stopped her game as she saw him, dropped the ball she was holding, and skipped towards her father.

'Daddy, Daddy,' she cried. David scooped her up in his arms as she reached him, and lifted her up high before bringing her down to sit on his shoulders.

'Giddyup, horsie, giddyup!' Joy heard her squeal, jiggling up and down as they came up the path towards them.

'Come on you two,' David called as he drew level with the verandah. 'We're going to check on Chipper. Come and join us.'

'You go, Joy.' Kitty smiled. 'I'll stay here and finish my tea.'

'Carrot,' Xandra sang out. 'I need a carrot for Chipper!'

'I'll get it.'

Joy stood up and headed into the house, returning a minute later with a carrot. She took handed it up to Xandra, who grasped it firmly before urging David on again.

Falling into stride alongside David, Joy walked with them down to the horse paddock, where Xandra demanded to be put down as Chipper ambled up to the fence.

David slid his arm around Joy's waist then, and dropped a kiss on the top of her head as they stood watching Xandra feed the carrot to Chipper.

'Happy?' He smiled down at her.

Looking up at him she saw the tenderness in his eyes, and a little bubble of joy rose inside her.

'Happy.' She nodded.

Joy's heart sang as she watched Xandra with Chipper, and she felt the pressure of David's arm around her. She had every reason to be happy now. The Redwoods' horses were doing well – Chipper had grown into a fine colt, and it wouldn't be long before he was ready to go to Jim Travers to commence training. Would he win races? Was it possible he could even perhaps match Thunderbolt, who had become the champion she'd wished for all those years ago at Ascot? After winning the Gold Cup he swept all before him, unbeaten in eight races since, and hailed by the Press as a wonder horse. Both Joy's Dream and Bonnie Doon had won a race each, and were placed in the first four more than once. Because of these successes Redwoods Stud was fast gaining in prestige.

But best of all was that she and David had regained the friendly and loving rapport they'd enjoyed earlier in their marriage. She had made the right choice.

The End
****

An Ambitious Woman
The old ways are changing, but they can't change fast enough for Joy Barron...

Praise for An Ambitious Woman
"Aussie author Kate Loveday's stories about independent women are wonderful stories. She has many twists and turns and surprises, good and bad, in her stories that a reader doesn't expect. She writes so smoothly it is like the pen in her writing hand touches the pages and the words just flow out of her pen onto paper with such ease. Ms. Loveday's writing is smooth and intelligent. She blends everything together very nicely and tells a wonderful descriptive story of different types of people, some you'll love and cheer on and some you'll dislike immensely. This story was not just a romance novel, Kate has imbedded a wonderful cast of true to life characters and many circumstances they went through. It would make a wonderful movie." Alice L Kent

"More Please!
I enjoyed reading Ambitious Woman as the last in this trilogy. It concluded the story with an interesting and satisfactory ending and if there was more I would love to keep reading." Wendy...Amazon

****

About Kate

Kate grew up in a beach area in Adelaide, South Australia and after an absence of almost twenty five years, spent mostly in NSW, she has returned to her home town with husband Peter.

She has worked as a freelance travel writer, has had many short stories published and is the published author of four novels, including the ***Redwoods Trilogy***, which are stories of historical romance and family sagas and have received 4 and 5 star reviews.

Her books, ***'Inheritance' and 'Black Mountain'*** are published by Escape Publishers and have received 5 star reviews. Kate now pursues her passions of writing, reading and listening to music, and is working on her next novel - ***The Necklace***.

Kate now writes Australian contemporary and historical fiction, and as long as you tell her, in reviews and emails, that you enjoy what she writes, Kate will continue doing so. Kate love chocolate, fine wines, dogs, music, and seeing new places.

An Independent Woman

The Redwoods series is a sweeping saga of romance, intrigue, and adventure, spanning many decades in a time when women have few choices, and life, and love, are not easy.

It is often a spur-of-the-moment decision that can become a turning point in life.

So it is for Kitty Morland, a young woman in London in 1878. Cheated of her birthright and condemned to a soul-destroying existence, Kitty yields to temptation one fateful day and commits a desperate, perhaps criminal, act. Realisation of its possible terrifying consequences forces her to flee to the other side of the world, to Australia, taking her widowed mother, Bella, with her.

Fearful that her past will catch up with her she marries William, an English aristocrat, and moves from Sydney to *Redwoods* in Bulahdelah, a remote logging area in the mid north of New South Wales – a place of red-cedar forests, wild rivers, and the loneliness of an early settlement.

Kitty needs all her courage and determination to survive a loveless marriage, dominated by a husband with a dark side to his character. She realises too late that the passion she feels for Rufe Cavanagh, a charismatic and entrepreneurial colonial, is reciprocated

Kitty finally has a chance for love and happiness but, torn between love and duty, she must make a difficult decision that will affect the lives of others. How will she decide?

Praise for *An Independent Woman*

"A brilliant read. I could not put this book down and the end left me begging for more."
~Sarah Cooke, Australian author

"A fabulous story! Well written and well told with colourful characters and finely drawn scenes. I give it 5 stars."
~Jacqueline Winn, Australian editor and author

"This has everything one could ask in a historical novel: clear,

compelling prose; engaging, well-drawn characters and complex, fast-moving plot involving domestic tragedy, diamonds, the perils of a logging camp and of a gold-mining town, a love banned by the time's laws of marriage, and a crime with results that span years and half a world. All taking place in a vividly realized setting of Australia with frontier Sydney, immense, exotic forests, wild rivers, and the loneliness of pioneer settlements."
~A. D. Byrd

A Liberated Woman

Can love be re-kindled after sixteen years apart?
This is the dilemma that faces Kitty Barron and Rufe Cavanagh. How much will the years have changed them? And what of their teenage daughters – important parts of their lives – would they accept sharing the love that has always been theirs alone?

While Joy embraces the idea of uniting their families, Lily burns with jealousy at the thought of sharing her father's affection, and schemes to keep them apart. When Joy and Lily go to London for a Season, the heady and exciting world of society London is a mixture of adventures and heartache for both Joy and Lily. They find that beneath the gaiety and excitement not everything or everybody is as it seems. Their romances bring problems that have far-reaching effects for Kitty and Rufe, and their happiness. London turns their world and everyone around them into chaos.

Love, seduction, intrigue, and greed all play a part in this tale. Part romantic story, part family saga, it sweeps from the village of Bulahdelah in New South Wales to pre-federation Sydney, and to the pomp and ceremony of Queen Victoria's court and a London Season.

Praise for A Liberated Woman

"Kate Loveday's writing is emotionally touching. The stories as they unfold on the different paths were done in a wonderful way while still tying the main threads together. I must say my emotions did become involved here for one of the story lines was heart rending for it is a portrait of life even in this day and age. The writer has a great way of telling her story in words. A historical romance that is not just Australia or London but a mixture of cultures and countries. This one is a good read for a long night where you wish good company. Only problem... It is somewhat of a cliffhanger!." Anna Swedenmom

"Great reading. Loved the series... Looking forward to the last book in the series. Great stories and the all the people in them." Amazon

"Wonderful historical romance with a feel of Australia that makes me want to experience it even though I know it would be different today. This sequel to the awesome An Independent Woman reunites Kitty and Rufe while it focuses on their daughters." Alice L Kent

"A Liberated Woman is a romantic tale of women, young and old, coming to grips with the evolution of a new social order forming at the beginning of the twentieth century. Kate Loveday has penned a story that flows well. Readers of this book will get enjoyment out of seeing how the protagonists overcome the different situations they find themselves thrust into."
    Warren Thurston, Australian Author
***

The Trophy Wife

Full of courage and resolve, this is a story about reinventing yourself, and the intrigues of Fate. A story of love, friendship, disillusion and retribution as a woman strives to change her life.

It seemed as if it would be a fairy tale existence...

When young and lonely Erin McDonald leaves Newcastle for a job in Sydney shortly after her mother's death she meets high powered business mogul Giles Brightman. He sweeps her off her feet, and she is thrilled when he proposes. Madly in love she marries him, but she soon realises he wants nothing more from her than to look beautiful and be compliant – ready to accompany him whenever he wishes, charming to his business associates, and ready to accommodate him in bed whenever he feels so inclined.

Slowly Giles' violent side emerges, and after an attack that makes her fear for her life, Erin knows she must get away. With little money of her own, and a platinum Amex card, she develops an audacious plan to give her a second chance in life – at Giles' expense. But Giles won't let her go easily.

When she consults lawyer Aden Marlowe the last thing on her mind is a new relationship. She tries to ignore her attraction to Aden, and throws herself into her efforts to create a specialised high fashion boutique. Aden is captivated from the start, but he has a secret, and must hide his feelings.

Giles tries to sweet talk Erin into returning to him, but when his pleading fails he threatens her and demands the return of documents that he accuses her of stealing. Undaunted by his threats, Erin ignores him and continues with her plans, but her home is ransacked and her store vandalised. Aden suspects a sinister reason behind Giles' actions, and he and Erin work together to find the secret of the seemingly innocuous *Phoebus* share documents.

**Can Erin overcome all the setbacks to find a new life...
and a new love?**

Praise for The Trophy Wife

"Second chance novel is too bland a term for The Trophy Wife.

I love women-of-strength novels and that is one on of the things Kate Loveday does so well. When young and lonely Erin McDonald leaves her home for a new job shortly after her mother's death, she is vulnerable to the practiced machinations of the urbane Giles Brightman and falls completely under his spell. Young, inexperienced, and loving does not equal weak, her love holds up under his growing busy-man routine but when he crosses a line, she walks. The tale of the rebuilding of her life, her soul, is the fascinating journey we travel with The Trophy Wife." *Jeanie W Jackson*

"Kate Loveday's stories of strong women are wonderful. Her writing is smooth and intelligent. She blends everything together very nicely and tells a wonderful descriptive story of different types of people, some you'll love and cheer on and some you'll dislike immensely. This story is not just a romance novel, Kate has imbedded a wonderful cast of true to life characters and the many circumstances they go through." *Alice L Kent*

Inheritance

An inheritance is usually a blessing . . . could it also be a curse?

An Australian rural romance about an unexpected inheritance that sends a city girl down deep into the country...

When Cassie Taylor inherits Yallandoo, a cattle station near Cairns in Far North Queensland, she is shocked.

What does she know about running cattle? But the property has been in her family for generations, and Cassie is not a quitter. She leaves behind her Sydney life and heads to the station, determined to make a go of it.

But a long drought and falling prices mean challenges Cassie doesn't expect. To save her heritage, she's going to have to come up with some new ideas — and fast.

Then the threatening letters start to arrive. Someone doesn't want Cassie to succeed, and they're willing to go to any lengths to stop her...

Praise for Inheritance

"*INHERITANCE is a great romantic suspense story, but also a chronicle of Cassie's life as she grows into a woman. I really liked her characters. I also enjoyed how she incorporated the lore of the Aboriginal people of Australia in the story. Ms. Loveday has created a wonderful setting in Yallandoo. Her characters are wonderfully developed and come alive off the page. This is a great book!*" Romance Junkies Reviewer: Lisa

"*Overall I found Inheritance compelling. Kate Loveday has a wonderful talent for getting into each and every character's head and telling the story from their point of view. The different twists and turns in the story retain the reader's interest. A very believable story; one that draws the reader in and leaves them feeling as though they have not only met these people but have really managed to get to know them all, very well.*" RRAH reviewed by Kay James

"*With her first novel 'Inheritance' ,Kate Loveday has created a fantastic read. I applaud her wonderful talent. Great work! Can't wait for her next book!*" Sarah Cook , Author

Black Mountain

An adventure set in the Australian rainforest, where the race is on to discover a precious plant – and an even rarer kind of attraction.

Elly Cooper's friend Jackson has gone missing – along with a journal that contains her dead father's lifelong work and the recipe for a product he described as the 'fountain of youth', potentially worth millions.

The catch is that the main ingredient is a rare plant found only in the Daintree Rainforest in Queensland. And only her father knew where to find it.

Elly enlists the aid of ex–policeman Mitchell Beaumont to help her find Jackson, the journal and the plant. But someone else is on the trail of the precious plant, and it seems they'll stop at nothing – even murder – to get what they want.

It's a race against time in the tropical heat as Elly and Mitchell battle the perils of the rainforest – and the feelings growing between them.

Praise For Black Mountain

"First time reading this author and thoroughly enjoyed her description of the country, characters and story line. Will be checking out her other books." *Net Galley*

"This is a fantastic short read that is fast pace and exciting. I really enjoyed this story as it was something different and really captured my attention. Elly is in a race against time to find the flower that holds the secret to her father's fountain of youth oil. Only problem is she's not the only one looking for the undiscovered flower. Elly isn't out searching the rainforest by herself.

Spending so much time with Mitchell, Elly might find more than just the flower." *Lost in sweet words*

'I really enjoyed this book as it had a hint of romance and bit of intrigue. Plus I have always found Australia fascinating from afar and for that reason found this read fun, and exciting. There are many unexpected things that happen in the story that you will miss out on if you don't take a chance on this enthralling read. 'Black Mountain' is the place where adventure, romance, and mystery abound; what more could one ask for? I would like to read more books by this author."

Lady P, Net galley

"Black Mountain is an exciting and complex adventure focusing on a race between greed and love." *Goodreads*

****

Connect with Kate Loveday

I really appreciate you reading my book!
The following are my Contacts:

Friend me on Facebook; **https://www.facebook.com/kloveday**
Follow me on Twitter: **https://twitter.com/LovedayKate**
Favourite my Smashwords author page:
https://www.smashwords.com/profile/view/PL
Subscribe to my blog: **https://kateloveday.wordpress.com/**
Visit my website: **http://www.kateloveday.com/**

*****

www.ingramcontent.com/pod-product-compliance
Lightning Source LLC
Chambersburg PA
CBHW031412290426
44110CB00011B/349